# A COMMENTARY
# ON *THE COSMIC DOCTRINE*

# A COMMENTARY
# ON *THE COSMIC DOCTRINE*
## Understanding Dion Fortune's
## Masterpiece of Spiritual
## Creation and Evolution

*John Michael Greer*

**AEON**

First published in 2023 by
Aeon Books

British Library Cataloguing in Publication Data

A C.I.P. for this book is available from the British Library

ISBN-13: 978-1-80152-010-2

Typeset by Medlar Publishing Solutions Pvt Ltd, India

www.aeonbooks.co.uk

# CONTENTS

PART II
SOLAR EVOLUTION

PART III
HUMAN EVOLUTION

# INTRODUCTION

Books on occultism come and go, but every so often a genuine classic appears. *The Cosmic Doctrine* by Dion Fortune is such a classic. The most important work of occult philosophy to emerge in the twentieth century, it sets out the principles of the Western mystery tradition with a clarity and depth that has rarely if ever been equaled. A foundational text within Dion Fortune's own esoteric order, the Society of the Inner Light, it has been required reading for students of the occult in the English-speaking world since it first became available to the general public in 1956.

*The Cosmic Doctrine* isn't an easy book to read, however. Its very conciseness makes it hard going, for every sentence requires close attention, but the challenge it offers to its readers goes well beyond this. In a phrase that has become famous in occult circles since its publication, *The Cosmic Doctrine* is intended to train the mind, not to inform it; it attempts to communicate to the reader an unfamiliar way of thinking, and so a great deal of patience and hard work are required to grasp what it has to say. Some of the difficulties, however, can be smoothed out by reframing and rephrasing the ideas Fortune presents, and this is what I have tried to do.

From ancient times through to the Renaissance, it was standard practice for scholars who had a certain amount of experience with a difficult text to write commentaries on that text for the benefit of the reading public. Examples such as Macrobius' commentary on *The Dream of Scipio* and Proclus' mystical commentary on the *Elements* of Euclid played important roles in the Western mystery tradition in earlier days. Since *The Cosmic Doctrine* is as rich and as challenging as either of these two examples, I thought it was high time to revive the commentary tradition. The following chapters accordingly appeared in monthly installments on my blog at ecosophia.net over a period of some three years, beginning late in 2018. The questions and comments of my readers helped me a great deal in revising and clarifying the commentary, and they are responsible for much of what is useful in this volume.

It's probably necessary to say in so many words that my views on the meaning of *The Cosmic Doctrine* make no claim to authority. I am not an initiate of the Society of the Inner Light, and my sole qualifications for writing this commentary are the years I have spent reading, studying, and meditating on this text, as well as Dion Fortune's other works and the literature of the Western mystery tradition generally. I've doubtless made many errors in what follows. If this volume helps students of the Western mystery tradition to understand one of its classic texts a little better, it will have done what I wanted it to do.

## Using this book

To make sense of what follows, you'll need to have a copy of *The Cosmic Doctrine* to hand. There are two widely available editions of the text, the Revised Edition, first published in 1966, and the Millennium Edition, first published in 1995, which reprints the original privately printed edition of 1949. Either one can be used to follow the discussion in this book. The text varies somewhat between the two editions, but the concepts and images are the same, and the commentary refers to both. In those places where the Millennium Edition refers to material not covered by the Revised Edition, I have outlined that material in the commentary.

As already noted, *The Cosmic Doctrine* is heavy going, especially for those who don't have any previous exposure to occult philosophy. It's useful to read through each chapter once or twice, trying to get an overview, but after that, it's best taken a little at a time. For most students, it is best to spend an entire month on each chapter, and to set aside five or ten minutes a day during that month to work on the text. During that daily session, take one short paragraph or half of a long one, read it closely, and think about what you've read, while picturing in your mind's eye the imagery that the text assigns to the concepts under discussion. Let images and ideas surface in response; it is helpful to write these down in a notebook and return to them at intervals. If you have already established a regular meditation practice, of course, exploring the text and its imagery as a series of themes for meditation is highly recommended—this is the method that Fortune herself assigned to the students who received the original version of *The Cosmic Doctrine*, and it has lost none of its value since her time.

## A note on authorship

Dion Fortune presented *The Cosmic Doctrine* to her students as a communication from one of the Greater Masters, a being whose soul had long since finished its pilgrimage through material incarnation and had risen to a very high level of spiritual advancement. I have no doubt that Fortune received the text through trance mediumship, as her considerable talents in that branch of occult practice are well documented. In her time, for that matter, receiving texts in that manner was common practice—a great many of the significant figures of the early twentieth-century British occult scene produced texts in this way, with Aleister Crowley's *The Book of the Law* (received 1904) and *A Vision* by Georgie Yeats and William Butler Yeats (received 1917–1925) as two of the most famous examples of the process.

Be that as it may, in the pages that follow I have treated the text as Fortune's own work. This is partly a recognition of the complex nature of trance writings, which (whatever their ultimate source) come through the mind of the individual who copies them down and are inevitably shaped thereby. Partly, however, it reflects the fact that *The Cosmic Doctrine* stands or falls on the value of the ideas that it communicates, not on the source of those ideas. We have had ample experience since Fortune's time, of writing that claimed to be from exalted spiritual personages and turned out to be nonsense or worse. *The Cosmic Doctrine* does not need the additional support of a claim to supernatural origin. Whether it was written by one of the Greater Masters or by Dion Fortune's own subconscious mind, its creator had things to say that are well worth hearing.

# PART I

## COSMIC EVOLUTION

CHAPTER ONE

# The Dawn of Manifestation

## Reading

Revised Edition:  Chapter 1, "The Dawn of Manifestation," p. 11–13.
Millennium Edition:  Chapter 1, "The First Manifestation," p. 19
through the first (partial) paragraph on p. 22.

## Commentary

Before we launch into the text, a couple of notes may be helpful. First, for those readers who haven't tackled a work of philosophy before, *The Cosmic Doctrine* is not light reading. You know the habits of reading you use when you're reading for pleasure—reading quickly and uncritically, letting the words weave someone else's daydreams in your mind? Those will emphatically not cut it here.

To grasp what a work of philosophy has to say, you need to go through it word by word, thought by thought, alert to the implications, watching for multiple meanings. That's why I recommend that you take an entire month to work through a chapter three pages long—and why it's going to take a long time to move out of what seems like profoundly abstract territory into something that seems more practical in nature.

3

(That's an illusion; the material we'll be covering in this first chapter has immense practical applicability, but that may not be evident for a while.)

Second, this is a work of *occult* philosophy. It's meant to teach you how to think in ways that don't come naturally to the untrained mind. What's more, everything you've absorbed from the habitual mental chatter of our society might as well be designed to stop you from thinking the way this book is meant to teach you to think. The habits of thinking taught by the habitual mental chatter of society also have their place, but if that's the only kind of thinking you know how to do, you're stuck with a very narrow range of cognitive options. *The Cosmic Doctrine* will give you a much more extensive mental toolkit, and there are things you can do with it that you can't do at all from within the stifling confines of modern materialist thinking.

To get anything at all out of *The Cosmic Doctrine*, though, you're going to have to work at it, and stretch your mind in ways it may not like stretching at first. The comparison with physical exercise is a useful one: if you happen to be out of shape, your first workout is going to leave you feeling pretty uncomfortable, but if you persevere you'll get past that discomfort and gain both enjoyment and a significant increase in health and strength.

The method this book uses to teach you how to think unfamiliar thoughts is one that was once very common in occult literature, though it's fallen out of fashion in recent decades. "In these occult teachings," says our text, "you will be given certain images, under which you are instructed to think of certain things. These images are not descriptive but symbolic, *and are designed to train the mind, not to inform it.*" If you've ever wondered why books of alchemy show enigmatic images and follow them with equally cryptic text, or why Manly P. Hall's famous *The Secret Teachings of All Ages* starts each chapter with an elaborate color plate which may or may not have anything obvious to do with the topic of the chapter—well, now you know.

The images in *The Cosmic Doctrine* aren't presented in the form of lavishly illustrated color plates, and there's a reason for that. Remember that this book was originally privately published, and issued only to members of Dion Fortune's magical order, the Fraternity (now Society) of the Inner Light, as an aid to training. Being able to imagine things clearly is one of the basic skills of the operative mage. Whether or not you have that skill now is immaterial. As with anything else, you get it by practicing, and *The Cosmic Doctrine* will give you plenty of opportunities for practice.

Let's begin. Take the paragraph at the beginning of the chapter (paragraph 3 of the Millennium Edition) that begins, "The Unmanifest is pure existence." Read through it once quickly to get the general shape of it, then again, slowly, thinking through each sentence. If you're puzzled by some of it, or even by all of it, that's a sign that you're paying attention!

Now follow the advice of the last sentence in the paragraph. Spend a while imagining interstellar space: pure empty vastness without stars or planets. Now go through a few sentences of the paragraph, keeping the image of interstellar space in mind. At every point, refer the thoughts back to the image. As you do—and it may happen quickly, or it may take repeated effort—you'll begin to get a clearer sense of what the text is saying about the Unmanifest.

The same method applies at every point in *The Cosmic Doctrine*. The images start off simple and obvious, and end up complex and subtle, but all the way through, if you picture the images in your mind and then think through the text in relation to them, you'll have a much better shot at getting what Fortune is trying to say to you, and the text will also accomplish its primary purpose—"to train the mind, not to inform it."

With that in mind, let's proceed. The first concept presented is the Unmanifest. Most occult philosophies, and a great many of the non-occult kind as well, include a discussion of what the ancient Greeks called the *archē*, the basic "stuff" of existence. In Fortune's account, that's the Unmanifest, "a state of pure 'being,' without qualities and without history," that is "best conceived of under the image of interstellar space."

One useful way to think about philosophies is to count how many basic realities they posit at the foundation of existence. Usually, the head count of realities comes to 0, 1, or 2. Philosophies that opt for 0, which can be called nihilist philosophies, see all apparent things as mere illusions and the sole reality as the void. Philosophiles that opt for 1, monist philosophies, see the universe in terms of some single "stuff" of which all things are modifications. Philosophies that opt for 2, dualist philosophies, hold that there are two kinds of "stuff" out of which all things are made—for example, spirit and matter.

Fortune falls squarely in the monist camp—but it's monism with a twist. For her, there's one fundamental "stuff," the Unmanifest, but its characteristics make it resemble the void that's the ultimate reality according to nihilist philosophies. The Unmanifest *is*, but its mode of being is so unimaginable to us that we can best think of it as the closest thing to nonbeing any of us can imagine, the empty vastness of interstellar space.

Is this true? Is the Unmanifest actually the basis for everything that we experience? Ahem. "These images are not descriptive but symbolic, and are designed to train the mind, not to inform it." It's one of the more embarrassing examples of human hubris to think that our brains, which evolved for such intellectually undemanding tasks as finding food and mates on the East African savanna, are capable of understanding the foundations of existence itself. This is why philosophy presents us, not with One True Answer, but with a variety of accounts of the world, some of which are more useful for certain purposes or more congenial to certain personalities than others. *The Cosmic Doctrine* is one account: an account very useful for certain purposes. What these purposes are will be explored in more detail as we go.

"The Unmanifest is the only Unity," our text goes on to say. "Manifestation begins when duality occurs." Duality—or, to give it another name, polarity—is the most important theme in *The Cosmic Doctrine*. The short paragraphs that follow outline our first sketch of polarity, by way of the usual interplay of image and idea. Imagine interstellar space, and then imagine some of it beginning to flow, forming a current—a current of space, in space, moving through space from space to space. Now imagine the two forces playing on the movement—the slightly stronger desire of space for momentum and the slightly weaker desire of space for inertia; imagine the second force pulling slightly on the first, making it curve; imagine the curve extended over immense distances until the current becomes a vast ring—the Ring-Cosmos.

There's your second image. The paragraphs that describe the formation of the Ring-Cosmos give you the ideas to think about under that image. All this is metaphor, as the text says; put another way, it's one account of the basic nature of things. Notice what it implies: that every act of creation unfolds from the intersection of two opposite and *un*equal forces.

This last point can be developed at great length. In his book, *The Power of Limits*, the architect and sacred geometer Györgi Doczi gave this interplay of opposed unequal forces the name "dinergy," and showed that beauty and creativity in nature and human art can best be understood as an expression of dinergy. Look at the exquisite arc made by a blade of grass bending in the wind: the arc comes into being from the interplay of the force of the wind and the weaker but still significant resistance of the grass. That's dinergy—and it's also what Fortune is talking about, as the two forces transform a current in space into a Ring-Cosmos.

With that in mind, let's go back to our text. Once the Ring-Cosmos is established, it begins to draw more empty space into its flow, and the Ring-Cosmos turns into a spinning disk. Think of it as the spinning wheel in a gyroscope, or an old-fashioned vinyl record spinning on a turntable. As it spins, it sets up stresses in the empty space beyond its outer edge, and those stresses eventually set another current of space in motion at right angles to the original current. If you picture the Ring-Cosmos as spinning horizontally, like an LP on a turntable, imagine the second current starting out vertically from a space beyond one edge of the Ring-Cosmos. The same paired forces have the same effect on the second current as on the first, so it curves as it flows, arcing over the Ring-Cosmos, descending vertically past it off beyond its far side, and then circling back beneath the Ring-Cosmos to return to its starting point.

That gives you two rings: the Ring-Cosmos and the Ring-Chaos, spinning at right angles to each other. The Ring-Cosmos is a disk; the Ring-Chaos is a ring outside the disk at right angles to the plane in which the disk spins—all, as our text says, to the nearest approximate metaphor. ("These images are not descriptive but symbolic ...") Once again we have a polarity, just as we did when space first started flowing ... and once again the dinergy between the two opposed but unequal forces gives rise to something new.

In the metaphor that Fortune uses, "something new" is represented by movement. What happens in the metaphor is that the Ring-Cosmos begins to pivot. Our text asks you to visualize the disk of the Ring-Cosmos as having an upper and a lower surface, and the upper surface on the outgoing arc (the first half of the original Ring-Cosmos, which it made by flowing away from its starting point) is attracted to the Ring-Chaos, while the lower surface is repelled by the Ring-Chaos; on the incoming arc, the attraction and repulsion are arranged the other way. This is metaphor, again, but it has quite a bit to teach; it's not only in cosmological metaphors, after all, that every attraction is balanced by a repulsion and every repulsion by an attraction, and that these alternate at various points of any creative process.

I've found that some students have a hard time visualizing the third movement that results, so we'll shift metaphors a bit. Imagine the Ring-Cosmos as a flat horizontal disk of metal. Imagine the Ring-Chaos as a ring of metal larger than the disk, positioned vertically so that the disk fits inside it, and the two touch at two points, where the ring passes just outside the disk. Imagine that the ring and the disk are connected at those two points by a pair of pins on which the disk can pivot. Now imagine the disk pivoting on those pins, one side rising up, the other dipping down, until the disk is in the same vertical plane as the ring—but the disk keeps pivoting, so that the side that rose is now dipping and that which was dipping begins to rise. The disk moves faster and faster, and as it moves its outer edge traces a sphere.

That sphere is the Ring-Pass-Not, the third of the Rings that define a Cosmos. The Ring-Cosmos is primary; the Ring-Chaos takes shape in response to it, as a function of the resistance of space; the Ring-Pass-Not takes shape out of the interaction between the other two rings, as a function of their mutual attraction and repulsion. Spend some time imagining the whole process as clearly as you can, all the way from the first movement of space to the formation of the Ring-Pass-Not. Then imagine it again, and think through each part of the text that describes the process, until you have some sense of how it all works.

Then apply what you've learned to something else—say, an interaction between two people. The Ring-Cosmos is set in motion by the initial action that brings them into contact. The Ring-Chaos is set in motion by the initial reaction to that first action. Over time, the interplay between action and reaction leads to the creation of a boundary— the Ring-Pass-Not—that defines the interplay between them. In the language of systems theory, these are action, reaction, and equilibrium; in the traditions of the Cabala, they are the three pillars of Force, Form, and Balance; in the symbolism of Masonry, they are the three pillars of Strength, Wisdom, and Beauty. Other symbolic systems have their own ways of talking about the same things.

It's crucial to understand the relative roles of the Ring-Cosmos and Ring-Chaos, and Fortune uses a deft bit of discussion to help you grasp that. The last paragraph of the chapter—in the Millennium Edition, this is the last paragraph on page 21, spilling over onto page 22—is the one to follow here. (In both, it begins "The secondary spin of the Ring-Pass-Not …") Here Fortune assigns several descriptive labels to the

Ring-Chaos. It's the prime stillness of the Cosmos; it's the thrust-block that resists the force of the Cosmos; finally, it's the Prime Evil.

The pun here ("primeval") is quite deliberate, of course, but so is the moral reference. From within the boundary of the Ring-Pass-Not, the Ring-Chaos represents everything the Cosmos is not; it represents the primal void out of which the Cosmos takes shape. It represents these things, but it is not these things. The Ring-Chaos, remember, comes into being *after* the Ring-Cosmos, and in relation to it. It is the reaction to its action, the pushback of the Unmanifest against that first movement of flowing space and everything that unfolds from it.

That pushback is also the original form of what we call evil. The question of evil has bedeviled philosophers for a very long time. It's especially challenging for thinkers who are committed to those monotheist faiths that claim the universe was created by one and only one almighty, omniscient, and infinitely loving deity; a vast number of unsatisfactory arguments have been deployed to try to explain why such a deity would have created a world as well-stocked with misery and brutality as the one we experience. *The Cosmic Doctrine*, as we'll see, does not posit deity in those terms, but it also proposes a distinctive vision of the purpose of evil.

Evil, in Fortune's account, is a thrust-block. It's the thing we resist and push off from in order to go somewhere else and do something else. The nature of evil, and the ways that the initiate uses it as a way to get traction, will be discussed in quite a bit more detail in the chapters ahead, and this will also involve an exploration of the difference between evil as inertia ("negative evil") and evil as actions on the part of conscious entities that follow the current of the Ring-Chaos rather than the Ring-Cosmos ("positive evil"). The point to take away here is that evil is the friction exerted by the Unmanifest, the resistance that allows the action to happen.

# CHAPTER TWO

# The Forces of (Negative) Evil

## Reading

Revised Edition:  Chapter 2, "The Forces of (Negative) Evil," p. 14–17.

Millennium Edition:  Chapter 1, "The First Manifestation," from the first complete paragraph on p. 22 through the end of the chapter on p. 25.

## Commentary

We pick up where we left off, with the Ring-Cosmos spinning in one plane, the Ring-Chaos spinning just outside it in a plane at right angles to the first, and the Ring-Pass-Not marking the boundary between them. In the diagram, the Ring-Cosmos is the light-colored ring, the Ring-Chaos the dark-colored ring, and the Ring-Pass-Not the dotted circle.

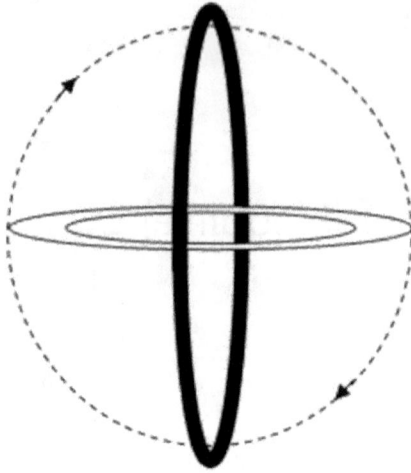

3Rings

When you imagine the three Rings for the purposes of this chapter, it's helpful to keep them in this orientation, with each of them at right angles to the other two. Yes, I know that the Ring-Cosmos pivots around as shown by the little arrows, but symbolically speaking—and these are symbols, remember, meant to train the mind rather than to inform it—the rings stand at right angles to one another. Much of the discussion in this chapter will make more sense if that's kept in mind.

The two versions of our text differ here in some details, but the basic concepts are the same in both cases. The first thing to work on, as you think your way through this chapter, is the series of distinctions between the Ring-Cosmos and the Ring-Chaos, or (which is the same thing) between evolution and devolution. (These aren't the words I would have used, but then I didn't write our text.) To Fortune, "evolution" means movement toward complexity and integration, and "devolution" means movement toward simplicity and disintegration. These two factors balance each other; they are the yang and yin of *The Cosmic Doctrine*'s Cosmos.

It's helpful to spend some time learning to think about the universe in this way—to see every existing thing as held in balance between the centripetal force of the Ring-Cosmos and the centrifugal force of the Ring-Chaos, between the pull toward complexity and the pull toward simplicity, between integration and disintegration. That balance has a cyclic component to it, but we'll be getting into that later in the text. For now, try to think of the world as the interplay of these two forces working at right angles to each other.

Fortune calls these forces "Good" and "Evil." Notice, though, that she immediately undercuts that seemingly straightforward statement by saying that they "are not 'good' and 'evil' as you understand these terms, but merely spinning circles of force at right angles to each other." This kind of paradoxical speech is of course immensely common in occult writings, and in the writings of every other branch of spirituality that deals with states of consciousness.

She's also doing a bait-and-switch job here, though that's only clear from the title of the chapter in the Revised Edition. We're talking about negative evil here. Negative evil? That's evil as inertia, evil as the force that resists the creative movement of the Ring-Cosmos. There's also positive evil, the actions of individual beings working along the same angle as the Ring-Chaos. This is much closer to the conventional notion of evil, but that's not discussed in this chapter. Negative evil is far more basic, and so it comes up for discussion first.

Here as elsewhere, Fortune is trying to jolt the reader out of habitual ways of thinking—in this case, the common notion that of course we know exactly what good and evil are, that they're whatever our cultural (or subcultural, or countercultural) presuppositions inspire us to love and hate respectively, and that we can get rid of evil (or we could, if only those bad people over there stopped being bad people, or simply stopped being). At the time *The Cosmic Doctrine* was written, such notions were just as fashionable as they are now, and just as counterproductive.

At the heart of those fashionable confusions, then as now, is the assumption that good and evil are objective universal qualities of things: in a word, they're facts rather than values. Let's take a moment to unpack that distinction. If I say, "it's raining here in East Providence this evening," that purports to be a statement of fact, and if you were standing on the corner of James Street and Taunton Avenue a stone's throw from my apartment on the evening in question, you would be able to tell whether it was actually a statement of fact or not.

Now let's imagine that you have a garden and I have a hay meadow next to each other on the outskirts of East Providence on the evening in question. It's shaping up to be a hot, dry summer, and as the clouds begin to spit down rain, you look at your garden and say, "Oh, good, it's raining." At the same moment, I look at my hay meadow, knowing that rain will spoil the newly mown hay, and say, "Oh, crap, it's raining." For you, rain is good; for me, it's evil.

That's where we cross the boundary between a fact and a value. Where a statement of fact says something about the objective properties of a thing, a statement of value says something about the subjective relationship of an observer to that thing. Good and evil are values, not facts, because something can never simply be good or evil; it must always be good or evil to someone, good or evil for something, and so on.

Does that mean that good and evil are whatever you say they are? This is where Fortune's analysis hits its stride. Good and evil, in her metaphor, are always relative to a Cosmos; good is the plane in which the Ring-Cosmos forms, and evil is the plane in which the Ring-Chaos forms. A different Cosmos will have its Ring-Cosmos and Ring-Chaos in different planes, and so good and evil may mean something completely different there. Note, though, that from within a given Cosmos, the original angles of its rings are absolutes. If you're part of that Cosmos, you can't change them; all you can do is respond to them.

As we'll see, furthermore, everything is a Cosmos. Your garden and my hay meadow are Cosmoi—yes, that's the plural of Cosmos—with their Rings at different angles, so that rain that evening is at the angle of your garden's Ring-Cosmos and my hay meadow's Ring-Chaos. Everything that exists has its own Ring-Cosmos, Ring-Chaos, and Ring-Pass-Not; put another way, everything that exists is in a state of equilibrium between a set of forces that tend to sustain it and a set of forces that tend to dissolve it. At every scale of being, the same pattern repeats.

This is one of many places where *The Cosmic Doctrine* does a remarkable job of anticipating a body of knowledge that didn't really come into being until after Dion Fortune's death. Systems theory was a product of the decade following the Second World War; it was newborn when *The Cosmic Doctrine* was first privately published in 1949, and didn't exist when Fortune penned the original manuscript in 1923 and 1924— and yet many of the core concepts in our text are also core concepts of systems theory. Did Fortune read some of the first tentative writings that laid the foundations of systems theory, such as Jan Smuts' *Holism and Evolution*? Or was Charles Fort right to argue that human creativity is subject to something like seasonal cycles, so that ideas crop up in various minds when it's time for them to appear? It's an interesting question.

One way or another, we can make good sense of Fortune's discussion of good and evil if we take the word "Cosmos" and replace it with the word "system." What is a system? There are various definitions in systems theory, but the most useful here is that a system is a set of self-sustaining interactions among a definable group of things. Quite a bit of systems theory talks about the way that systems find an equilibrium between anabolic processes (those that move toward complexity and integration, i.e., the Ring-Cosmos) and catabolic processes (those that move toward simplicity and disintegration, i.e., the Ring-Chaos), but I want to focus on a different point here.

Systems unite into greater systems and subdivide into smaller systems. From the viewpoint of systems theory, you are a system; you are made up of systems (your nervous system, your digestive system, etc.), which are made up of systems called tissues, which are made up of systems called cells, and so on. Going the other direction, you are part of a system called a community, which is part of a system called a nation, which is part of a system called humanity, and so on. Each of those systems, in Fortune's terms, is a Cosmos with its own set of rings.

So those labels "good" and "evil" can be applied to a great many rings going at a great many angles. You are part of some of those systems, and how much influence you have over them varies dramatically from case to case. Some of those systems, of course, are also part of you, and your digestive system (for example) may well have its own ideas about what is good and what is evil! Then there are other systems that are distinct from you, and exist independently in one of the larger systems to which you already belong. Each of these are Cosmoi. Each has its own good and evil, just as you have, and your interactions with all of these nested systems define your life.

Good and evil in the usual moral sense of the words are simply the Ring-Cosmos and Ring-Chaos of the culture (or subculture, or counterculture) in which you happen to have been born, or in which you now live. Notice how this works: if you do the things that your culture (etc.) considers good, you will end up more deeply integrated into it; if you do the things that your culture (etc.) considers evil, you will probably end up either removing yourself from it or being removed from it—in either case, you're following the Ring-Chaos, which is a suction toward outer space.

If you've had the experience of leaving one subculture and ending up in another, as so many people do these days, you know what it's like to drift quickly or slowly out of line with the rest of the subculture, to spiral out to the edge of the Ring-Pass-Not, and then one day to find that you're on the outside looking in and nothing inside really makes sense to you any more. Take Fortune's metaphors and apply them to that experience, and the abstract structure of Rings and angles may be a little less abstract thereafter.

Let's move on. In the last page and a half or so of the chapter we're studying, Fortune takes her analysis of evil and builds on it in a way that many people find counterintuitive, even threatening. She suggests that there are basically two ways of dealing with negative evil: you can oppose it in order to lock it into place and make it permanent, and then do something with that; or you can draw back from it in order to let it follow its natural trajectory to the Ring-Pass-Not, where it will dissolve back into raw substance and go away.

We don't think like this in modern Western cultures. Our basic assumption is that if you want any kind of evil to go away, you fight it and destroy it, and if you want it to stick around, you back away from it and let it follow its trajectory. That's deeply ingrained into our thinking, and probably explains why we're so bad at dealing with evil.

Evil in the terms we're using, remember, doesn't mean whatever you happen to hate. Negative evil, which is what we're discussing, is the circle of force at right angles to the current of evolution, the suction toward dissolution and the void. There are certainly things you and I don't like that can't be met with the strategies Fortune offers, but then they're not what she's talking about when she speaks of negative evil.

I'd like to ask every reader to go over the paragraph above at least three times, and make an effort to remember it. I've noticed that in studying *The Cosmic Doctrine*, this is one of the places where brain cramps hit the largest number of people. They read the concept I've just reviewed, they seem to understand it, and then five seconds later they start babbling about Nazis: Nazis this and Nazis that and the Nazis couldn't have been stopped by letting them follow their trajectory to the Ring-Pass-Not, blah blah blah.

Ahem. We're not talking about Nazism, or any of the manifestations of positive evil. We're talking about negative evil, the Cosmic principle of disintegration and devolution in terms of a set of abstract symbols; the practical applications of those symbols, and the discussion of positive evil, will follow in due time. As it happens, Dion Fortune took on Adolf Hitler and his Nazi minions in magical combat, and won; what's more, she did it using the exact strategy she laid out in the chapter you're reading. You can find the details in the book *The Magical Battle of Britain*, which makes a good sequel to our present text.

You can do the same two things noted above when you have to deal with positive evil, i.e., with persons or forces within a Cosmos that are moving in harmony with the Ring-Chaos of that Cosmos. You can use them as a thrust-block, something to push against so that you have traction for something you want to do. Alternatively, you can evade them, and let them follow their own trajectory right out to the void. Both of those work, though they work in different ways. Both of them also require skill and a good sense of timing.

Interestingly, this is something that martial artists know well. If you're a competent martial artist and somebody throws a punch at you, you can do one of two things. You can block the punch, and use that moment of hard contact between your bodies as a thrust-block to give power to your own response. Alternatively, you can evade the punch so that the other guy wastes his energy in empty air, and then do something while he's flailing. Different martial arts (and different martial artists) specialize in one or the other of these, and take it in various directions; one may use a hard block to stop the other guy's fist and then kick him in the face while the impact has him off balance; another may slip neatly out of the way of the punch and then add a graceful push at exactly the wrong moment, so that the other guy loses his balance and has a sudden face-first encounter with the ground. Either way, Fortune's rules work.

Either way, too, you're using evil for your own purposes. That doesn't mean that you move in harmony with it, in the plane of the Ring-Chaos; that's what Fortune has in mind when she warns about working dynamically with evil. Instead, you use evil as a static presence, either to propel yourself along the track of the Ring-Cosmos, or to take something out of existence for you. That's one of the secrets of the initiates: since negative evil is always present, you might as well do things with it, and this is how you do things with it without getting caught up in it.

It helps, by the way, if you make sure that you're actually moving in the same plane as the Ring-Cosmos of your system. Few things are so common in human life as a person or a group of people who are so sure they're on the side of the angels that they never bother to check, and it's quite possible for two parties in bitterest contention with each other—at right angles to each other, in Fortune's symbolism—to be equally far from the Ring-Cosmos. That's common in situations when a conflict remains stuck in place for a long time; since they're equally balanced between the two primary Rings, neither side wins, and neither side dissolves. Their opposition remains as solid as concrete.

You oppose something when you want to lock it into place in order to build on it; as some schools of psychology like to point out, "what you resist, persists." You evade something when you want to send it spinning out past your Ring-Pass-Not. Choose carefully which of these you want to do, because the results will not be the same.

# CHAPTER THREE

# The Twelve Rays and the Seven Cosmic Planes

## Reading

Revised Edition: Chapter 3, "The Twelve Rays and the Seven Cosmic Planes," p. 18–22.

Millennium Edition: Chapter 2, "The First Trinity," pp. 26–31, and the first three paragraphs of the following chapter.

## Commentary

This is an extremely complex chapter in which a great many concepts are covered very briefly, so we'll take things a step at a time. We pick up again where we left off, with the three great Rings—the Ring-Chaos, the Ring-Cosmos, and the Ring-Pass-Not—all in place. As mentioned already, it's useful for what follows to imagine them at right angles to one another, as shown in the diagram in the last chapter.

The text summarizes the points already made about the three Rings, and stresses that only the Ring-Cosmos can create anything, because the forces of the Ring-Chaos diffuse outward into infinity. The Ring-Cosmos has a limit—the Ring-Pass-Not—which prevents its forces from diffusing. Instead, they act and interact among themselves and produce complexity. Notice here one of the fundamental principles of esoteric philosophy: creation requires limitation. To bring something into being is to accept limits. To reject limits is to guarantee that whatever you do will dissolve uselessly into the void.

This is a very difficult concept for most people nowadays to grasp. Now, as in Dion Fortune's time, a great deal of pop spirituality fixates on the notion that limits are always bad and that you can and should free yourself of all limits. There's a certain value to these teachings, since a great many people limit themselves in an assortment of self-defeating ways. Believing that there are no limits can help people shake off limiting beliefs that they've absorbed from their parents, teachers, or culture, and accomplish things they didn't believe they could do. The difficulty here is, first, that unfairly limiting beliefs aren't the only kind of limits that exist, and second, that believing that there are no limits itself imposes certain very sharp limits on those who hold this belief.

One of the many cats Dion Fortune let out of the bag in *The Cosmic Doctrine*—discussed in Chapter 25—is the reason why the fixation on limitlessness became so widespread in twentieth-century pop spirituality: it was one way for occult groups to create a readily accessible pool of force that could be directed by the group's adepts. There were a number of gimmicks that will do this, and most of the big public occult groups of the time used one or more of them relentlessly, teaching exercises to the largest possible number of novices that mostly functioned as ways to charge the pool of forces, and then selecting from among the novices the few who had the discipline, intelligence, and commitment to become adepts themselves and work with the pool of forces.

This doesn't have to be done in a secretive and abusive manner. The more reputable occult schools, Dion Fortune's among them, were quite open about what they were doing, and explained to participants how their contributions of force would be used. Churches by and large used to do the same thing. Read Christian writings about group worship from before the First World War, and very often the concept of group prayer as a source of energy is all but spelled out. Of course, you then have to have priests or ministers who know what to do with the energy thus collected, and that's become increasingly rare as today's churches embrace modern, up-to-date, cutting-edge notions of clergy training that guarantee that the clergy thus trained will have no clue about the magical dimensions of the ceremonies they perform.

It doesn't help that many of the ceremonies in question have been revised by people who were guided by fashionable notions of relevance rather than any grasp of magical principles, and that many of the practices given to the laity to guide their end of the work have been abolished or neglected due to reforms with similar motivations. In some denominations, as a result, the services no longer bring in any energy at all, and you get at best a pleasant gathering with some moral platitudes thrown in for seasoning, and at worst one of those undead churches that would not feel noticeably different if the minister and congregation had all been expertly embalmed.

In other denominations, the energy still comes in, but since no one knows what to do with it any more, it sits unused and turns stagnant. It usually ends up discharging through the clergy using the normal outlet of the life force, and another sexual scandal is the normal result. I'm not sure how many people realize that the decrease in miracles and the increase in sexual scandals among clergy have an identical cause, but from the point of view of occult philosophy, it's obvious.

*The Cosmic Doctrine*, though, was written for those who want to work with power, not for those who simply want to sit in the congregation and contribute power for the person up front to work with. If you want to work with power, you need to understand what, in a later chapter, Fortune will call the Law of Limitation. The principles that underlie that law are the ones we've been covering in the two chapters we've read already.

You embrace limitation when you want to create and sustain something; you release limitation when you want something to dissolve into the void. As you create and sustain something, though, it takes on unexpected qualities. In the metaphoric language of our text, the forces we're discussing are movements of empty space, but as movement reaches its maximum complexity it produces a second kind of activity, which our text describes as light; when light, in turn, reaches its maximum complexity it produces a third kind of activity, which our text describes as sound.

This is one of the places where it's crucial to remember that *The Cosmic Doctrine* is a system of metaphors meant to teach occult philosophy, not a physics textbook. In physics, movement doesn't create light, and light doesn't create sound, except in certain jerry-rigged instances. In the metaphor we're using—a metaphor Fortune took from early twentieth-century Rosicrucian sources—things are otherwise, and it's worth spending time imagining movement creating light and light creating sound, and then considering what this might mean. One point of the metaphor is that movement, color, and sound comprise the three primary tools of the operative mage, and are combined in even the simplest magical working. Another point of the metaphor, more broadly applicable than the first, is that activity of one form can cause activity in other forms, and if you're not paying attention, this can blindside you.

As force begets force, and the movements of the Ring-Cosmos flow back inward toward the center of the spinning disk, the simple spinning movement described earlier breaks apart into a cascade of more complex movements, accompanied by light and sound. The first set of these complex movements are the twelve Rays, which radiate from the center to the circumference and return to the center again. Our text calls them "a set of revolving spirals," which may be confusing unless you know that the words "spiral" and "helix" were treated as interchangeable by a great many authors in Dion Fortune's time. The Rays are streams of force that spin around their own axis of movement as they flow out from the center and return to it, and the meeting of the Rays in the center turns the center into a great cauldron of energies—in Fortune's language, the Central Sun.

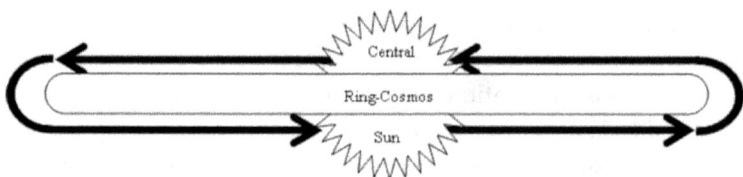

Central

Ring-Cosmos

Sun

RayMotion

Each Ray is paired with the Ray that flows out in the opposite direction. For the purpose of the metaphor, the energies of the Ring-Cosmos are imagined as a disk spinning around the Central Sun. Of each pair of Rays, one flows out along the upper surface of the disk and returns along the lower, while the other flows out along the lower surface and returns along the upper.

"This is a very deep truth, closely related to practical occultism," notes Fortune. When she says something evasive and portentous like this, by the way, you can take it for granted that she's hinting at polarity magic, the mode of magical working with sexual energies that was central to her inner teachings. You'll find the basic theory, including an explanation of what she's hinting at here, in her book *The Esoteric Philosophy of Love and Marriage*.

So we've got the spinning disk of energies with Twelve Rays flowing out from the Central Sun and returning to it. The movements of the Rays then set up stresses in the disk that divide it into seven concentric rings. These are the seven Circles, which are also the seven Cosmic Planes. It's important not to mistake these for the seven planes discussed in practical occultism; as we'll see, the Cosmos is the whole of which individual solar systems (in Fortune's terms, "universes") are tiny parts, and the seven planes that you and I can work with belong to our own solar system, which exists in its entirety on the seventh Cosmic Plane.

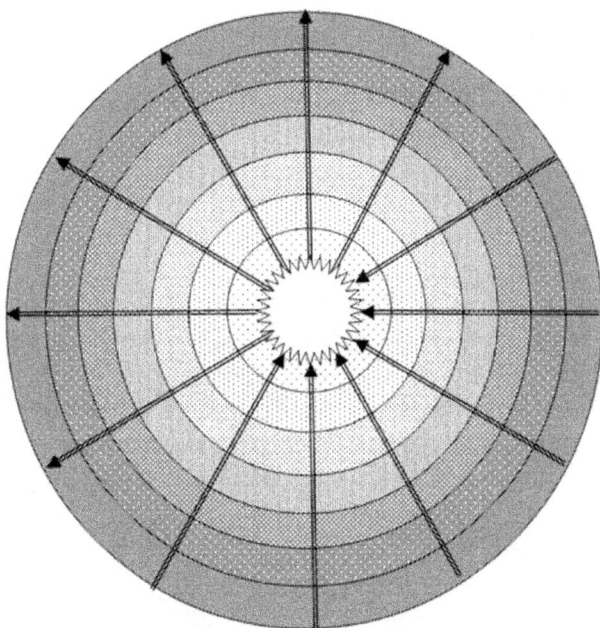

Rays and Circles

With the development of the seven Cosmic Planes, the evolution of the Cosmos is complete. The three Rings, seven Cosmic Planes, and Twelve Rays form the background to everything else that happens. (Those of my readers who know anything about the Cabala know exactly where these numbers come from and what they refer to; those who don't, can find the details in Dion Fortune's book *The Mystical Qabalah* or my book *Paths of Wisdom*.) It's what happens within that framework that will concern us from here on in.

What happens within that framework, first of all, is that the movements of the Rays as they cross the spinning Circles set off additional movements in space, which our text calls "Tangentials." The Tangentials are brief movements of space that flow off at various angles, and when there are enough of them in a given region of the Cosmos, they collide with each other. (In Chapter 4, Fortune explains that this happens where the Rays intersect with one another to form the Central Sun.) When two Tangentials set in motion by different Rays collide, they deflect each other's motion, and start spinning around each other, forming a stable unit. Notice here another of the fundamental principles of esoteric philosophy: when you oppose something, you lock it into place, and you lock yourself into a relationship with it.

Two tangential movements spinning around each other, locked into relationship with each other, and forming a single vortex: this is a prime atom. This is another of those places where it's important to remember that *The Cosmic Doctrine* is not a physics textbook; the atoms we're discussing aren't the kind that physicists study. They are metaphors, remember, meant to train the mind rather than inform it.

The prime atoms are the building blocks from which everything else in the Cosmos is made. Some of them, as we'll see, remain prime atoms, but others interact with other prime atoms and form composite atoms. The process is the same as the one that formed the prime atoms: two prime atoms collide, deflect each other's motion, and start spinning around each other, forming a stable unit. The process continues as the composite atoms absorb more influences and become more complex. Eventually, in place of a simple spinning, you get a pattern of motion that approximates an angular figure, with from three to ten sides.

The atoms, prime and composite, then sort themselves out through something not too far from centrifugal motion. Those prime atoms that remain unattached stay in the Central Sun. Those that have become composite begin to drift outwards, and settle out into one of the seven Circles: the three-sided composite atoms into the circle just outside the Central Sun, the four-sided atoms into the next circle out, and so on, out to the nine-sided atoms, which fill the seventh Circle. And the ten-sided ones? We'll get to those in a later chapter.

Toward the end of the chapter, Fortune drops two broad hints. The first is the recapitulation that assigns the numbers 1 through 5 to five different movements covered in *The Cosmic Doctrine*, and thence to five basic concepts. Those concepts are among other things the first five of the ten Spheres of the Tree of Life, seen from a particular point of view, and those of my readers who know their way around Cabalistic symbolism may find it interesting to explore the Tree of Life from this standpoint.

The second is one of the few places she gets close to explaining a concept that pervades *The Cosmic Doctrine* but is never quite explained in so many words. You will remember from Chapter 1 that the Ring-Cosmos rotates relative to the Ring-Chaos, and that this rotation forms the Ring-Pass-Not. You will also remember from Chapter 2 that the angle in which the Ring-Cosmos starts moving originally defines "good" for that Cosmos, while the angle of the Ring-Chaos, which is perpendicular to the original angle of the Ring-Cosmos, defines "evil."

As the Ring-Cosmos rotates, in other words, it gradually approaches the angle of the Ring-Chaos, then passes through that angle and out the other side, diverging from it until it returns to its original angle (though it's turned over and is therefore upside down and spinning in the opposite direction). Then, as it turns further, it approaches the angle of the Ring-Chaos again, passes through it, and returns to its original angle in its original orientation.

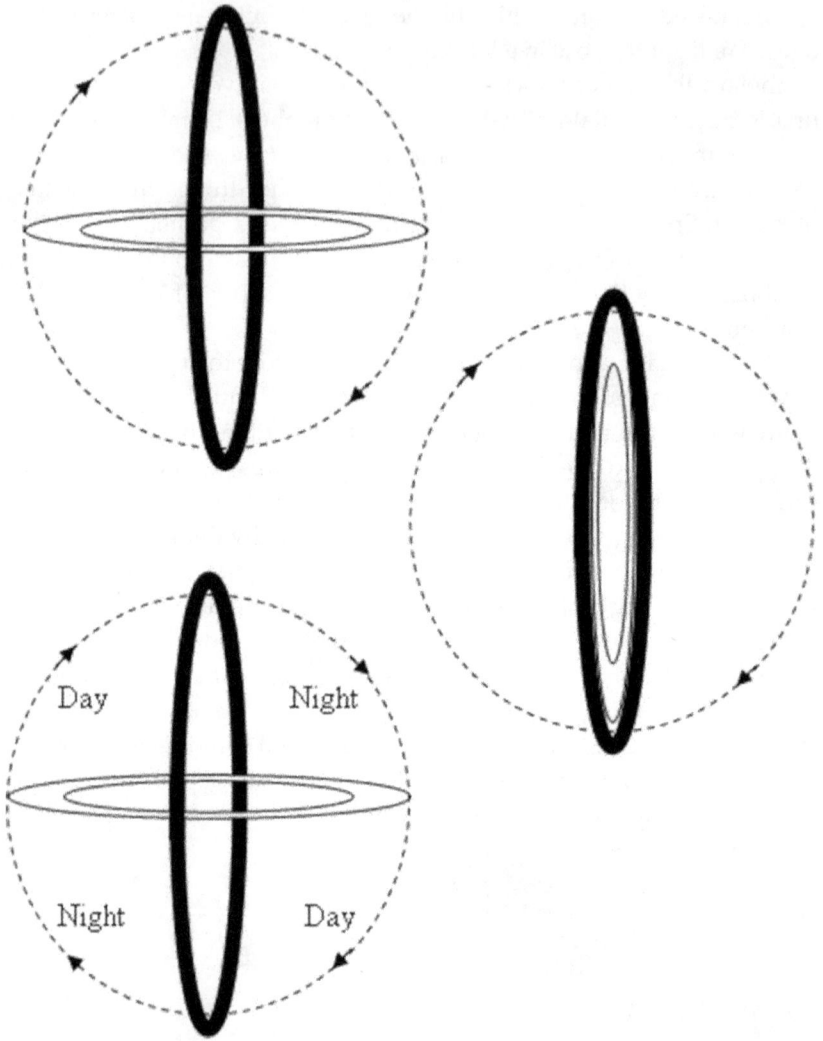

Days and Nights

This is the basis for what occult philosophy calls the Days and Nights of Manifestation. This is the vastest of all the cycles that shape the Cosmos, the one that governs the rise and fall of universes. The rule here is simple: when the Ring-Cosmos is rotating toward the angle of the Ring-Chaos, that's a Day of Manifestation, and when the Ring-Cosmos is rotating toward its own angle, that's a Night of Manifestation.

Why? Because the Ring-Chaos is what sets things in motion. If the Ring-Cosmos were to rotate at its original angle forever, nothing would ever change or grow or evolve; as mentioned in Chapter 2, the Ring-Cosmos unchecked is static in the present moment. The Ring-Chaos provides the force that tips the balance and sets the Cosmos moving. So there are two Days and two Nights of Manifestation in each full rotation of the Ring-Cosmos. Each Day begins as the attraction of the Ring-Chaos overturns the static balance of the previous Night, and ends as those forces set in motion that haven't established an equilibrium with the rest of the Cosmos are drawn out to the Ring-Pass-Not, the boundary of existence, and dissolve into the Unmanifest. Every Night begins as the remaining forces start to settle into their equilibrium, and ends as the wholly balanced and equilibrated Cosmos is disturbed anew by the attraction of the Ring-Chaos.

In itself, even if it wasn't a metaphor, that would be of limited use to human occultists, who exist in an eyeblink of Cosmic time. What makes this useful is that every smaller cycle in the Cosmos has similar phases. This is true, for example, of the cycles of the day, the lunar month, and the year. Take the lunar month for an example. The period between the New Moon and the First Quarter is favorable for beginning anything new; the period between the First Quarter and the Full Moon is favorable for strengthening and consolidating things; the period between the Full Moon and the Last Quarter is favorable for making changes; the period between the Last Quarter and the New Moon is favorable for ending and letting go.

The reference to "the numbers of the secret calendar" is a reference to this. There are various systems for tracking tides of the sort just set out, ranging from relatively simple methods, such as watching the phases of the Moon, to maddeningly intricate numerological and calendrical systems that take a lot of study to grasp. The point remains the same, which is that time is not just an undifferentiated flow; it cycles through different phases, and some of those phases are more favorable for certain activities than others.

# CHAPTER FOUR

# The Building of the Atom

## Reading

Revised Edition:   Chapter 4, "The Building of the Atom," pp. 23–26.
Millennium Edition:   Chapter 3, "The Building of the Atom," pp. 32–35,
and the first two pages of the following chapter.

## Commentary

The material in this chapter is easy to misunderstand, so it's probably wise to revisit two points before going on. First, it's essential to keep in mind the basic rule Fortune puts at the beginning of the text—"These images are not descriptive but symbolic, *and are intended to train the mind, not to inform it.*" Second, this is a textbook of occult philosophy, not of physics. When Fortune discusses atoms in this chapter, she's using the concept of the atom as a metaphor, not talking about atoms as imagined by the scientists of her time, or for that matter of ours.

Too many students of *The Cosmic Doctrine* lose track of this basic rule somewhere in these early chapters, and end up trying to force Fortune's metaphor to fit current scientific notions of atomic structure, or vice versa. This isn't helpful at all when you're trying to make sense of the basic concepts of occult philosophy expressed in terms of visual metaphors—which is after all what we're doing here.

Yin-Yang symbol

With this in mind, let's proceed to the text. The chapter begins with a crisp summary of the nature of Fortune's (metaphorical) atoms: they consist of two opposing movements locked into a relationship with each other, so that they spin around each other. I suspect Fortune had the Yin-Yang symbol in mind when she wrote this; whether or not this is true, it makes a good visual emblem of the concept in question. While the two movements that form the atom are locked into their relationship, the vortex they form by their spinning isn't frozen in place; it can move.

Fortune's metaphor likens this to a waterspout drifting over the sea, but another metaphor comes forcefully to mind: as a write these words, a hurricane is bearing down on the east coast of the United States. Just as the Cosmos in *The Cosmic Doctrine* consists solely of movements in space, a hurricane consists solely of movements in warm wet air; a hurricane is a vortex surrounding a Central Stillness; and it moves according to a complex logic of its own, veering this way and that in response to the atmospheric conditions around it. Replace atmospheric conditions with movements in space, and the same is true of the vortices Fortune describes.

Left to themselves, given the principles we've already covered, the atoms would probably move in circles, but they're not left to themselves. They're formed in the seething cauldron of energies of the Central Sun, in the angles where the Twelve Rays interpenetrate, and so as they're born they're jostled and shoved and flung from side to side, and so they end up moving in sudden, jerky, angular patterns. These settle out into geometric patterns—triangles, squares, pentagons, and so on up to decagons (ten-sided figures).

Just as a planet has two motions—it spins around its own axis, and it also revolves around its sun—an atom has two motions. The two movements that form it spin around each other, and the vortex created by that spin moves through an angular pattern. Once they have each settled into a stable pattern, the atoms can then begin to interact with each other. This takes time, but eventually atoms moving in parallel interact with each other and become linked together in a common pattern of movement. The more atoms gather together in this way, the more of an attraction the resulting mass exerts on other atoms—and the more the mass is affected by the tides of the Cosmos, the great patterns of movement set in motion by the Rings, Rays, and Circles.

Our text finishes sketching this out, and then plunges straight into one of the most important concepts of *The Cosmic Doctrine*. Back at the beginning of the first chapter, you were asked to imagine empty space flowing, and told that since space is frictionless, once it starts flowing, it keeps flowing forever. Again, this is a metaphor, but it's one of immense power and importance.

Every movement of space persists forever. If you move the point of a pen an inch across a sheet of paper, that movement sets space in motion, and the motion never goes away. In the normal way of things, such a motion quickly gets absorbed in some larger pattern of movement, but the Cosmos is never quite the same as it would have been if the movement hadn't happened. This is true of every action, every word, and every thought.

Each movement lays down what our text elsewhere calls a "track in space." When another movement more or less parallel to the first takes place, it will tend to be drawn into that track in space, and to the extent that it follows the track, it reinforces it. As more movements repeat the same motion, following the track left by the original movement, the track becomes more and more strongly fixed, so that any movement that even roughly approximates the original movement will be drawn into the track and follow along the original movement.

We all know this in a personal sense. Repeat the same action over and over again, and it becomes a habit; reinforce the habit often enough, and it becomes fixed. An old but still valid maxim from the New

Thought movement phrases it elegantly: "Sow a thought and reap a deed; sow a deed and reap a habit; sow a habit and reap a character; sow a character and reap a destiny."

The same rule also applies, however, beyond the personal level. Some years back, a scientist named Rupert Sheldrake ran experiments that demonstrated this effect. He showed, for example, that English schoolchildren who didn't know a word of Japanese were able to learn a Japanese children's song faster than they learned a sequence of nonsense syllables set to the same tune. Why? Because generations of Japanese children, learning that song, laid down tracks in space that the English schoolchildren could follow half the world away. Sheldrake's book *A New Science of Life* was duly denounced in the scientific literature—the dogma that material effects can only have material causes is deeply entrenched in scientific thought—but nobody ever proved that his experimental evidence was invalid.

To students of occult philosophy, however, Sheldrake's book came as no surprise, not least because *The Cosmic Doctrine* discussed the same effect half a century in advance. It's precisely because repetition has the effects it does that so many occultists perform a single ritual daily, and permit changes in important ceremonies only for very good reasons. Spontaneity has its own gifts to offer, but far more often than we realize, when we think we're being spontaneous, we're simply following a set of tracks in space laid down by others in the past.

The implications of this principle reach very far indeed. Several of the implications are discussed in the next few paragraphs of our text. First, we learn that as the prime atoms come into being and organize themselves, they are drawn into patterns of movement already set in motion—the great patterns of the Rings, Rays, and Circles that form the Cosmos. Over time, as a result, each of the great composite atoms that emerge from the Central Stillness takes on the form of a miniature Cosmos. Much of the rest of *The Cosmic Doctrine* focuses on what happens within those smaller Cosmoi, which Fortune and the scientists of her time called universes, and which we now call solar systems.

The same rule then applies to the things that come into being within those solar systems, including you and me. Everything that exists is conditioned by the larger system in which it exists. In the words of the Emerald Tablet, the great foundational text of ancient alchemy: "That which is above is as that which is below, and that which is below is as that which is above, to perform the miracles of the One Thing."

That rule applies at all levels. Any pattern of movement establishes itself as a steady rhythm and becomes a foundation on which later realities must build.

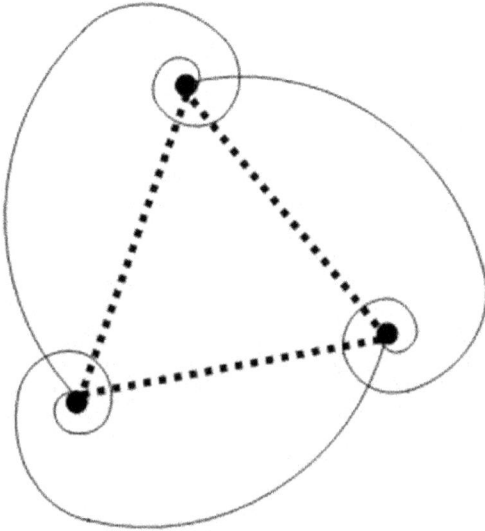

Three-sided tangential

The text asks us to imagine a prime atom that moves in a triangular pattern because of the influences acting on it at the time of its formation. As it interacts with other forces, the basic triangular movement becomes modified into a pattern of three interwoven spiraling movements, a little like that shown in the diagram. Behind that complex pattern lies the simple geometry of the equilateral triangle, shown by the dotted lines. Take this metaphor and apply it, and it becomes possible to see how, behind the intricately interwoven spirals of life, a scaffolding of basic patterns can be traced. Understand the patterns, and you understand where the spirals are going and why.

Each primal atom, in Fortune's metaphor, consists of just such a pattern of spirals traced around one of eight possible geometrical figures, from the triangle to the decagon. Each primal atom forms connections with other atoms that have the same geometrical basis—as our text says, "whose angles of stress are similar"—and the composite atoms that result begin to drift outward from the Central Stillness, following the lines of one of the Rays and passing from the center into the first of the

Circles. There the composite atoms unite with other composite atoms of the same basic geometry to create even more complex composites, and these then drift out into the second Circle, where the process repeats with similar results. Eventually, the whole Cosmos, right out to the Ring-Pass-Not, is full of atoms, ranging from prime atoms in their pure state in the Central Stillness to unimaginably complex atoms in the seventh Circle.

It's when some of these extremely complex atoms take on one more level of complexity that the process of Cosmic evolution proceeds to its next phase.

# CHAPTER FIVE

# Atomic Evolution upon the Cosmic Planes

## Reading

Revised Edition: Chapter 5, "Atomic Evolution upon the Cosmic Planes," p. 27–30.

Millennium Edition: Chapter 4, "The Evolution of the Atom," beginning with the first complete paragraph on p. 38 (which starts with the words "Evolution on the Cosmic Planes ...") and the beginning of Chapter 5, "The Genesis of a Solar System," ending with the second paragraph on p. 43 (which ends "... start back up the spiral to the Central Sun.").

## Commentary

As with previous chapters, it's probably wise to revisit two points already made before we go on. First, it's essential to keep in mind the basic rule Fortune puts at the beginning of the text—"These images are not descriptive but symbolic, *and are intended to train the mind, not to inform it.*" Second, this is a textbook of occult philosophy, not of physics.

When Fortune discusses atoms in this chapter, she's using the concept of the atom as a metaphor, not talking about atoms as imagined by the scientists of her time, or for that matter of ours.

With this in mind, let's proceed to the text. At this point in the development of the Cosmos, an immense number of atoms have been generated by the interplay of the forces of the Twelve Rays, and begin to drift outward under the influence of centrifugal force. (My copy of the Revised Edition, dated 1966, ornaments this chapter with one of my all-time favorite typos: in place of centrifugal, it has "centrifrugal." I decided many years ago that this refers to people who are too cheap to want to live in the big city.)

Our text gives us two accounts of the way this works, and they aren't entirely compatible. According to the first account, the primal atoms, which are vortices of repeated movement with from three to ten angles, emerge from the Central Sun and fill the first Circle. They then combine with one another to form composite atoms, which are influenced by centrifugal force and drift out to the second Circle. The composite atoms then unite with one another to form more complex atoms, which drift out to the third Circle, and the same process continues until all seven Circles are filled with atoms. The fantastically complex atoms of the seventh Circle then proceed along the evolutionary track we'll be discussing next.

The second account focuses not on the complexity of the atoms but on the number of angles in the prime atom around which each composite atom takes shape. In this version, the atoms sort themselves out among the circles based on their number of angles. The three-sided atoms settle in the first Circle, the four-sided atoms settle in the second Circle, and so on out to the nine-sided atoms, which take up their station in the seventh Circle. And the ten-sided atoms? Those are the ones that go on to follow the evolutionary track we'll be discussing next.

Both these accounts are stated in so many words in the text, and there are specific passages that fit one and not the other—for example, in some places the traveling atoms (the ones that follow the evolutionary track) are described as forming around prime atoms of all different numbers of sides, and in others the traveling atoms are described as forming around ten-sided prime atoms only. This isn't accidental; Dion Fortune has laid a trap.

It's a trap you can evade with perfect ease so long as you remember that all the things we're talking about are metaphors. When Robert

Burns wrote the following lines, he was using two different similes to communicate the same emotion from different angles.

> O my Luve's like a red, red rose
> That's newly sprung in June:
> O my Luve's like the melodie
> That's sweetly play'd in tune.

he was using two different similes to communicate the same emotion from different angles. I've yet to hear of anyone getting outraged by this and insisting that Burns' lady friend couldn't be like a rose *and* like a melody, since one's a flower and the other's a sequence of sounds. Unfortunately, such squabbles are far too common when we're dealing with the intricate metaphors human minds need to use to make any kind of sense of spiritual realities.

That's the trap. Those who are too prone to take *The Cosmic Doctrine* as a textbook of physics or cosmology will run into the deliberate contradiction between the two metaphors we're discussing, and either fling the book across the room because it contradicts itself, or get into a fight with some other student of *The Cosmic Doctrine* over whether or not the seed-atom at the core of a traveling atom can have less than ten sides. It's painfully easy, especially at this moment in history, to imagine Decimalists and Multinumerists shrieking denunciations at each other for falling away from the One True Interpretation of our text, and spending so much time wallowing in the quarrel that they never get around to studying the text. The thing has happened so often!

Fortunately, we can sidestep this whole issue by remembering that these are metaphors, and that they can both be good metaphors for a truth that, like all spiritual truths, cannot be grasped by the human mind by any means except metaphor. Here's one metaphor; here's another; imagine them both as clearly as possible, think about them, see what sense they make, and then try to get as much of a sense as you can of the structure of consciousness that both metaphors represent.

In both metaphors, we have atoms gradually working their way out from the Central Sun to the seventh Circle, on the edge of the Ring-Pass-Not. So at any given point during this phase of the formation of the Cosmos, you have certain atoms that have settled into their final places, and certain others that have worked their way out from the Central

Sun but haven't yet stopped moving. As they move outward along the tracks of one of the Rays, they absorb the influences of each of the Circles they pass through. Eventually, most of them settle into a stable orbit—but not all of the atoms do this.

Whether it's sheer density or a ten-sided prime atom at the center of their structure that does it, some atoms keep on moving even after they've reached the seventh Circle. Beyond the seventh Circle, though, there's nowhere for them to go but the Ring-Pass-Not, and except in certain very special circumstances to be discussed later on, When they reach the outer edge of the seventh Circle, the Ring-Pass-Not sends them spinning back down the Ray toward the Central Sun, and they go straight through and out the other side along the opposite Ray.

When the Ring-Pass-Not sends them back along that Ray, in turn, they reach the Central Sun, veer a little and go out on a different Ray. This continues until each of the ten-sided traveling atoms has passed out and returned along all twelve of the Rays. They go outward along each Ray in a straight line, but the Ring-Pass-Not imparts a spin to them, and they make a circular movement on the seventh Circle, and repeat it on every subsequent Circle as they return to the Central Sun, absorbing the influence of each Circle from every side. (All this, remember, is still more metaphor.) Since the atoms themselves consist of nothing but movement in space, and each movement of an atom lays down a track in space that pulls further movement along its trajectory, the result is another immense increase in the complexity of the traveling atoms.

Once a traveling atom has completed the full circuit of twelve Rays, its evolution is finished for the time being, and it settles into temporary stillness in the Central Sun. Once all the traveling atoms have finished the full circuit, a phase of evolution is finished, and the Cosmos as a whole settles into a temporary stillness. As our text points out, this is the third phase in the evolution of a Cosmos. The first is the formation of the Ring-Cosmos, Ring-Chaos, and Ring-Pass-Not; the second is the transformation of the Ring-Chaos into a disk and the genesis of the twelve Rays, the seven Circles, and the Central Sun; the third is the creation of the atoms and their sorting out by complexity.

In each case, we have an active phase of construction, and then a passive phase of equilibrium in which the patterns of movement created in the active phase settles down into a stable structure. As explained in an earlier chapter, these are governed by the rotation of the Ring-Cosmos relative to the Ring-Chaos.

As the Ring-Cosmos turns toward the plane of the Ring-Chaos, the static condition established at the end of the last cycle breaks up and a new phase of development begins. As the Ring-Cosmos passes the Ring-Chaos and begins to move away from its plane, the patterns set in motion during the phase of development settle into stability and move toward equilibrium. Then the Ring-Cosmos reaches and passes the point of maximum distance from the Ring-Chaos, and the influence of the latter sets the cycle in motion again.

Apply this same pattern to everyday life, to magical training and practice, or to the cycles of history, and you will find that it makes sense of phenomena that the ordinary linear thinking of our culture leaves unexplained. There is always the period of change in which fresh combinations, permutations, and rhythms of action and reaction unfold, and there is always the subsequent period of rest in which the new forces find their equilibrium and settle into a relative stillness. If you want to make a change in any context, you need to allow for intervals of calm between bursts of change.

Lacking those, instead of a rhythm of change and repose, you can count on setting up a rhythm of change and counter-change, in which the imbalances set in motion by too prolonged a movement to one extreme generate an equally prolonged and unbalanced movement to the other extreme—a pendulum motion going nowhere. To avoid this, stop the movement you desire while it still has room to run, so that the rest of the Cosmos can settle into stability around it in its new position, rather than dragging it back the other way. That stability then becomes the thrust-block against which a new round of change can push.

Having reviewed the process by which the turning of the Ring-Cosmos sets the great cycles of the Cosmos in motion, the text briefly notes the previous teachings about the three Rings, and starts drawing connections between the metaphors of *The Cosmic Doctrine* and a variety of other concepts from religion, occultism, and science. First, the interactions of the three Rings are briefly discussed, and compared to the Athanasian Creed, the longest and most intricate of the creeds used in Western Christian churches. Here's the part of it that Fortune is referencing:

> We worship one God in Trinity, and Trinity in Unity; neither confounding the Persons, nor dividing the Essence. For there is one Person of the Father; another of the Son; and another of the Holy

> Ghost. But the Godhead of the Father, of the Son, and of the Holy
> Ghost, is all one; the Glory equal, the Majesty coeternal. Such as the
> Father is, such is the Son, and such is the Holy Ghost.

Apply the same logic to the three Rings and Fortune's point is clear.
From the initial movement in space, all three Rings come into being;
while the Ring-Cosmos is in some sense first, the Ring-Chaos second,
and the Ring-Pass-Not third, all of them are implied in that original
motion, and you can't have any one of them without the others. Each is
an essential part of the whole system that frames the Cosmos.

Fortune's reference to the Athanasian Creed, though, may also be
intended to hint at another part of that document:

> The Father is made of none; neither created, nor begotten. The Son
> is of the Father alone; not made, nor created; but begotten. The
> Holy Ghost is of the Father and of the Son; neither made, nor cre-
> ated, nor begotten; but proceeding.

Notice here that the structure of the Christian Trinity is mirrored in the
structure of the three Rings. The Ring-Cosmos, like the Father, comes
into being out of nothing—"made of none" is quite an expressive way
of putting it; the Ring-Chaos, like the Son, is begotten by the motion of
the Ring-Cosmos; and the Ring-Pass-Not proceeds from the interaction
of the two other Rings as, in Western Christianity, the Holy Ghost proceeds from the other two members of the Trinity.

(Dion Fortune was herself an Anglican Christian; her book *Mystical Meditations on the Collects* is a good introduction to that end of her
thought. She was also a careful student of early twentieth-century Rosi-
crucianism, a widely practiced form of Christian occultism, which she
absorbed from her teacher Dr. Theodore Moriarty. Those of my readers
who are familiar with either or both of these traditions will find plenty
of points of contact in the chapters ahead.)

So the Rings are compared, if not quite equated, to the Christian
Trinity. The Rays are equated to the twelve signs of the Zodiac. The
Circles are equated to the seven Cosmic Planes of Theosophical and
Rosicrucian teaching. Then, in a sudden leap that seems to leave all
talk of metaphors in the dust, it places the Central Sun in astronomical
space, at a point somewhere off beyond Alpha Centauri. Once again,

Fortune has laid a trap for the unwary; this also is a metaphor, and can and should be explored as such.

Notice, more generally, what our text has done in these paragraphs. Over the last five chapters, Fortune has sketched out an abstract image of the genesis of a Cosmos without connecting it explicitly to any other body of spiritual, philosophical, occult, or scientific ideas. Now, in a few short lines, she hints at a galaxy of connections—to Christian theology, to astrology, to occult philosophy, and to science. She doesn't work out these connections in any detail; she simply shows that they are possible, and leaves the rest to her readers—that is to say, to you.

# PART II

## SOLAR EVOLUTION

CHAPTER SIX

# The Beginnings of a Solar System

## Reading

Revised Edition:   Chapter 6, "The Beginnings of a Solar System,"
pp. 31–34.

Millennium Edition:   Chapter 5, "The Genesis of a Solar System," from
the second complete paragraph on p. 43 (which
starts with the words "You have heard how these
atoms...") to the end of the chapter.

## Commentary

Once again, it's crucial here to remember the metaphoric nature of what
we're discussing. One of the easiest ways to misunderstand *The Cosmic
Doctrine* is to forget that this is a textbook of occult philosophy, not of
astrophysics. When Fortune discusses solar systems in this chapter,
she's using concepts borrowed from astronomy as a set of metaphors,
not trying to compete with the astronomers of her time (or ours) by
offering up a physical theory of the formation of solar systems.

There's a further level to the metaphor, however, and it's one that
will become increasingly important as the book proceeds. From ancient

times onward, it's been common in Western esoteric writings to identify the sun as the representation, the habitation, or even the material body of the principal divine power active in the world we know. That habit almost certainly has Egyptian roots, tracing its origins to the veneration of the sun god Ra; you can find the same solar vision all the way through classical Western occultism from the emperor Julian's hymns to Helios the sun god straight through to Robert Fludd's identification of the sun as the habitation of the Logos, the second person of the Christian Trinity.

Fortune's work is squarely in this tradition. For her, the Solar Logos—whom she also identifies as the second person of the Christian Trinity—is the god of this solar system, the Great Organism who organizes and conditions everything on Earth and the other planets that orbit our sun. In the chapters we've already studied, Fortune has sketched out in metaphoric terms the evolutionary process by which the Solar Logos (and countless other Great Organisms of the same type) comes into being; we now proceed to the chapters in which she explores how the Solar Logos creates a solar system in the image of the greater Cosmos.

That process begins as the traveling atoms discussed in the previous chapter find their way back to the Central Sun. Each traveling atom has gone out and back again along each of the twelve Rays, absorbing the influences of each Ray on each of the seven Circles or Cosmic Planes of existence. Each of these atoms started out as a vortex of movement in space based on a simple geometrical pattern; each finishes its journey as a fantastically complex structure of forces in equilibrium, having experienced every possibility the Cosmos has to offer and made each one of those possibilities part of its internal structure.

These Great Organisms, as we may now call them, started their outward journey when the Ring-Cosmos was turning toward the Ring-Chaos. As they complete the journey, they come to rest in the Central Sun and stay there as the Ring-Cosmos begins pivoting away from the Ring-Chaos and the Cosmos sinks into its negative phase. Once the Ring-Cosmos begins moving toward the Ring-Chaos again, the Great Organisms leave the Central Sun again, following the lines of the twelve Rays.

In the previous phase of activity, the atoms moved outwards to fill empty space, and some of them became complex enough to go all the way out to the Ring-Pass-Not and begin their career as a traveling atom that would transform them into Great Organisms. In this new phase of activity, the atoms that didn't become traveling atoms are still there, distributed by density or geometrical structure among the seven Circles. As the Great Organisms go out along the Rays, they gather up as many of the atoms of each plane as their mass can attract, and their outward movement slows down accordingly. Eventually, each of the Great Organisms, with its cloud of accompanying atoms, comes to rest in one of the Circles and begins to revolve around the Central Sun at a fixed distance, passing through each of the Rays in turn.

What determines the Circle in which any given Great Organism settles down to stay? Here again, we have the trap mentioned in the last chapter, the one Fortune laid with exquisite care for would-be fundamentalists. Remember how an earlier chapter had only the ten-sided atoms becoming traveling atoms, while all the other atoms settled out to stay in one or another of the circles, from the three-sided atoms in the first Circle, all the way out to the nine-sided atoms in the seventh. Here, all of a sudden, the Great Organisms can have atoms of any shape at their core, and each one settles out into a circle determined by the number of sides of its basic form. "If the vortex set up in the angles of the Rays moved in a three-sided path, it could go no further than the first plane beyond the Central Stillness," our text says; "it would have to be a ten-sided figure to reach the seventh plane and evolve there."

Did you hear the click? That was the trap closing shut.

The difficulty Fortune has placed in the way of a simplistic literalism here is straightforward enough: the numbers don't work. If atoms based on three-sided figures settle out in the first Circle, atoms based on four-sided figures in the second Circle, those based on five-sided figures in the third Circle, and so on, then the atoms assigned to the seventh Circle would be nine-sided, and ten-sided atoms would have no place to go. Try to turn *The Cosmic Doctrine* into an allegedly infallible sacred scripture, and you crash headlong into that obvious problem. Accept instead that it's a set of metaphors meant to train the mind, and you're fine; sure, the numbers don't work, but they don't need to.

You can imagine, with perfect serenity, the Great Organism that created our solar system having a ten-sided figure at its core. You can see it drifting out along one of the Rays, gathering a cloud of other atoms with it as it goes, and settling into its permanent orbit on the seventh Circle. Since the rest of the book focuses on events inside our solar system, that's as much as you need. Since all this is metaphor, getting bent out of shape because every detail doesn't mesh precisely with every other detail is like responding to Robert Burns' claim that his love is like a red, red rose by wanting to know if she has thorns and green skin.

With that in mind, let's return to the metaphor. Once each Great Organism settles into its permanent orbit, the cloud of atoms that surrounds it sorts itself out into a miniature Cosmos, with the Great Organism at the center and a disk of less complex atoms around it, reflecting the Central Sun and the disk of the Ring-Cosmos. That's a newborn solar system, as Fortune comments elsewhere, to the nearest approximate metaphor: the Great Organism as the sun-to-be, and the cloud of atoms surrounding it as the great swirling cloud of Cosmic dust and debris that will eventually coalesce into planets, asteroids, and comets.

With this picture sketched out, Fortune proceeds to drop several important hints. The first is that the solar system we happen to inhabit is nothing special. Even the subset of them that settle into orbits on the seventh Cosmic Plane are so numerous that the stars known to human beings are but an infinitesimal fraction of the total, and each of the other Cosmic Planes has a comparable number of Great Organisms building solar systems there, outside the reach of our awareness in this phase of our evolution. The point being made here is one that nineteenth- and twentieth-century occultism liked to stress: human beings are not the be-all and end-all of existence, and the Cosmos does not exist solely for our benefit.

We have a place in the scheme of things. As we'll see in more detail later on, it's by no means a shabby place, all things considered, but it's not unique to us, and there are other beings who rank far above us on the scale of things *and will always do so*. The sort of giddy anthropocentric arrogance that claims vast Cosmic importance for human beings, and only for human beings, was already far too common when the nineteenth-century occult revival got under way, and it's become even more so since then. Where Renaissance occultists such as Giovanni Pico di Mirandola spoke of the dignity and potential power of humanity, to try to counter the contempt for the human condition so common in the Middle Ages, modern occultists have had to grapple with the opposite problem, and labored to deflate the overblown collective ego of our species.

That's the first hint. The second one is another of those remarkable prefigurations of systems theory that pop up all through *The Cosmic Doctrine*. In Dion Fortune's time, the very first tentative efforts toward systems theory were trying to find a way to describe the way that every system divides itself into subsystems structured like the original system, and these subsystems do the same thing in turn. When I studied systems theory in college in the early 1980s, systems theorists had assigned that property a variety of names, such as self-similarity and recursive structure.

Not long thereafter, though, a branch of mathematics that had begun to explore the same process in numerical and geometrical forms got its fifteen minutes and more of fame, and gave the rest of us a straightforward way to talk about the property in question. Were Dion Fortune to reincarnate now for the purpose of bringing out an enlarged and Revised Edition of *The Cosmic Doctrine*, she could sum up half a dozen lengthy paragraphs with a single sentence: the Cosmos is fractal.

In a fractal picture, each part of the image—all the way down to the smallest—duplicates the overall structure of the picture, and vice versa. That same dynamic structures the relationship between the Cosmos, individual solar systems, and individual beings that exist within a solar system. That's what Fortune is getting at in the last half dozen paragraphs of this chapter. The Cosmos has Rings and Rays and Circles, and so each solar system develops its own Rings and Rays and Circles; within each solar system, in turn, the atoms that got scooped up with the Great Organism that is that system's Solar Logos go through a reflection of the same experience that made a Solar Logos out of a traveling atom, and themselves become Great Organisms, and the process continues.

The Cosmos is fractal, and so everything we have discussed in terms of the overall structure of the (metaphorical) universe is also part of the structure of each individual human being, and each human society, and each ecosystem, and any other whole system you want to understand. As a human being, a microcosm of the macrocosm, you have your own Ring-Cosmos, Ring-Chaos, and Ring-Pass-Not; you have your own Rays (the cusps of your natal horoscope) and your own Circles (the various bodies, dense and subtle, of the human being); your actions spiral outward from your Central Sun to your Ring-Pass-Not and back again, evolving into habits that find their proper orbit and continue in it thereafter. As above, so below: the great axiom of the Hermetic tradition is a continuing theme of *The Cosmic Doctrine*, and this is one of the places where it's central.

Though the Cosmos and the individual have the same basic structure, in turn, there's a crucial difference between them: the Cosmos forms the environment that conditions and influences the individual, not the other way around. At every moment, your consciousness and your life are being shaped by the forces of the Cosmos; some of the ways in which this happens are obvious, but a great many more are not. The essence of the Secret Wisdom—that is to say, the essence of occultism, since "occult" simply means "that which is hidden"—is the knowledge of those hidden influences, and of the times and places and forces that cause them to change. To know those influences is to attain wisdom. To wield them in harmony with the innate patterns and directions of the Cosmos is to become the equivalent of a traveling atom: in a phrase traditional among occultists, it is to enter onto the Path.

# CHAPTER SEVEN

# The Evolution of a Solar System

## Reading

Revised Edition: Chapter 7, "The Evolution of a Solar System," pp. 35–38.

Millennium Edition: Chapter 6, "Cosmic Influences upon a Solar System," pp. 49–54.

## Commentary

At this point, we've completed the first six chapters (or five, if you're using the Millennium Edition) and the first six months of work with *The Cosmic Doctrine*. Those readers who have followed along have put in six months of heavy philosophical lifting, learning to make sense of the magical vision of the Cosmos as expressed to the nearest approximate metaphor. The basic structures and concepts of Fortune's symbolic philosophy have all been set out in emblematic form, and what follows will draw on symbols and metaphors a little easier to relate to the world as we experience it.

It's important to keep the Cosmic background in mind as we go on, though, and there are two reasons for that. First of all, a solar system in its structure and evolution reflects the Cosmos that gave birth to it. Each of the stages of the process of Cosmic evolution we've discussed over the previous chapters has its equivalent in the stages of evolution that a solar system follows in turn. The stages are equivalent rather than identical, since each solar system starts out in a complex, intricately structured Cosmos rather than in a vast emptiness representing the Unmanifest. Still, as we proceed, it will be simple enough to point out how the evolutionary phases of the Cosmos are mirrored in the evolution of the solar system.

The second reason is that solar systems aren't isolated from the Cosmos. Beings within a solar system are influenced mostly by factors internal to that system, but influences from without still have a secondary role. It's a subtle role—it works primarily by way of the influence of Cosmic processes on the Solar Logos, the Great Organism at the center of a solar system, and secondarily by way of the Star Logoi, who come into being within the solar system and will be discussed later—but it has its effect. The great phases of expansion and contraction driven by the movement of the Ring-Cosmos relative to the Ring-Chaos, the influence of the twelve great Rays as they stream out from the Central Sun to act on each of the seven Cosmic Planes, and the influence of Great Organisms and their solar systems on one another, are thus all significant in the life of a solar system. It's by being aware of these factors that we can understand some of the oddities in our own collective evolution.

Since it's crucial to recall the Cosmic context as we proceed, this chapter is a recapitulation of the material covered in the previous chapters, with a few additional notes of interest. It sums up the genesis of the Cosmos from the first flowing movement in empty space to the establishment of solar systems on the seven Cosmic Planes. From here on in we're going to be talking about the evolution of one particular solar system—the one you and I happen to inhabit, one of countless solar systems to be found on the seventh Cosmic Plane.

One of the things stressed in this recapitulation is the role of numbers in this philosophy. Motion in space—the basis for the whole system—is represented by the number 1. The great Cosmic forces—the Rings, the Rays, and the Circles or Planes—are represented by the numbers 3, 12, and 7, respectively. These four numbers are the Primaries. Each of the Circles collects atoms whose orbits have a particular geometry, and thus a particular number—the three-sided atomic orbits settle out on the first plane, the four-sided on the second plane, and so on out to the seventh plane, where the atoms have nine-sided orbits. The numbers three through nine inclusive are therefore the Secondaries. Finally, the number 10 is the Prime Tertiary, the number that guides and shapes evolution once the Primaries and Secondaries are in place.

Those readers who know their way around traditional occult philosophy will recognize these numbers at once. The numbers of the great Cosmic forces, 3 and 12 and 7, added together make 22, the number of the paths of the Cabalistic Tree of Life. Ten, of course, is the number of spheres in the Tree of Life. It's more common in occult philosophies to make ten the primary number and 22 dependent on it, but Fortune's making a specific point here. Her Cosmos of metaphors is made entirely of motion in space, and so she makes the paths, the currents of moving force on the Tree, Primary. The spheres, which in one sense are stages of spiritual unfoldment, are dependent on the soul's movement along the paths.

The Secondaries also have their importance in occult philosophy, but they do so individually rather than collectively. If you add them together, you get 42; this will doubtless delight Douglas Adams fans, but the number 42 has only a modest role in occult symbolism. The numbers 3 through 9 are the numbers of the great planetary forces, from Saturn (which has a threefold symbolism and a magic square of three times three cells) to the Moon (which has a ninefold symbolism and a magic square of nine times nine cells). One, finally, is the number of divinity and, in a solar system, represents the influence of the god of that solar system, the Great Organism who, as the solar system is born, becomes its Solar Logos.

Notice that two numbers have obviously been left out of these categories: the numbers 2 and 11. There is of course nothing in the least accidental about this exclusion. The number 2 equates to negative evil, the force of inertia or resistance against which every other force in the Cosmos and the solar system alike must test its strength. As a number, it represents nothing internal to the Cosmos or the solar system—it represents, rather, the background against which the Cosmos and the solar system unfold their possibilities.

By contrast, 11 in this system of thought is the number of positive evil. We haven't talked much about that so far, and quite a few more chapters will have to be studied and understood before Fortune's way of talking about positive evil will make sense. For now, think of it as the *refusal* of evolution, where negative evil is the *resistance* to evolution. While positive evil certainly exists in our solar system, it's not a necessary part of things. It comes into being as a result of unforced choices on the part of individual beings, and thus it's conceivable that there might be some solar system somewhere in the Cosmos where none of the individual beings happened to make those choices, where negative evil was a reality, but positive evil remained a theoretical possibility and nothing more.

These numbers, therefore, provide the framework for the new solar system. The Great Organism at its core started off with a tenfold structure, and then developed reactions corresponding to each of the other numbers in the course of its journeys up and down the twelve Rays of the Cosmos as a traveling atom. It then continues to respond to each of the forces represented by these numbers as it settles into place on its plane with its cloud of static atoms around it. This is the basis for what Fortune calls sidereal astrology.

In some ways, that's an unfortunate label, since it has also been taken up by a school of astrology that uses the constellations rather than the equinoctial and solstitial points to set out the wheel of the Zodiac. Still, there's a connection. The tropical Zodiac—that's the technical term for the Zodiac used in classic Western astrology, in which the sign Aries starts at the point where the Sun is at the moment of the spring equinox—is based on factors entirely internal to our solar system. The sidereal Zodiac tries to take into account forces from outside the solar system, and what Fortune calls sidereal astrology is all about those outside forces. The influence of those forces shifts over vast intervals of time, and can be tracked by a number of means, starting with the precession of the equinoxes.

History offers interesting reflections on what Fortune is saying here. It's an interesting detail of the history of astrology, for example, that in the early days of Western astrology, when it was practiced by astronomer-priests standing on mud-brick ziggurats along the banks of the Tigris and Euphrates Rivers, Venus was a planet of war as well as love. Recently deciphered Mayan inscriptions show similarly that the movements of Venus were used in Mesoamerican astrology to choose good times to declare war and to predict victory in battle.

I don't know of any astrologer at present who would try to read the placements of Venus with that in mind, since that's not the way the energies of Venus influence people's lives today. The most likely explanation for the difference is that the energies have changed over the last several thousand years—that the Cosmic influences flowing in from the fifth Cosmic Plane, and brought into focus in our solar system by way of the planet Venus, have shifted over time, downplaying the violent aspect of Venerean passions and amplifying the gentler aspects.

Keep in mind, though, that these changes are in some sense cumulative. In the chapters we've already studied, a central theme is that the changes set in motion by one phase of Cosmic evolution become the foundation on which the next phase of Cosmic evolution builds. This same principle remains in effect as we move into the evolution of the solar system, and also as we go from there to the evolution of individual beings within the solar system. Our text summarizes this in a crisp phrase: "you start where God leaves off." You come into the world, in other words, with the entire past of the Cosmos implicit in you, and then you add to it through your own actions. Those actions are directed by something that usually gets called "free will," though Fortune notes that this is an unhelpful label for it; her own label—epigenesis—will take quite a bit of explanation as we go further.

There is more going on here than unforced choices in an otherwise deterministic Cosmos, though. Fortune asks us to imagine our solar system in its formative stages, as the Great Organism who will become its Solar Logos sweeps outward from the Central Sun all the way to the seventh Cosmic Plane, gathering up as many of the static atoms of each plane as it can draw with it by a metaphoric equivalent of gravitational attraction. Once it reaches the seventh Circle, it settles into its orbit, and the static atoms it brought with it sort themselves out into great belts of Cosmic atoms of different kinds, each belt consisting of atoms of one kind, orbiting the Solar Logos at a distance set by its (metaphoric) density. As the Logos and its attendant atomic belts sweep around the vast arc of the seventh Circle, they pass through each of the Rays in turn. All this is perfectly orderly.

At the same time, something much less orderly is also going on. All the other Circles are also full of solar systems of their own, which differ from ours in that they lack atoms from the seventh Circle, the Circle that corresponds to the plane of physical matter. Those other solar systems move at different speeds, and as they swing close to our solar system, their influence affects the atoms in our solar system that come from the plane where the passing solar system exists. If a solar system on the sixth Circle swings past, all the atoms in our solar system that have eight-sided orbits and originally settled on the sixth Cosmic Plane will be affected. Think of this influence as gravity, first pulling the eight-sided atoms back along the track of our solar system's orbit, then pulling them in toward the Central Sun, and then pulling them forward as the sixth-plane solar system speeds past ours.

The same is true, in turn, of atoms in our solar system with three-sided orbits whenever a solar system of the first Cosmic Plane swings past. As the solar system proceeds with its evolution, in other words, it's constantly being pulled and pushed and buffeted in complicated ways by the influence of other solar systems on the Circles further in. As we'll see, this makes things challenging for the Solar Logos, and also for the individual beings who arise within the solar system and pass through their evolution there.

One measure of that complexity can be judged from one of Fortune's passing remarks in the Revised Edition. Since it's not in the Millennium Edition, I'll quote it in full:

> You can see that there are times when the Lower Astral would receive a stimulus and times when the Upper Spiritual would likewise, although this is not so strong as the corresponding Cosmic Plane is not so near. This is one of the things that check evolution and often set up trouble in a system.

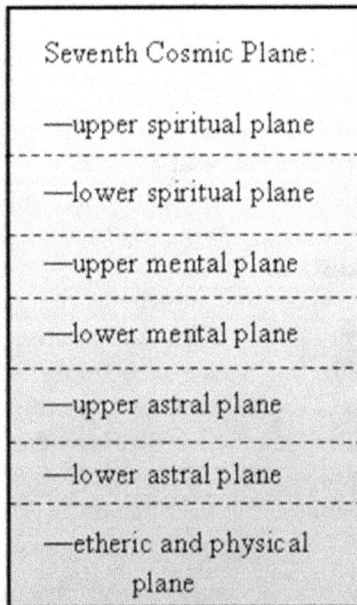

Seventh Cosmic Plane:

—upper spiritual plane

—lower spiritual plane

—upper mental plane

—lower mental plane

—upper astral plane

—lower astral plane

—etheric and physical plane

Planes of Being 2

This may take some unpacking. Here, as she usually does, Fortune is using a taxonomy of the planes of being in our solar system, which identifies seven planes: upper spiritual, lower spiritual, upper mental, lower mental, upper astral, lower astral, and physical/etheric. These exist on our plane, the seventh Cosmic Plane, but all of them but the last also reflect the influence of one of the other Cosmic Planes—thus, the upper spiritual plane reflects the influence of the first Cosmic Plane, the lower spiritual plane that of the second, and so on. Since each of us exists on every plane from the physical to the upper spiritual, we are subject to influences from outside our solar system whenever a solar system on one of the higher Cosmic Planes passes by. When human beings act collectively in very strange ways, this can be one of the causes.

We'll be exploring those complexities further as we proceed. For the time being, it's most important to get a clear sense of the way that the opening phases of solar evolution unfold. The last two paragraphs of our chapter sketch out the emerging solar system in a clear visual image, which is meant to remind you of the corresponding stages in the emergence of the Cosmos. Take the time to build up that image in your imagination; from it, a great deal will unfold as we go further.

# CHAPTER EIGHT

# The Evolution of a Great Entity

## Reading

Revised Edition:   Chapter 8, "The Evolution of a Great Entity,"
pp. 39–43.

Millennium Edition:   Chapter 7, "The Evolution of a Great Entity,"
pp. 55–57, and the first half of the following
chapter, to the bottom of p. 60.

## Commentary

With this chapter the text shifts in an important way. Up to now, *The Cosmic Doctrine* has made use of physics as a basis for its "nearest approximate metaphors." The images that we've been presented all have to do with space and movement. Within that framework, a kind of visionary astronomy has been unfolded, setting out the principles of occult philosophy as though we're talking about the formation of suns and planets.

There are good reasons for that approach. For most people in the industrial world, the narratives of modern science provide the raw material for our thinking, in exactly the same way that the mythic

narratives of ancient Greece, let's say, provided the raw material for
Classical thought. Many Americans who grew up when I did will recall
the glorious Chesley Bonestell paintings of the newborn Earth commis-
sioned by *Life* magazine and published in a very widely read coffee-
table book, *The World We Live In*; equivalent images were commonplace
in Fortune's time and today as well. These are our creation myths, and
it was a wise choice on Fortune's part to use them to provide a half-
conscious mental background for her teaching.

The challenge that has to be faced by any set of metaphors that relies
on physics, though, is the barrier that materialist science has tried to
raise between matter and mind. That's the barrier Fortune needs to get
past in order to make her account of the Cosmos relevant to magic—the
art and science, to use her definition, of causing change in consciousness in accordance with will. She does the job with considerable aplomb
by the straightforward tactic of driving an argument right through the
middle of the barrier, sending fragments flying in all directions.

Let's see how this works. She starts by asking us to imagine the consciousness of a Great Entity, one of the traveling atoms of the Cosmos
that has passed through the whole process of Cosmic evolution and settled down on one of the seven planes of being to create a solar system of
its own. At first, the consciousness of that Great Entity would simply be
a dim sense of whirling, reflecting the movement of the Ring-Cosmos.
That becomes established, and fades from awareness in the same way
that any repeated stimulus does. (Pay attention to your tongue. Before
I mentioned it, were you aware of the sensations it was receiving?)
Then the secondary movement of the Ring-Chaos follows, entering consciousness and then fading out as the Great Entity becomes habituated
to it. From there, step by step, every other phase in the evolution of the
Cosmos is reflected in the consciousness of the Great Entity.

Why? *Because the consciousness of the Great Entity is nothing other than
these patterns of habituated movement.* Fortune points out: "(T)here is an
unbroken line of development from movement to thought. Tangential
movement is a simple form of reaction. Thought is an infinitely complex
form of reaction. It is a question of difference of degree, not of difference of kind" (p. 40, Revised Edition; p. 56, Millennial Edition). Think
of your consciousness as an extremely complex set of movements that
have worked out all their interactions and whirl smoothly and silently
on, until disrupted by some new influence.

It's common for people to treat this sort of understanding as though it's a dismissal of the very idea of consciousness—as though Fortune is saying, "consciousness is nothing more than very complex movement." It would be just as accurate to say that movement is nothing less than very simple consciousness, and that physics studies those forms of consciousness that are simple enough that their results can be predicted by mathematical formulas. To say that movement and consciousness are the same thing doesn't mean that consciousness doesn't exist—it means that everything is conscious to one degree or another.

The point to take from this discussion is that Fortune's account doesn't set out two separate realms of mind and matter (philosophers call this dualism); nor does it see mind as an effect or product or illusion created by matter (in philosophers' jargon, materialism); nor does it see matter an effect or product or illusion created by mind (to philosophers, this is idealism). Rather, to Fortune, mind and matter are the same thing experienced in different ways—or, in modern industrial society, chopped in half to make the universe fit an ideology with a covert agenda. (This makes Fortune's account, in philosophers' language, a variety of monism. As we'll see, however, Fortune shows that philosophical monism and religious theism are perfectly compatible if you approach them both in the right way.)

We'll get to these latter points as we proceed. For now, let's turn back to the text and watch the slow dawning of complex consciousness in the mind of a Great Entity. As it finishes the process of Cosmic evolution and settles down into a stable orbit on one of the planes of being, and the other atoms that accompanied it out to that plane settle into their own stable orbit, the Great Entity repeats the motions that it absorbed from the Cosmos, and imparts those same motions to the swarm of atoms that surround it. These motions, which are implicit in the momentum of the Great Entity, can also be thought of in a psychological sense as will: "a Cosmic Will," as our text specifies, since it is based on the movements of the Cosmos. The swarm proceeds to sort itself out into the miniature Cosmos we call a solar system and Fortune, like the astronomers of her childhood, called a universe. (The term "universe" didn't get its modern meaning until the discovery of other galaxies in the mid-twentieth century; the term literally means "that which rotates together," and was already being used in the Middle Ages for the Earth-centered Cosmos imagined in those days.)

Fortune talks about this same process in two ways, once in terms of motion, and once in terms of consciousness; these are the same thing, but our habits of thought make it difficult to grasp that, thus the repetition. The Great Entity repeats the motions of the Cosmos, and thus—this is simply another way of saying the same thing—formulates the *concept* of those motions. The repetition of a motion, after all, is the simplest form of reflection on that motion. So we can begin to see the Great Entity meditating on the conditions of its being, the vast movements of the Cosmos it absorbed during its long pilgrimage through time. As they respond to these motions, the atoms surrounding the Great Entity recapitulate that pilgrimage in a reflected form. They absorb the fruits of the Great Entity's experience; we might even say that they receive an initiation from the Great Entity, and are introduced to the modes of consciousness of the Great Entity. Certain aspects of religion can be understood in this way; others—well, we'll get to those further on.

The solar system doesn't simply settle down into habituated motion and unconsciousness, though, because it isn't isolated. Three main sets of influences from the Cosmos, as noted in previous commentaries, affect the solar system as it sweeps around the Central Sun in its orbit. First of all, the great phases of the Rings continue to affect it. When the Ring-Cosmos is moving toward the Ring-Chaos, all the solar systems within the Cosmos are stirred into new activity and the generation of novelty; when the Ring-Cosmos moves away from the Ring-Chaos, all the solar systems settle down to the elaboration and synthesis of the new influences absorbed in the previous phase.

Second, the Great Entity and its solar system pass through the twelve Rays one after another. These Rays are far from interchangeable; each one has its own distinctive influences, which are reflected within the solar system in the form of the twelve zodiacal influences. Think of the way that the Earth passes through each of the twelve forces of the Zodiac as it circles the sun; the same thing happens, on a vastly greater time scale, as the Great Entity in the sun follows its own orbit around the Central Stillness. This is the Cosmic factor behind the astrological ages marked by the precession of the equinoxes: the change from one age to another happens when our solar system, in its orbit around the Central Stillness, passes from one Ray to another.

Third, other solar systems are sweeping around the Central Sun on their own orbits, and those on each plane move at a different rate of speed—the closer to the Central Sun, the faster the rate of movement.

Here in the seventh Cosmic Plane, we're subject to the influences of solar systems on every other plane of being. Those influences have two parts, one of which we've discussed already and one of which we haven't.

The one we've discussed is the (metaphorical, remember) gravitational attraction exerted by systems of each plane on the atoms that share the same geometric keynote of that plane. A Great Entity on the seventh Cosmic Plane has the matter of every other plane in its solar system, and so when a Great Entity on the sixth Cosmic Plane goes past, all atoms that have an octagonal keynote are influenced by it; when a Great Entity on the fifth Cosmic Plane goes past, it's the turn of atoms with a heptagonal structure to be affected, and so on. (Remember that the first Cosmic Plane has three-sided atoms, and every other plane has atoms with a number of sides two greater than the number of the plane.) Only the atoms of dense matter, which belong to the seventh Cosmic Plane alone, are unaffected by these influences.

The form of influence we haven't discussed so far is what happens when a solar system of a higher plane passes (metaphorically) between our solar system and the Central Sun. That weakens the gravitational influence of the Central Sun. Thus every atom of the plane corresponding to the interrupting system tends to move inward toward the solar system moving past, but every atom of every other plane tends to drift further out toward the Ring-Pass-Not, the boundary of the Cosmos. Our solar system doesn't fly apart when this happens, because it has its own gravitational attraction, and a complex network of stresses in equilibrium holding it together. Those keep it in one piece, but the pressure of the contending forces puts strains on the structure of the solar system and sets up various unbalanced patterns of movement.

These, in turn, are the origin of positive evil. We've talked already about negative evil and positive evil—the basic inertia and resistance that provides a thrust-block for creative action, on the one hand, and the actions of individual beings that follow the momentum of the Ring-Chaos rather than that of the Ring-Cosmos, on the other. Negative evil is necessary for anything to come into existence—if there were no inertia, no thrust-block against which the forces of the Ring-Cosmos can push, there would be no Cosmos at all. Positive evil, by contrast, isn't built into the structure of existence. It's accidental, though in a sufficiently complex Cosmos the accidents that bring it into being are statistically inevitable.

Fortune gives us two new labels for negative evil and positive evil; she calls the former Cosmic evil, and the second universal evil. (A universe, again, is what early twentieth-century astronomers called what we call a solar system.) Negative or Cosmic evil is always present in every solar system, forming the background inertia against which the solar system's evolution unfolds.

Positive or universal evil, by contrast, comes and goes; it appears when a set of discordant stresses moves through a system, and disappears as the discords are gradually brought back into balance. Positive evil thus takes the most extreme forms in the early phases of any evolutionary process, when the patterns of force that will eventually bring the whole system into balance haven't yet become habituated. Over time, the balance becomes harder to disrupt, until finally the entire system has settled into perfect balance—and then, of course, a new Cosmic phase begins and the process starts over again.

Positive evil takes two forms, which Fortune calls by indicative names. Perverted force she calls sin; perverted form she calls disease. (Remember that the word "perverted" means simply "turned aside from its normal course"—the common sexual meaning of the term is secondary to that basic meaning, and isn't what Fortune is talking about here.) While the term "sin" is unpopular these days, it does a better job of communicating the particular kind of imbalance Fortune is discussing here than any of its partial synonyms. Sin and disease, unbalanced force and unbalanced form, are the tangles that work their way into a solar system and have to be pulled out straight again in the course of evolution.

There's a subtle point here that we'll be exploring in more detail later on. In one sense, as we've just seen, positive evil is the product of forces from outside the solar system setting discordant patterns at work within it. In another sense, as discussed earlier on, positive evil is the product of unforced choices on the part of individual beings. That seems like a contradiction, doesn't it? As we'll see, though, that apparent contradiction resolves itself as we begin to come to grips with the process Fortune calls epigenesis and less careful philosophies call free will.

# CHAPTER NINE

# The Creation of a Universe

## Reading

Revised Edition: Chapter 9, "The Creation of a Universe," pp. 44–47.

Millennium Edition: Chapter 8, "The Relation of a Great Entity to the Cosmos," from page 61 to the end of Chapter 9, "The Projection of the Concept of the Universe," p. 66.

## Commentary

To understand the material in this chapter, it's important to remember one of the crucial points made in the last chapter: the concept that motion and consciousness are two ways of talking about the same thing. When one pool ball hits another pool ball and the second ball moves in response, that response is akin—in a very, very simple way—to what happens when an idea enters your mind and interacts with the ideas already in place there. Is that a metaphor? Of course; everything in *The Cosmic Doctrine* is a metaphor. As we'll see, though, it's a metaphor that has a great deal to teach.

This is especially important to keep in mind as our text shifts focus from the Cosmos as a whole to the individual solar system we live in. As the protagonist of our tale gradually changes from traveling atom to Great Entity to Solar Logos—or to say the same thing in different words, as we move from that entity's relationship to the Cosmos, through its relationship to the solar system it creates, to its relationship to those beings who inhabit that solar system—the metaphors Fortune uses change gears from physics to astronomy to psychology. Those are all ways of talking about the same things, but "the nearest approximate metaphor" changes as the context changes. It's well to keep that in mind, to avoid the sort of fundamentalism that fixates on the words and loses their meanings.

With that in mind, we plunge at once into the inner brooding of the Great Entity. That being has gone spiraling outward to the seventh Cosmic Plane to take up an orbit there, and swept along with it a vast number of other atoms of all seven basic types. It does this while the Cosmic cycles are in their negative or destructive phase. Why? Because it's in the destructive phases that a settled order is shaken apart and change becomes possible. Once this is over, the Great Entity sorts itself out—we can think of this in terms of movement, as the vast and intricately tangled pattern of "tracks in space" that form the Great Entity settling into a stable equilibrium, or we can think of it in terms of psychology, as the Great Entity brooding over what it has experienced in its long pilgrimage through the Cosmos.

It doesn't brood over the Cosmos. The Great Entity is entirely unconscious of the Cosmos, in much the same way that you and I are unconscious of the deep processes of our own minds. The Cosmos forms the foundation or, as Fortune says, the conditioning background of the Great Entity. What the Great Entity broods over, rather, is itself. It becomes aware, not merely of this or that sensation within itself, but of itself as a whole. (In terms of motion, we can describe the same process as the achievement of a state of equilibrium in which every motion balances, and is affected by, every other motion.)

That act of self-knowledge brings a universe into being. That's easy to say and just as easy to misunderstand. Remember that in *The Cosmic Doctrine*, consciousness is movement, and everything that exists is space moving. The universe that the Great Entity creates is a pattern of movement in space, set in motion by the intricate movements of the Great Entity itself. The pattern of movement gathers up the atoms that have accompanied the Great Entity out to the seventh Cosmic Plane and begins to move them the way the original traveling atom was moved by the great wheeling currents of the Cosmos.

The universe brought into being by the Great Entity's knowledge of itself isn't static. While the Great Entity isn't directly aware of the Cosmos, it is aware of changes in its own state that are caused by the great Cosmic tides. So the Great Entity comes to know itself as a being in time, changing in long slow cycles as the Cosmic tides shift, and also changing in less predictable ways as other Great Entities on other Cosmic Planes sweep past in their own orbits and briefly come between our Great Entity and the Central Sun at the heart of the Cosmos. All these changes become part of the Great Entity's understanding of itself, and shape the pattern of movements in space that surrounds the Great Entity.

The Great Entity is therefore, in Fortune's words, the Creator and Sustainer of the universe it has brought into being. It is the god of that universe, if you're a monotheist, or the chief and parent of the gods if you're a polytheist. Druids in the Revival tradition who work with *The Cosmic Doctrine* thus tend to identify the Great Entity with Hu the Mighty, and the tale of his leading the Cymry from Deffrobani to the Island of Britain with the Great Entity's journey from the Central Sun to the seventh Cosmic Plane; readers who prefer other myths and other theologies will likely have no trouble finding something suitable to their needs in their own tradition's resources.

To say that the Great Entity is the god of the solar system is to court certain misunderstandings, and Fortune does her best to confront those. Is such a god infinite and omnipotent? From the point of view of the universe, it creates, yes, because from within that universe the Great Entity defines and maintains everything there is. From the Cosmic point of view, though, the Great Entity is finite and subject to Cosmic conditions; while from the point of view of the Unmanifest, the entire Cosmos and everything in it is a pipsqueak phenomenon not worth noticing.

In the space around the Great Entity, though, are the atoms of all seven Cosmic Planes that the Great Entity swept along with it as it went out to the seventh Cosmic Plane to take up its orbit. Like the Great Entity, these atoms are complex vortices of movement in space, born of the same Cosmic processes as the Great Entity. Unlike the Great Entity, though, they didn't do the rounds of the Cosmos, moving through the Rings and Rays and absorbing every Cosmic influence from every angle. Think of them as the wallflowers of the Cosmos, waiting nervously for someone to invite them to dance. That's what the Great Entity did, and now they're dancing with it, pirouetting around it as it makes its more dignified way around the inconceivably vast arc of the seventh plane.

Those atoms will take on considerably more importance in our narrative as it proceeds. One thing that Fortune mentions a little later on may make them a little more interesting right now, and that's the far from minor point that you, dear reader, are one of those atoms.

More precisely, the essential spiritual core of you is one of those atoms. Just as the Great Entity started out as a single atom and became a vast and intricate structure of movements in space (that is, of consciousness) over immense ages of evolution, you started out the same way and are heading in the same direction. The Great Entity is the Creator of the solar system in which we exist, the parent and great conditioning force of that solar system, but at the heart of each being in that solar system is something that has its origins in the Cosmos. The Solar Logos is in Fortune's view not our father but our elder sibling.

(It's probably worth taking a moment here to remind those of my readers with strong theological opinions that nobody is required to believe *The Cosmic Doctrine*, in the sense of "believe" normally heard in churches. *The Cosmic Doctrine* is not a scripture. It's a set of metaphors designed to teach certain ways of thinking that are otherwise very difficult to grasp. I'm fairly sure that Fortune did believe that the metaphors of *The Cosmic Doctrine* were true, to the extent that any statement that can fit inside a human mind can be said to be true, but I'm just as sure that she didn't make a fuss about that. If you believe other things about God or the gods, bracket Fortune's claim as a misplaced metaphor; the rest of the story works just as well if you identify the Great Entity as a mighty angelic being, for example.)

Let's take a moment to follow the Cosmic atom that became you as it moves through the first phases of its existence. Like the traveling atom that became the Great Entity, it came into being in the seething cauldron of forces at the center of the Cosmos, but its basic geometry was such that it drifted out to one of the seven Cosmic Planes and stopped there, settling into an orbit while the traveling atoms were preparing for their great adventure along the Rays. For ages it circled around, absorbing the influences of the Rays passively, until finally the Great Entity invited it to dance and the music started to play.

As the Great Entity settled into its orbit on the seventh Cosmic Plane and began to bring itself into conscious equilibrium, so did the atom. Since the atom had been through a much narrower range of experiences, that process was much simpler, but your atom and all its companions ended up with their own modest bits of self-knowledge, or to put the same thing another way, their own sets of tracks in space, laying out the range of reactions possible to each. If you like, you can think of the individual atom as the very first and simplest form of soul, and the pattern of reactions in space surrounding it as the very first and simplest form of body.

So we have the Great Entity brooding over its experiences, and the individual atoms that have accompanied it doing the same thing, forming a vast cloud surrounding the Great Entity; and we have the thoughts of the Great Entity becoming movements in space, and drawing the atoms of that cloud into patterns of motion (and thus of consciousness). Since the only things in the consciousness of the Great Entity are patterns of movement/consciousness that came from the Cosmos, the Great Entity's brooding draws the cloud of atoms into a replica of the Cosmos.

So seven planes appear, each one stocked with atoms drawn from the corresponding Cosmic Plane—the first plane with atoms from the first Cosmic Plane, and so on out to the seventh plane with atoms of the seventh Cosmic Plane. Each of the planes divides in turn into seven sub-planes; these are called Regions in the Rosicrucian teachings from which Fortune seems to have derived some of her cosmology, but we'll stick to her term "sub-planes" here. Each sub-plane represents one set of possible reactions on the part of atoms of that plane, and—since substance in *The Cosmic Doctrine* is always and only movement in space— as the atoms of each plane act out those reactions repeatedly, they create substance.

From this point on, as a result, it's necessary to draw a distinction between the original atoms of the seven Cosmic Planes, on the one hand, and the patterns laid down by their movements within the solar system, on the other. Fortune calls the first set Cosmic atoms, reasonably enough, and uses the bare term "atoms" hereafter for the latter.

The Cosmic atoms ultimately belong to the Cosmos, not to the solar system in which they dance. They are younger siblings of the Great Entity, and while they dance in the pattern the Great Entity's brooding sets in motion, that's not the only force that influences them.

That's where the idea of the Great Entity as an infinite and omnipotent god becomes complex, because the Great Entity may be infinite and omnipotent in terms of its solar system, but it's not quite either of these in relation to the Cosmic atoms. They know nothing outside the solar system, but they are still influenced by the background of the Cosmos.

Each Cosmic atom, to be specific, is influenced by the Cosmic Plane where it orbited for all those ages, and when Great Entities of that plane come close, the Cosmic atoms that came from that plane are affected by it. Thus the Cosmic atoms aren't simply puppets of the Solar Logos, the Great Entity at the heart of their solar system. They have their own independent reactions. At times they will contend with the Solar Logos, and the Logos will contend with them—and out of this intricate fabric of contention, compromise, and ultimately cooperation, the solar system takes shape and seeks its destiny.

# CHAPTER TEN

# The Beginnings of Consciousness

## Reading

Revised Edition:    Chapter 9, "The Beginnings of Consciousness,"
pp. 48–51.

Millennium Edition:    Chapter 10, "The Relation Between the Projected
Image and the Logoidal Consciousness," and
Chapter 11, "Auto-Reactions and Cosmic
Memory," pp. 67–72.

## Commentary

This chapter's section from *The Cosmic Doctrine* goes further along the
path sketched out in the last chapter—the trajectory that leads from one
set of metaphors based on physics to another based on psychology. It's
an unfamiliar route in today's world for two reasons. First, our habitual
way of dealing with knowledge is to break it up into separate sciences,
so that—to borrow one of Buckminster Fuller's jokes—nature has to
call an interdepartmental meeting any time a kid throws a stone into
a lake, to figure out how to resolve this unwarranted intrusion of one

discipline on another that proceeds from psychology through anatomy to physics.

The point of the joke, of course, is that divisions between sciences have to do with the limits of human understanding, not with the thing that's being understood. Psychology and physics exist in the same world, subject to the same habitually repeating sequences of events that modern materialist thinkers like to call "natural laws." At least in theory, it should be possible to start from either science and move step by step to the other, making only the changes required by shifts in complexity or scale. That's exactly what Fortune is doing in this section of *The Cosmic Doctrine*. Having built up an elaborate set of metaphors relating to motion in space, she shows how increasing complexity gradually transforms motion into mind—and, of course, vice versa.

That's where we enter into the second source of unfamiliarity, because the gap between physics and psychology, between matter and mind, has been turned into a no man's land full of smoking craters and barbed wire by centuries of bitter quarrels between science and religion. For a long time, it was standard practice in the Western world to split the Cosmos down the middle, handing the material world over to the scientists while turning the world of subjective experience over to the clergy. It's the attempt to overcome this division and claim the whole of existence for one's own that drives the efforts of scientific materialists to insist that mind is "nothing but" something matter does, if mind exists at all; the same attempt drives the efforts of Christian fundamentalists to insist that the Bible ought to be treated as a geology textbook.

One of the things that makes occultism so controversial in today's society is that the subject matter of the occultist is the realm where physics and psychology impinge on one another. To be an occultist is to deal with the places where mind affects matter and matter affects mind— where a symbolic image held in the mind and filled with emotional energy can make things happen in the world of outward experience; where the positions of the stars at the moment of birth reveal an individual's character and destiny; and so on through the roll call of the occult sciences.

It's not unheard of for occultists to engage in the same sort of imperial thinking as scientific and religious fundamentalists, and try to impose occult explanations on the whole of existence. That's why H.P. Blavatsky's first big book, *Isis Unveiled*, spends one thick volume lambasting the science of her time and another lambasting to the mainstream religions of Western Europe and the Americas. (Her critiques didn't age well, which is why even among Theosophists, you won't find many people who've put a significant amount of study into *Isis Unveiled*.) More often, the occultists of Fortune's time placed their discipline in the gap between science and religion, and tried to maintain good relationships with both sides—an attempt that got no more encouragement from either side, to be sure, than it does today.

By and large, this latter approach was Fortune's way of dealing with things. That's why she encouraged her students to study the sciences and to participate in whatever religion made sense to them. (She practiced what she preached; she published books on psychology and soybean cultivation, and most Sundays you could find her at her Anglican parish church.) *The Cosmic Doctrine*, though, took a subtler tack. By presenting metaphors for meditation that move elegantly from physics to psychology, she provided a mental toolkit for bridging the gap between mind and matter without trying to impose any one set of explanations on either. That, to conclude this somewhat lengthy prologue, is the project that this chapter is meant to further.

We are dealing at this stage in her cosmology with the mind of the Solar Logos, the god of this solar system, whose physical body is the sun and whose aura embraces the planets. This is a metaphor that reveals much, though readers who don't have the kind of occult training Fortune's students got may need some help following out its implications. In occult teaching, the aura or Sphere of Sensation is a roughly egg-shaped body of subtle energies that surrounds the physical body. It's the body of consciousness, and its outer surface is both the sense organ by which we perceive patterns in consciousness and the organ of action by which we create such patterns and radiate them outwards for others to perceive. (In modern English, we confuse these two processes by lumping them together under the single word "imagination.")

The solar system is the aura of the Solar Logos. It is the screen on which the influences of other Logoi and of the twelve great Rays of the Cosmos are projected. So—and this is where the metaphor becomes extraordinarily useful—everything Fortune says about the relation between the Solar Logos and the solar system is also being said about the relation between your consciousness and the realm of images and ideas reflected from other minds or created by yours.

So we begin with some developmental psychology. The Solar Logos, remember, has settled into its orbit on the seventh Cosmic Plane after eons of journeying, and the atoms swept up with it in its outward journey form a vast formless cloud around it. The Logos and its companion atoms all go through the various changes and reactions possible to them in their new setting. Think of it as settling into a new neighborhood, meeting the neighbors and figuring out where to shop and what pub's going to be your local from now on, and you've got a decent metaphor for this process. The companion atoms, being much simpler than the Logos, get settled in much faster and then begin a process that's going to play a very large role in what follows.

Fortune's term for this process is "epigenesis." Another term for it, which Fortune also uses and which expresses one of its core aspects very well, is "play." The companion atoms have finished settling in long before the Solar Logos has finished brooding over its experiences, and so they find ways to fill the time until the Logos begins to act on them. That's the first phase of Logoidal evolution—the creation, by the Cosmic atoms, of new possibilities through play—and it's also the seed from which free will, in a certain nuanced sense, eventually unfolds.

The second phase of Logoidal evolution happens as the Logos reflects on its experiences, and those reflections shape the cloud of companion atoms around it. Since the Cosmos is what the Logos has experienced, the solar system is drawn into the image of the Cosmos, with seven Circles or Planes surrounding the Logos and twelve Rays streaming outward from his solar body.

The third phase begins as the Logos begins to reflect on the solar system around it. It has been conscious of the Cosmos, and then of itself; now, it becomes conscious of its surroundings. The differentiation between subject and object now shapes its awareness, and since its broodings are reflected outward into its aura, the Cosmic atoms that form its aura reflect this, and begin to perceive themselves as subjects and other things as objects.

This is an immense shift. Think of what you experience when you wake up from a dream. You move from a state of consciousness with no center, in which "you" can mean a dozen different things in as many moments, to a state in which your own consciousness becomes the center of your experiences. You become a subject, and other things become objects. This allows you to know the things that surround you, but it also allows you to know yourself. That's what happens in the third phase of Logoidal evolution.

It's important to remember that none of this takes place in a vacuum. We've already learned that as the Solar Logos and its companion atoms move in their orbit, they're affected by the forces of the twelve Cosmic Rays, and also by the influences of Logoi and their solar systems on other planes. Once the Logos has awakened to objective consciousness, it is no longer directly aware of these things. They become the exact equivalent of the subconscious influences that affect each of us, and work their way out into the brooding of the Logos and the answering movements of the solar system in exactly the same way that subconscious influences on the human mind reflect themselves first in our thoughts and feelings, and then in the events we experience around us.

Since the Logos isn't deliberately repressing the influences of the Cosmos, they work their way into consciousness in a roundabout fashion—the same way, in turn, that each of us can come to terms with our own subconscious patterns. A Cosmic influence shapes the brooding of the Logos, and causes certain modifications in the solar system. The Logos perceives these, reflects upon them, and integrates them into its own understanding of itself and its solar system. In words, Fortune borrows from the Book of Genesis: it "sees that it is good." This is the process by which the great creative periods take shape: the Days of Creation in Christian esotericism, for example, or the periods of geological history understood by science.

Implied here, of course, is the idea that the Solar Logos learns and grows. It is the god of its solar system—we'll see a little later on where the other beings worshiped by polytheist religions come from and how they relate to the Logos—but neither it, nor they, nor any other being in Fortune's vast metaphor, exists in a static condition of perfection. Everything is learning, growing, exploring new possibilities.

The Cosmic atoms are also learning and growing. Like the Solar Logos, they are conscious of the patterns of tracks in space they have created around themselves, and of the similar patterns that other Cosmic atoms have created around themselves. We call these patterns, in their present extremely complicated form, "bodies," and call the tracks in space that form them "matter." At first, their consciousness is of a very simple form, like the bodies that are its objects, and both grow more complex as the solar system ripens. We'll get to that in future chapters.

Notice, though, that the Cosmic atoms are not conscious of the Solar Logos. Instead, the Logoidal consciousness becomes the subconscious background of the newborn minds of the Cosmic atoms, in exactly the same way that the Cosmos forms the subconscious background of the Logoidal consciousness. As the Cosmic atoms ripen and engage in further epigenesis, they will each develop a personal subconscious, but the Logoidal consciousness remains as the deeper background to their acts and awareness. If you want to borrow a turn of phrase from another occultist with a strong background in psychology—yes, that would be Carl Jung—you can call these the personal unconscious and the collective unconscious, respectively. The implication, as Jung and Fortune would both have agreed, is that the collective unconscious that humans experience is identical at its deepest level to the mind of God.

But what is this thing that we're calling "consciousness"? It's to Fortune's credit that she does not try to dodge this difficult question. She starts by pointing out that consciousness does not belong to the Cosmos; it is not a reaction of the Cosmic atoms in and of themselves; it does not originate from and return to the Logos. It is a modification that affects the Logos and the Cosmic atoms, and it is the first such modification that comes into being as a result of conditions in the solar system as distinct from the Cosmos. It is, to be precise, a matter of tracks in space.

Tracks in space, as my readers will doubtless remember, are how the Cosmos got started in the first place. The same principle gives rise to the solar system as we experience it, but there's a difference, of course. The tracks in space that gave rise to the Cosmos were set in motion by the movement of empty space itself; the tracks in space that become a solar system are set in motion by the movement of Cosmic atoms, whether we're talking about the immensely complex Cosmic atom which has become the Logos of the solar system or the far simpler Cosmic atoms which were swept up in the outward movement of that Great Organism. It's all tracks in space, but within the context of a solar system, there's a point to drawing a distinction between tracks in space that have a Cosmic origin and tracks in space that originate within a solar system, as a result of the actions of things that have a Cosmic origin. That distinction is in fact drawn very often; we call things of the Cosmos by the term "spirit," and things of the solar system "matter."

Between these lies a third kind of thing, which also originates within the solar system and is also a matter of tracks in space. A Cosmic atom reacts to something, and that reaction leaves a track in space that continues to flow even when the Cosmic atom is doing something else. That ongoing flow is memory. As reaction follows reaction and more tracks in space are formed, memories flow together into patterns of pure movement that we can, without too much confusion, call "thoughts" and "images." Over time, the Cosmic atom develops a rich network of movements in space surrounding it, expressing all the potential for reaction that it has gained. We normally call this network "mind."

So we have the Cosmic atom, or spirit; the network of tracks in space surrounding it, which is mind; and the specific repeated movement-patterns the Cosmic atom acts out at any given time, which is body. It can be helpful to try to imagine these in some simple form—say, a Cosmic atom as a single point of light tracing out the pattern of a tri-angle repeatedly, going from angle to angle to angle and around again, while all around the point of light whirl the faint tracks of other possible motions the Cosmic atom isn't making just at that moment. The point of light is spirit, the tracks whirling around it is mind, and the triangle is body. Then imagine yourself as a far more complex version of the same thing: a glowing point of light, which is your spirit; a whirl of possi-bilities tumbling through your consciousness, which is your mind; and a pattern of movement which has swept up billions of other, smaller lives—the cells of your body—into its dance. Meditate on this and you'll find that Fortune's metaphor is the key to much.

CHAPTER ELEVEN

# The Evolution of Consciousness

## Reading

Revised Edition: Chapter 11, "The Evolution of Consciousness," pp. 52–54.

Millennium Edition: Chapter 12, "The Birth of Consciousness in the Universe," pp. 73–76.

## Commentary

This is a difficult chapter for many students, but it's also a very important one, for in it Fortune develops her set of metaphors for consciousness in directions that will have important practical implications. We'll take it a little at a time.

It's important, to begin with, to remember the definition of consciousness Fortune uses, which she introduced in the previous chapter: "consciousness is reaction plus memory." Think about that for a moment. If you had reactions, but no memory, the sensations of each instant would erase the sensations of the previous instant. What's more, none of the sensations would mean anything to you, because meaning is what occurs when you connect a present reaction to a memory from the past: when we say the letter A means a particular sound used in speech, or the word "cat" refers to a four-legged creature that meows, what that indicates is that you connect the shape of the letter or the word to the memory of a sound or an animal.

Alternatively, if you had memory but no reaction, your awareness would be fixed on whatever happened to be in your memory, if anything was, and you would be completely oblivious to what was happening to you at the moment. Combine reaction and memory, though, and you have consciousness; you can perceive at least a little of what is going on around you, and what you perceive can be linked to past perceptions so that it means something to you.

That's one of two definitions of consciousness that Fortune provides. The other is included again in the present chapter: "consciousness is an integration of reactions, so that any change in any part is responded to by the corresponding adjustments of the whole." This definition approaches the same subject from a different angle. Those corresponding adjustments of the whole are the basis of memory; something happens, and the whole system becomes a little different. It is affected by the change: that's reaction. Its structure is changed in an enduring way by the thing that has happened: that's memory.

Human consciousness is this same process made complex by billions of years of evolution, but the same patterns can be seen at work in the brain. Sensory organs respond to specific ranges of stimuli: that's reaction. The brain responds by laying down complex electrobiochemical patterns that enable the reaction to be recalled at a later date: that's memory. Combine the two and you've got the material basis for consciousness. These same two processes can be seen at work in many things other than human beings, some of them not even defined as living by our current notions of what life is. Does that suggest that these things are also conscious, each in its own way? Why, yes, this is indeed what it suggests.

Fortune goes on to differentiate between two levels of consciousness, one of them in the background and the other in the foreground. Each conscious being, whether we're discussing a Solar Logos or one of the countless beings who inhabit the solar system the Logos has created, has some capacities for reaction that have already been worked out in all their permutations over past cycles of experience, and other capacities for reaction that have just been developed by contact with new experiences and have not yet settled into stable relationships. In the case of the Solar Logos, the first of these categories—the background of capacities for reaction that have settled into stable patterns—are the results of its experiences as a traveling atom journeying out and back along the twelve Rays. The second of these categories—the new capacities for reaction still needing to be integrated into a balanced whole—are the results of its experiences as it reflects on itself, and notices its own reactions to the great Cosmic tides.

Human beings, like all other beings in the solar system, also have these two levels of consciousness or, to put things another way, these two parts of the self. The background of capacities for reaction gained in previous lives is called the Individuality, or the Higher Self; the foreground of new capacities being sorted out by conscious action in this life is called the Personality, or the Lower Self. These can be called, without too much inaccuracy, the unconscious and the conscious selves.

It's important to understand how these two parts of the self relate to each other. The Personality in each life lays down reaction-capacities that become part of the Individuality in future lives. In each new life, in turn, the Personality unfolds from the reactions of the Individuality to new experiences. We don't experience the Individuality directly, because our attention is fixed by the foreground of new reactions to new experiences, but it forms the enduring background to the mental activities we perceive.

It would not be going too far, in fact, to speak of the Individuality by using that old-fashioned term "character." Your Individuality is the basis of your character, the source of those enduring habits of thought and action that frame the way you relate to the world. Your Personality can be thought of as a set of potential additions to your Individuality, which you are trying out in the changing conditions of your present life. "That which is the Personality today will be part of the Individuality tomorrow," Fortune writes. Readers who know their way around the literature of Freudian psychology, which Fortune studied, will recognize this as a wry commentary on Freud's overconfident dictum "where Id was, there shall Ego be."

The Solar Logos or Great Entity goes through the same process on a much vaster timescale. Its Personality comes into being as it contemplates the effects of the changing Cosmic tides on itself, and this Personality is built up along the lines already laid down by the Great Entity's experience of the Cosmos. So, in this Personality, there are currents of motion that arc around after vast ages to become three vast Rings; there are twelve Rays that stream out from a center and return to it; there are atoms born of tangential movements set in motion by the Rays, which are caught up and swept along in the currents of motion. All told, there is a mirror image of the Cosmos, reflected in the consciousness of the Great Entity, and this becomes a universe of its own—but the Solar Logos is not the only inhabitant of that universe.

There are also the Cosmic atoms that were swept up by the Great Entity on its way out to its orbit on the seventh Cosmic Plane. They sort themselves out into orbits surrounding the Great Entity according to their own Cosmic Plane of origin. As the Great Entity evolves a Personality—or, to put the same point in a different way, as the Great Entity brings its solar system into being, for the Great Entity's Personality and its solar system are one and the same thing—the other Cosmic atoms are caught up again in the patterns of movement laid down by the Great Entity in its dance. They become the Higher Selves of the beings who will inhabit the solar system, and in over the vast cycles of the solar system's evolution they evolve too, developing their own capacities for reaction and memory.

In the period we are discussing, the period of the first stirrings of consciousness, all this is far in the future. The first development of consciousness in the newborn solar system does not take place in individual Cosmic atoms, although it affects them. Instead, the patterns of movement in space laid down by the Solar Logos in his contemplation become organized among themselves, forming a whole system in which a change to any part affects all the other parts. Consciousness is born, in the form of a vast Oversoul that links everything in the solar system. Eventually, individual souls will emerge from that Oversoul, but the time for that has not yet arrived.

Two points deserve to be noticed here. First, since the solar system is projected as a thought-form by the Great Entity, the solar system and every being in it contain all the reaction-capacities of the Great Entity in latent form. The Cosmic atoms and the embodiments they create around themselves go through the same stages of evolution as the traveling atom that became the Great Entity, but they do so much more quickly, because they are recapitulating rather than breaking new ground. "And God made man after His image, according to His likeness," says the Book of Genesis; *The Cosmic Doctrine* agrees entirely with this statement, but interprets it in a way that draws an unexpected kind of sense out of it.

Second, in the relationship between pure movement in space and the stable atoms generated by movement we have the first sketch of the relation of soul to body. Fortune asks the reader to imagine that each atom, as it moves through space, leaves an invisible "track" of pure movement which remains behind it, frictionless and therefore persistent. If a second atom gets drawn into the same "track" as the first, the "track" deepens and strengthens, while at the same time the track is changed at least a little by the vagaries of the atom. Repeat this countless times, and the track in space becomes a rut along which atom after atom moves.

This is the way the Oversoul affects the individual atoms it overshadows. As the atoms develop new capacities for movement from their encounters with the Oversoul, they lay down their own internal patterns of tracks in space, simple at first and then mounting to dizzying levels of complexity. In this way, the atom begins to develop its own mental dimension, and from the Oversoul emerges an individual soul capable of passing through the cycles of evolution itself.

# CHAPTER TWELVE

# The Beginnings of Mind

## Reading

Revised Edition:   Chapter 12, "The Beginnings of Mind," pp. 55–58.
Millennium Edition:  Chapter 13, "The Beginnings of Mind and Group
                       Consciousness," pp. 77–81.

## Commentary

This chapter is trickier than most, and has to be read carefully in order
to dodge a pitfall or two and find the trail Dion Fortune has marked out.
I suspect, for what it's worth, that this is entirely deliberate. Whenever
the text of *The Cosmic Doctrine* comes close to certain of the secrets of
practical occultism, Fortune becomes evasive. That was standard practice
among occult authors in her time, and she herself defended the practice in her writings. Times have changed, and a great many things that
were secret in her time can be found splashed all over the internet in ours;
that was one of the reasons I decided it was time to write a commentary
on *The Cosmic Doctrine* that's noticeably less reticent than the original text.

    Fortune starts out by drawing a distinction between objects, on the
one hand, and the tracks in space left by the movements of objects,

on the other. An object moves and then comes to rest, but the track in space left by the movement keeps on flowing. These two things, concrete objects and abstract movements of space, form the two halves of the universe we experience. Atoms in motion form the half we call matter, substance, and manifestation; pure movements apart from atoms and other objects form the half we call spirit, mind, and consciousness.

Did you spot the trap? Atoms are themselves pure movement, as Fortune explains repeatedly in the first part of this book. Movement and space, between them, are all there is. Thus the distinction between objects and tracks in space is more apparent than real. Objects are tracks in space that, through repetition, have settled down into a stable condition. The tracks in space that still look like pure movement apart from objects are those that haven't yet gone through all their changes.

One important implication is that what is spirit, mind, and consciousness today, if it sustains itself over time, becomes matter, substance, and manifestation tomorrow. We explored that same point earlier in a different context, when talking about the difference between the Individuality (the part of the self that endures from life to life) and the Personality evolved in each life. The point applies more generally, though. Understand it in its fullness and you grasp the necessity of repetition and rhythm in operative occultism.

With that point made, or rather hinted at, Fortune turns at once to the narrative of the solar system's development she's been tracing out since Chapter 7. On the Cosmic side of things, we have the Solar Logos, once a traveling atom moving through the Cosmos and now the center of a solar system, and we have the Cosmic atoms that were swept up with the Solar Logos on its journey out to the seventh Cosmic Plane, and now circle around the Logos. From this point on references to the Cosmic atoms will be relatively sparse in our text.

This is because we have passed from the Cosmos to the solar system: in effect, into the dream the Solar Logos dreams as it orbits the Central Stillness. That dream is our reality. Though each of us has a Cosmic atom at the core of our being, we don't wake from the dream until we have passed through an entire cycle of evolution.

Within the dream, the phenomena of the solar system take center stage. Those consist, first, of the tracks in space laid down by the uncoordinated movements of the Cosmic atoms, which (since any repeated movement ends up becoming a manifested reality) become atoms in their own right, the raw material out of which the solar system will take shape. Second, we have the tracks in space laid down by the dance of the Solar Logos, which reflect the Logoidal experience of the Cosmos and draw the atoms of the solar system into their pattern.

Those are the ingredients of a solar system. Because the consciousness of the Solar Logos has been imprinted with the rhythms and patterns of the Cosmos, its dance imitates the Cosmos, and everything else in its solar system is drawn into that imitation and becomes part of a Cosmos in miniature. At the center, in place of the Central Stillness of the Cosmos, is the Solar Logos, and the same pattern of Rings, Circles, and Rays discussed in the commentary to the first part of *The Cosmic Doctrine* is recreated anew on a smaller scale.

That process doesn't happen all at once. Remember that the Solar Logos is still part of the Cosmos, and is constantly being influenced as it follows its orbit on the seventh Cosmic Plane around the Central Stillness by the Rays through which it passes and by other Great Entities on higher Cosmic Planes. Each of these things causes adjustments in the movements of the Logos—that is to say, in the Logoidal consciousness, for in Fortune's metaphor mind and movement are the same thing—and these adjustments cause corresponding adjustments in the dance of the atoms about the Logos.

Thus the Logos moves in its immense and intricate dance; one after another, the movements of the dance lay down tracks in space; through repetition, the tracks become enduring currents of space, and begin to influence the movements of objects that encounter them. One after another, the structures of the Cosmos are mirrored in the newborn solar system, and every object in the solar system is drawn into those patterns and begins to absorb the imprint of the Cosmos to at least some degree.

The objects that matter most at this stage of the process are the secondary atoms—the atoms created by repeated movements in the solar system, not the Cosmic atoms that existed before the solar system was born. As in the Cosmos, so in the solar system, some atoms are more complex than others. They sort themselves out in exactly the same way, most of them settling out into seven planes, which can be imagined as great concentric circles orbiting the Solar Logos.

(A note on planes is probably in order here. In the Rosicrucian philosophy that underlies Fortune's grand metaphor, there are seven great Cosmic Planes, six of which are completely outside our knowledge and understanding; everything we are capable of knowing about exists on the seventh Cosmic Plane. The seventh Cosmic Plane is divided into seven planes, which are the planes on which our spiritual evolution takes place. Each of the seven planes is divided in turn into seven sub-planes or regions; the physical plane, for example, is divided into the solid region, the liquid region, the gaseous region, and four etheric regions, the chemical ether, the life ether, the light ether, and the reflecting ether. Fortune's students learned all this material from the standard occult literature of the time, and some of the details of *The Cosmic Doctrine* make more sense if you keep the Cosmic Planes, the planes, and the sub-planes separate in your mind.)

There's an interesting reversal between the Cosmos and the solar system that needs to be kept in mind. In the Cosmos, the seventh Cosmic Plane, where the most complex Cosmic atoms settle out, is the plane furthest from the Central Sun. In a solar system, by contrast, the seventh plane is the one nearest the center, and thus closest to the Logos. This is one of the ways that a solar system is a Cosmos turned inside out.

This is crucial here because not all the atoms of the solar system settle out into the seven planes. Some are too complex and become traveling atoms, like the traveling atoms of the Cosmos but on a far smaller scale. The traveling atoms, like their Cosmic equivalents, have a more complex destiny than their simpler cousins; they are imprinted by the Logoidal consciousness—and since this has been conditioned by the Cosmos, the traveling atoms of the solar system receive at second hand the same Cosmic imprint as the traveling atoms of the Cosmos.

In the metaphor, of course, that's expressed in terms of motion. So you have great numbers of secondary atoms that are too complex to settle out in any of the seven planes of the solar system, and each of these dances in rhythm with the Solar Logos. The dance, as it repeats itself, becomes a track in space echoing the thoughts of the Logos. So these traveling atoms become twofold entities: a complex atom, with a track in space laid down by its attunement with the Logos, which governs the motion of the atom.

Since that track in space is pure motion, it is of the same nature as the motions of the Logos and can interact in some sense with the Logoidal consciousness. Since it has been shaped by the motions of the Logoidal consciousness, it contains in embryonic form all the possibilities for reaction that the Logos itself evolved during its long ages as a traveling atom of the Cosmos. The secondary atoms that settle into place in the seven sub-planes have that same potential, but since they don't come into direct contact with the Logos the potential remains unfulfilled for the time being. In the traveling atoms, that potential becomes a reality. In this way, as already noted, God makes man in His image and likeness.

So we have our secondary traveling atoms. Each one is a set of movements that has become stereotyped through repetition and now acts like an object. Each one also picks up a new set of movements absorbed from the dance of the Solar Logos, which gives it a set of new possibilities for reaction and memory—which, as my readers will recall, is Fortune's definition of consciousness. Finally, each of these atoms begins to attract other atoms into its dance. These latter are not traveling atoms but ordinary stay-at-home atoms of the seventh plane. These form a body, the seventh-plane body of a new kind of entity.

The original traveling atom is called the seed-atom, and Fortune calls it "the beginnings of a vehicle." The term "vehicle" was much used in the occultism of her time, whereas nowadays most occultists prefer "body." The seed-atom is overshadowed by the track in space that guides its motions and those of its seventh-plane body. As we'll see, this track in space has a special destiny. If the seventh-plane atoms attracted by the seed-atom are the first foreshadowings of a body, the track in space is the first foreshadowing of a spirit, and the composite being made up of these three things is an entity capable of evolution.

Each such entity is a reflection, within the solar system, of a Cosmic atom which is the spiritual essence of that entity. As already noted, Fortune will have little to say about the Cosmic atoms in much of what follows, but they should not be forgotten. The Cosmic atom was there before the solar system was born and will be there after it has dissolved; it enters into manifestation in a solar system for an entire evolution the way a soul enters a body for a single incarnation—and the composite form made up of a seed-atom, a track in space, and a seventh-plane body is the most basic form of its embodiment, the form you had at the beginning of your own journey through the realms of manifestation.

That's a key theme to keep in mind as we proceed. We are not talking about things that happened to some other kind of being in some other Cosmos far, far away. What Fortune is trying to communicate, using the nearest approximate metaphor, is your own spiritual biography, the immense journey that brought you to the beginning of this life: as Iolo Morganwg's *Barddas* puts it, "through every form capable of body and life to the state of man." As we proceed further, the applicability of Fortune's great metaphor to our individual lives will become increasingly clear.

*CHAPTER THIRTEEN*

# The Evolution of the Divine Sparks

## Reading

Revised Edition: Chapter 13, "The Evolution of the Divine Sparks," pp. 59–64.
Millennium Edition: Chapter 13, "The Seed Atom Building a Seventh Plane Body," pp. 82–89.

## Commentary

In the last several chapters, Fortune has discussed the emergence of the raw materials of a solar system and their organization into a swarm of individual beings, each of them composed of three parts: a seed-atom that began as one of the traveling atoms of the solar system, a shell of seventh-plane atoms that gather around the seed-atom and form the first and simplest kind of body, and a set of tracks in space marked out by the rhythms of the Solar Logos, which form the first and simplest kind of mind.

There are also vast numbers of atoms not yet organized into individual beings, circling the Solar Logos like clouds of dust around a newborn sun. That's the image Fortune wants you to think of, because her grand metaphor draws extensively on the astrophysics of her time. If you keep in mind accounts of the solar system's origin from popular scientific literature, you'll have an easier time following along with the material in this chapter.

The individual beings, though, are the ones who matter just now. The seed-atom and its shell of seventh-plane atoms go through their various changes and gradually settle down into a stable rhythm. The tracks in space are another matter. From here on, Fortune calls these the Divine Sparks, as they are reflections of the Solar Logos' own consciousness—in terms of the metaphor, patterns of movement that echo the movements of the Logos. The Divine Sparks don't settle down to a stable rhythm, because they're constantly being influenced by three sets of movements from outside themselves. First, each Divine Spark is pulled this way and that by the movements of the seed-atom to which it relates; second, each Divine Spark is jostled by all the other Divine Sparks around it; third, each Divine Spark is constantly influenced by the Solar Logos itself.

So the Divine Sparks remain nimble and capable of learning, and what starts out as a random jostling of one Divine Spark by another gradually settles into something far more complex: a reflection of the Solar Logos made up of all the individual beings that have come into existence, held in balance by their Divine Sparks. Think of it as a spherical mass of atoms—a planet—orbiting the Solar Logos in the seventh plane. As the Divine Sparks and their atoms interact, they establish a rhythm and form a set of tracks in space, which—since movement is consciousness—becomes the collective consciousness of the newborn planet.

Dion Fortune engages in another bit of trickery here, and those readers who know their way around geometry, sacred or otherwise, will doubtless have caught it already. The symbol of the Solar Logos is a sphere, she notes, and the number of primary manifestation is three; therefore the symbol of the first satellite is a three-sided pyramid in a sphere. She might as well have said a three-sided pentagram, since there are of course no three-sided pyramids; the pyramidal figure with the smallest number of sides is a tetrahedron, which has four sides. (Did you forget to count the bottom?)

Again, as long as you remember that all this is metaphor, you're fine. For practical purposes, the symbol of the first satellite is a circle surrounding a triangle; just keep in mind that the circle represents a sphere, and the triangle represents a threefold pattern in space.

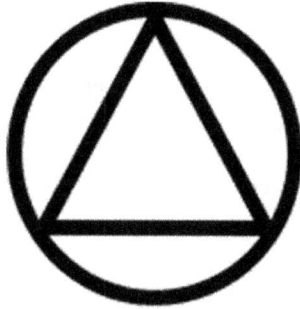

Symbol of the First Satellite

So we have the first satellite orbiting the Solar Logos. The Solar Logos is aware of it, and each of the Divine Sparks is aware, to some degree, of the Solar Logos. The collective consciousness of the planet—the Planetary Spirit, as Fortune will call it in the next chapter[1]—is not aware of the Solar Logos, but she is aware that the Divine Sparks are aware of something that she cannot perceive itself. She knows herself and the conditions of her existence, and she knows the atoms whose motions in space have brought her into being; as the Divine Sparks are influenced by the Solar Logos and change accordingly, she learns indirectly of the Solar Logos that conditions them.

As the consciousness of the Divine Sparks becomes more and more coordinated, the collective consciousness of the planet gets a clearer and clearer understanding of the Logos as reflected through the minds of the Sparks, and so she achieves an awareness of the Solar Logos. Meanwhile, the Solar Logos has something new to think about; the experiences of the atoms and Divine Sparks on the first satellite are unfamiliar to the Logos, and it turns inward, contemplating these, until it has absorbed those experiences and integrated them into its understanding of things. While that happens, the Divine Sparks keep doing what they were doing, and the Planetary Spirit keeps doing what she was doing, and the resulting repeated movements build up tracks in space that form a template for the first satellite.

---

[1]Fortune had trouble making up her mind about what to call this entity. In the first published version it was the Planetary Spirit; in the revised version, it was the Planetary Being. I prefer Planetary Spirit, as this is the term used in other occult literature, and so that's the label we will be using in this commentary.

Then the Solar Logos finishes its contemplations and turns its attention back to the solar system. Its dance has changed, the dances of the Divine Sparks change accordingly, the pattern of balanced stresses that holds the first satellite together breaks up, and so does the first satellite. All the individuals that composed it go spinning away into the great dust cloud of atomic matter that surrounds the Solar Logos, and a cycle of involution comes to its end.

Two things happen thereafter, though. The first is that the individual beings, having absorbed the possibility of integrating themselves as a planet, do the same thing again. Since they've worked through all the possibilities of their seventh-plane bodies, they have enough (metaphoric) mass to attract atoms of the sixth plane, and so they add a shell of sixth-plane atoms to the seventh-plane body they already have. They proceed to form a new satellite on the sixth plane, and work through all the changes there that they worked through on the seventh, gradually evolving a collective consciousness that becomes a new Planetary Spirit.

At the same time, the Planetary Spirit of the first satellite didn't go away; she remains, an intricate pattern of tracks in space, just waiting for atoms to fill it. There are plenty of seventh-plane atoms drifting around aimlessly, and over time enough of them get drawn into the tracks in the space of the Planetary Spirit that a new planet is born.

These atoms, though, have a conditioning influence the first swarm of traveling atoms didn't have. The Planetary Spirit absorbed all the influences of the traveling atoms, was conscious of their consciousness, and gradually reached the point at which she could contemplate the Solar Logos. Her rhythmic dance thus includes all the capacities of the first swarm of seed-atoms, including their ability to gather a seventh-plane body and the pattern of tracks in space that linked them to the Solar Logos. The atoms gathered by the Planetary Spirit accordingly pick up all these capacities, and become individual beings with Divine Sparks and seventh-plane bodies. Thus the traveling atoms of the first swarm are the makers of the Planetary Spirit, but the Planetary Spirit is the mother of each of the subsequent swarms.

The whole process then repeats. The Divine Sparks of the first swarm, on the new planet of the sixth plane, integrate themselves to the point that the new Planetary Spirit can experience the Solar Logos; the Divine Sparks of the second swarm go through their own changes on the first planet under the guidance of its Planetary Spirit; the Solar Logos retreats into contemplation, absorbing all the new experiences of the atoms of the first two swarms; then it turns its attention outward again, and the two planets dissolve.

The first swarm then moves out to the fifth plane, and begins building a new planet there. The second swarm moves to the sixth-plane satellite, and gets to work building its own sixth-plane bodies under the guidance of the second Planetary Spirit. Meanwhile, another batch of seventh-plane atoms gets swept up into the embrace of the first Planetary Spirit, which teaches them to build seventh-plane bodies and endows them with Divine Sparks.

The process continues, until there are seven planets revolving around the Solar Logos, each one with its own Planetary Spirit, each one inhabited by individual beings who have a number of bodies appropriate to the plane they have reached. The process doesn't end there, but what happens when all seven planets are in existence will be the subject of a later chapter.

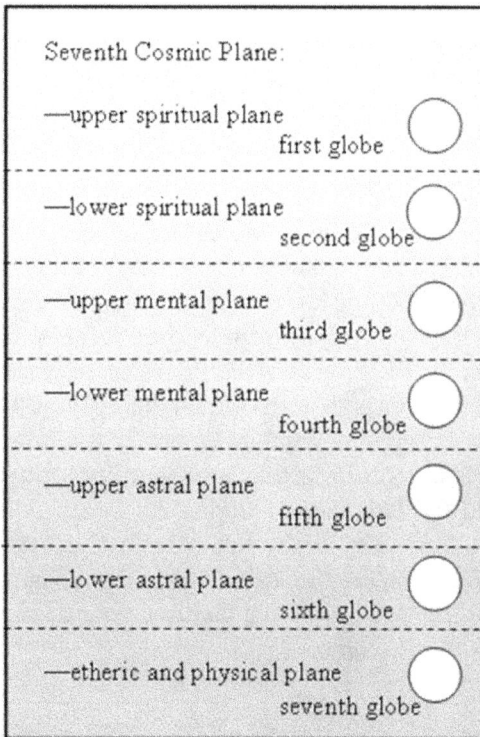

Seventh Cosmic Plane:

—upper spiritual plane
first globe ◯

—lower spiritual plane
second globe ◯

—upper mental plane
third globe ◯

—lower mental plane
fourth globe ◯

—upper astral plane
fifth globe ◯

—lower astral plane
sixth globe ◯

—etheric and physical plane
seventh globe ◯

Planes of Being 3

(It's probably worth putting in a caution here, because many readers who reach this chapter jump to the conclusion that since the Earth is the third planet from the Sun in our solar system, it must be the third planet to be created in the process we're discussing, and thus exists on the fifth plane. Not so; as will be explained later on, the planets came into being in a specific order, which is not the order they form going outward from the Sun. For the time being, though, think of the swarms moving outward from the Solar Logos and then back again; this will make it easier to make sense of the process, and you can adjust your understanding later as we get to the true order of the planets.)

Something else has been going on all this time, though, while the swarms have been taking shape and proceeding down the planets. Remember that the Solar Logos is aware of the Divine Sparks, just as they are (in a much more limited way) aware of the Logos. Every time a swarm of individual beings finishes its evolution on a planet, and the Solar Logos turns inward to contemplate the new experiences of that evolution, it integrates all those experiences into its consciousness—in the metaphor, it expresses them in the motions of its dance. As each swarm of atoms in the first planet acquires a Divine Spark, that Divine Spark moves in harmony with the dance of the Solar Logos at the time when it is formed.

As a result, each swarm of atoms comes into being on the seventh plane with all the lessons of its predecessors embodied in abstract form in its Divine Spark. The first swarm, composed of the traveling atoms of the solar system, does the heaviest of the heavy lifting in creating the planets; each of the next two swarms, as we'll see, also has a particular task to take care of in the genesis of the solar system. The beings of these three swarms have names in each of the religious traditions Dion Fortune drew on in shaping her great metaphor. In the language of Jewish Cabala and Christian theology; they are identified with the hierarchies of the angels; in the language of traditional Pagan religion, they are called gods and goddesses. In the Rosicrucian philosophy that underlies *The Cosmic Doctrine*, they are called the Lords of Flame, the Lords of Form, and the Lords of Mind. We'll be discussing them in much more detail in the chapters to come.

CHAPTER FOURTEEN

# The Evolution of a Planetary Spirit

## Reading

Revised Edition:   Chapter 14, "The Evolution of a Planetary Being,"
pp. 65–69.

Millennium Edition:   Chapter 15, "Evolution of the First Planetary
Form," pp. 91–96.

## Commentary

This chapter continues the discussion of planetary evolution started in the previous chapter, "The Evolution of the Divine Sparks," adding additional details to this phase of Dion Fortune's grand metaphor. Fortune begins by briefly recapitulating the themes of the previous chapter, and then spends several paragraphs reviewing the structure of the individual entities that have come into being at this stage of the evolutionary process. It's worth taking the time to work through what she's saying here, because it provides—in metaphoric terms, of course—a key to that very large branch of occult philosophy that deals with the subtle bodies of the individual human being.

Fortune sorts out the different parts of the entity as follows:

**The Cosmic atom or traveling atom:** this is the essential core of the entity, the one part that partakes of the reality of the Cosmos and does not simply belong to the dream-body of the Solar Logos—or, as we call it, the solar system. Like the Solar Logos, it came into being out of the play of energies in the Central Sun of the Cosmos, but was insufficiently complex to set out as the Solar Logos did on the long journey up and down the twelve Great Rays, and settled down instead on one of the seven Cosmic Planes surrounding the Central Sun. It then was gathered up by the gravitational attraction of the Great Entity as that being swept out to the Seventh Plane to become the Solar Logos of our system. The traveling atoms, then, by their uncoordinated movements, created the patterns of movement in space that became the atomic raw material of the solar system.

As Cosmic entities, the traveling atoms are real in a way the atoms of the solar system are not. They are also far more primitive, because the atoms of the solar system, once the Logos begins to coordinate them, receive the imprint of the Logoidal awareness and absorb some of its complexity. The long history of the soul, in Fortune's metaphor, is the process by which a Cosmic atom not yet prepared to make the journey through the twelve Cosmic Rays is prepared for that journey through its initiation by the Solar Logos.

**The seed-atom:** this is the atom within the solar system created by the steady rhythmic movement of the traveling atom at rest, and therefore is most directly connected to the traveling atom. You can think of it as the representation of the traveling atom within the dream-body of the Solar Logos. You can also think of it as the Lower Self or Personality in relation to the traveling atom as Higher Self or Individuality.

**The Divine Spark:** this is the pattern of abstract movement set in motion by the Solar Logos, which affects the seed-atom and functions as the first template of its mind. Each seed-atom has such a pattern linked with it, created by the movements of the seed-atom in response to the vast and complex dance of the Solar Logos. If the seed-atom is the Lower Self and the traveling atom is the Higher Self, the Divine Spark is the guardian angel, which is set to watch over the Lower Self until such time as it is able to contact and unite with its own Higher Self, and begin to act on the Cosmic level.

**The seven shells:** these are the bodies the seed-atom gathers around itself by its own repetitive movements, and are made of the atomic matter created by the traveling atoms in the early days of the solar system. Each traveling atom has its own ordinary rhythmic motion, which forms its associated seed-atom, but each traveling atom also makes other movements in response to the various influences imping-ing on it from the Logos and from other traveling atoms, and when these become rhythmic they create atoms. From the mass of unorga-nized atomic matter thus produced, each seed-atom gathers up a certain number of atoms in its dance, and those form its body on whatever plane it then inhabits.

As we saw in the previous chapter, the seed-atoms make their way outward through the seven planes of the solar system, and in each plane they evolve the capacity to build a body of the matter of that plane. Those bodies are the seven shells Fortune discusses. In her taxonomy, they belong to the physical-etheric (1st), lower astral (2nd), upper astral (3rd), lower mental (4th), upper mental (5th), lower spiritual (6th), and upper spiritual (7th) planes. Each seed-atom evolves the capacity to build a seventh-plane body first, and then adds the others one at a time as it descends the planes to the plane of dense matter, the one we perceive with our senses.

Note the phrasing above: each seed-atom evolves the capacity to build a body of the matter of each plane. In terms of Fortune's meta-phor, that capacity consists of a network of tracks in space laid down by repetitive motion, into which atoms of the appropriate plane are then drawn. Exactly the same process leads to the emergence of another cat-egory of beings, the one with whom this chapter is chiefly concerned: the Planetary Spirits.[2]

The Planetary Spirits are "creations of the created," to use a term Fortune deploys extensively in other parts of her writing. They are not, as the Solar Logos and the Cosmic atoms are, realities on the planes that transcend the solar system; they exist entirely within the solar system, and they are not created not by the Solar Logos, the god of the solar system. They are independent beings in their own right, however, and as waves of evolution pass over them, they themselves evolve, becom-ing vast and complex thinking beings, far greater than the beings that inhabit the planets they rule. The Planetary Spirit of the Earth is the being that systems ecologists call Gaia, the natural philosophers of an earlier time called Nature, and the natural religions of the world describe as

---

[2] As already noted, these are called Planetary Beings in the revised edition of Fortune's text, but I prefer the original term "Planetary Spirit," as it refers usefully to older occult traditions.

the goddess of the Earth. She passed through immense cycles of evolution long before you and I started on our own evolutionary journey, and our lives on Earth are conditioned by her consciousness.

As already hinted, the evolutionary process that brought her and the other Planetary Spirits of this solar system into being echoes the process by which the seed-atoms acquire bodies. As we saw in the previous chapter, the Planetary Spirits are created by the activities of the swarms of seed-atoms guided by their Divine Sparks. Each swarm, as it forms itself into a planetary mass and goes through its evolution on the resulting planet, creates a set of tracks in space that will affect all other entities, and all atomic matter, that come into contact with it. Thus the first swarm builds the planetary forms as it proceeds on its way from the seventh to the first plane; every subsequent swarm is drawn into the form already established. Once it has finished absorbing the influences left behind by previous swarms, it elaborates the pattern of tracks in space further, taking the evolution of the Planetary Spirit further. In the process, each swarm gives the Planetary Spirit the capacity to build the same body the swarm itself is learning how to build in that phase of its evolution.

Did you catch Fortune setting another of her traps for the literal-minded here? The way the metaphor was set out in the previous chapter, each planet exists on its own plane, and each swarm comes to the planet, learns how to build new bodies of the matter of that plane, and then goes on. In the next chapter, we'll be given a different metaphor, according to which the planet of the seventh plane just has seventh-plane matter, the planet on the sixth plane has matter of the seventh and sixth planes, and so on down to the planet on the first plane, which has matter of all seven planes. In this chapter, by contrast, each planet gradually picks up the capacity to build bodies of all seven kinds of matter, until each planet has the capacity to take a swarm of Divine Sparks all the way through the process of evolution right there, on its own surface.

Fortune stresses that the Divine Sparks don't have to go from planet to planet to gain the ability to take on an additional body, since atoms of all types are everywhere—another shift from the metaphor in the previous chapter, in which the atoms of each type form separate rings extending outward from the Solar Logos. Which of these is the truth about the way the solar system was built? Ahem. "These images are not descriptive but symbolic, and are designed to train the mind, not to inform it." *The Cosmic Doctrine* is not a textbook of astrophysics. It's a set of metaphors meant to teach you to think in certain ways, so that you can understand the universe in a way that furthers the process of initiation.

Of the various ways to think about Planetary Spirits and the Solar Logos, for what it's worth, the one that comes closest to the way astrophysicists currently talk about the genesis of planets and the Sun is the one given in this chapter. There are, in fact, eight planets circling the Sun—Mercury, Venus, Earth, Mars, Jupiter, Saturn, Uranus, and Neptune—along with a flurry of moons, another flurry of dwarf planets such as Ceres, Pluto, and Sedna, not to mention the asteroid belt, the Kuiper belt, and the Van Oort Cloud out there at the solar system's blurry edges. Getting all this to fit into some kind of sevenfold order would require enough stretching and chopping to put Procrustes to shame.

Thus, if you want to think about the genesis of the actual planet you're standing on, you can think of each planet as starting out as a pattern of stresses created on the upper spiritual plane by the actions of the first of the swarms—the Lords of Flame, as we'll be calling them shortly—and being given additional bodies by each of the subsequent swarms, until they each finally sweep up their quota of dust and gases and become physical planets. That said, thinking about the genesis of the actual planet you're standing on is not the only thing Fortune has in mind here, and the other metaphors also have their place in the structure of ideas Fortune is building.

In terms of this chapter's metaphor, however, we have a sequence of planets, each with its own Planetary Spirit. These beings are far from identical, for each one is powerfully shaped by the stage of evolution the Lords of Flame had reached when they were building the Planetary Spirit's initial structure. Here we have the basis, in terms of Fortune's metaphor, for the differing influences of the planets in astrology. On these planets, various beings go through the process of evolution, taking on forms of increasing complexity so that they can absorb the patterns of abstract movement that underlie the forms, and so develop their own capacities.

And the goal of this whole process? That's the last theme Fortune develops in this chapter.

Each of the entities we've been discussing, as already noted, consists of a Cosmic atom linked to a series of movement-patterns within the aura or dream-body of the Solar Logos—the seed-atom, the Divine

Spark, and the seven shells forming its bodies on each plane. The seed-atom is a creation of the Cosmic atom, the Divine Spark is a creation of the Solar Logos, and the atoms forming the seven shells were created by the Cosmic atoms collectively through their uncoordinated movements at the dawn of the solar system.

The Cosmic atom itself, though, was not created at all—not created, at least, in any sense relevant to the things of the solar system. The Cosmic atom is a younger brother or sister of the Solar Logos, born as the Logos was, out of the surging energies of the Central Sun of the Cosmos. As the seed-atom linked with it goes through the mighty dance of evolution with the Solar Logos, the seed-atom gradually increases in complexity and power until it can identify itself with the Cosmic atom that created it. Once this happens, the Cosmic atom attains a level of complexity and power sufficient to become a traveling atom in the Cosmos, and go through the long journey up and down the twelve great Rays that will eventually prepare it to become the Logos of a solar system of its own.

"These last details have never been revealed before," Fortune says. In making that claim, she's prevaricating, because they may have been new to the British occult scene when *The Cosmic Doctrine* was first published, but they were far from new in any other sense. A nearly identical scheme of Cosmic evolution has played a central role in the theology of the Mormon church since well before the death of Joseph Smith in 1844. Where Smith came by it is an interesting question, and I'm by no means prepared to dismiss out of hand the claim that he got it from the angel Moroni—John Dee, very much to his dismay, was introduced to the concept of reincarnation by an angel named Madimi in 1586—but similar ideas can be found all through American occultism and alternative spirituality in the nineteenth century, and Smith was far from being the illiterate farm boy who sometimes features in both pro- and anti-Mormon literature.

How literally should this part of the metaphor be taken? Any of my readers who happen to be Mormons, or find themselves entranced by such grand visions of Cosmic evolution, are welcome to take it as literally as they wish. My own take, for whatever that's worth, is that if evolution has some kind of goal—which is frankly an open question—and if that goal is the same for every single being in the Cosmos—which strikes me as a very uncertain bet at best—then the nature of that goal would inevitably be far beyond the reach of the very modest mental capacities possessed by human beings in our current stage of evolution.

What remains to us is metaphor. Christian evangelists in the eighteenth century, trying to find a way to talk about the bliss of Heaven to audiences of working-class people exhausted by sixteen-hour days in the shrieking clamor and smoke-filled darkness of early industrial factories, got the idea across by picturing a realm of luminous clouds and unbroken rest where the loudest sound was the soft plucking of harp strings. In much the same way, the idea of each individual soul becoming the Solar Logos of a future solar system and presiding over the process by which more souls take the same path is, among other things, a potent way to talk about the way that each initiate becomes capable of passing on initiation, whether in the formal setting of a magical lodge or in casual interactions in the course of ordinary life. What other meanings might be extracted from this aspect of the metaphor, and whether to give Fortune's proposal any credence at all on a less metaphoric level, is up to each individual student of *The Cosmic Doctrine*.

## CHAPTER FIFTEEN

# Evolution of the Lords of Flame, Form, and Mind

### Reading

Revised Edition: Chapter 15, "Evolution of the Lords of Flame, Form, and Mind," pp. 70–75.

Millennium Edition: Chapter 16, "Evolution of the Lords of Flame, Form, and Mind," pp. 97–103.

### Commentary

The construction of the solar system in Dion Fortune's metaphor continues in this chapter. Over the last two chapters, we've watched the first swarms of individual entities begin their pilgrimage down the planes of being. We've seen how their activities on each plane bring a planet into being, and we've watched each planet develop its own Planetary Spirit, which conditions each of the subsequent swarms of entities as these descend the planes in turn. Now it's time to look a good deal more closely at the three original swarms—the Lords of Flame, Form, and Mind.

Here Fortune is enriching her metaphor with material that has deep roots in the Western occult tradition. I doubt that many of my readers will have encountered the technical terms *epiphaniai*, *epiphonomiai*, and *ephiomai*—literally "appearances," "voices," and "acclamations"— which were used for these beings by Renaissance occultists such as Robert Fludd, though I suspect that Fortune knew the terms. To summarize a great deal of lore too quickly, though, the Lords of Flame are the beings that both occultists and more orthodox believers call angels. The Lords of Form are the beings that occultists of various traditions call devas. The Lords of Mind are the beings that many occultists call intelligences. The capacious logic of polytheism tends to give these and other beings such labels as *numina* or *kami*; "gods" will do in English, if you happen to be a polytheist, or are comfortable contrasting "gods" with a small "g" to God with the capital letter.

Let's begin with the angelic Lords of Flame, the first swarm to set out from the Solar Logos and descend through the seven planes of the solar system the Logos has dreamed into existence. (Remember that in our text, when Fortune writes "universe," she means "solar system"—that was standard usage in her day, at a time when other galaxies had not yet been discovered.) This first swarm is made up of those atoms that became complex enough in the solar system's first phases of evolution to take part in the journey up and down the solar system's twelve Rays; they are equivalents, in the smaller scale of the solar system, of the traveling atoms of the Cosmos—one of whom is now the Solar Logos, the god of our solar system. So they come to the work of creating a solar system with much more experience, and much more complexity, than subsequent swarms.

That's the first thing that sets the Lords of Flame apart. The second is that they begin their work when the solar system consists solely of the Solar Logos and a formless cloud of atoms around it, dancing to the rhythms the Logos sets in motion. The sole influence on their evolution is the Solar Logos. Later swarms also receive the influences of the Planetary Spirits; the Lords of Flame don't.

Those are the things that make life easy for the Lords of Flame. The thing that makes life hard for them is that they are the first. If you will, they boldly go where no Divine Sparks have gone before. They have to build bodies out of the raw material of the seventh plane, using atoms that have never before been organized into a body. Since atoms are nothing more than habitual tracks of motion, this means that the atoms have to be reshaped comprehensively to make their movement-tracks fit the needs of a seventh-plane body. That's just the individual side of the work the Lords of Flame must accomplish. They also have to work together to build the body of a planet on the seventh plane, and the atoms that are their raw material have never been part of a planet, either.

Thus the Lords of Flame have their work cut out for them. When they arrive on each plane, they are surrounded by a mass of unorganized atoms. When they leave it, they leave behind a pattern of forces so intricately coordinated that all subsequent swarms are drawn into it and formed by it. To use a metaphor from esoteric Masonry, they have the role of Solomon King of Israel, setting out the fundamental patterns and proportions that subsequent workers on the planetary Temple will follow.

The second swarm has a different task and a different destiny. The Lords of Form or devas of nature begin as ordinary atoms of the seventh plane that are drawn into the archetypal form of the seventh-plane planet once the Lords of Flame leave it. They gather up bodies of other seventh-plane atoms and attune themselves to the Planetary Spirit in the same way that the Lords of Flame did, but they don't have to do it all from scratch; the tracks in space laid down on the planet of the seventh plane make building a body easier than it was for their predecessors, and they don't have to create the Planetary Spirit, they just have to learn to work with her.

Both of those advantages come with corresponding drawbacks. The tracks in space that help the Lords of Form build their bodies were laid down by the very different consciousness of the Lords of Flame, and so the Lords of Form have to balance out the resulting vagaries. The same thing on an even larger scale happens when they deal with the Planetary Spirit. On each plane, the Lords of Flame condition the Planetary Spirit, but the Lords of Form and all subsequent swarms are conditioned by her. Each Lord of Form thus has to balance the sometimes conflicting influences of the Solar Logos and of the Planetary Spirit of the planet on which the Lords of Form are then incarnate.

The Lords of Form also have a unique function as they work their way down the planes. They come into being on the seventh plane when the Lords of Flame have gone on to the sixth, and build seventh-plane bodies; when the Lords of Flame go on to the fifth plane, the Lords of Form proceed to the sixth, enter into the planet that has been built there, and get to work building sixth-plane bodies and attuning with the Planetary Spirit of that plane. Then the Lords of Flame go on to the fourth plane, and the Lords of Form are caught between the gravitational attraction of the fifth and seventh-plane planets. The conflicting pulls are strong enough that the seventh and sixth-plane bodies they've built dissolve into their component atoms, and those atoms are caught up in the structure of the sixth-plane planet and remain there.

Meanwhile, the Lords of Form circle back to the Solar Logos, pick up the Logoidal vibration again, and start out anew. Since they've already built seventh and sixth-plane bodies, they do this quickly, and land on the fifth plane while the Lords of Flame are still busy with their pioneering work on the fourth. When the Lords of Flame go on to the third plane, though, the same thing happens to the Lords of Form; their seventh, sixth, and fifth plane bodies dissolve, and the atoms of which those bodies are made become the raw material of the fifth plane planet, and back the Lords of Form go to the Solar Logos to repeat the same process, bringing atoms of higher planes to each planet as they go. In the language of esoteric Masonry, the Lords of Form have the role of Hiram King of Tyre, who provided the raw materials for the building of the Temple.

Meanwhile, the third of the three primal swarms is getting underway. When the Lords of Form move from the seventh plane to the sixth, another batch of seventh-plane atoms are drawn into the Planetary Spirit on that plane and form a new body for her. Like the Lords of Form, they take on the patterns already laid down, becoming individualized beings, building seventh-plane bodies, and entering into rapport with the Planetary Spirit. This third swarm has an easy time of it on each plane, since the atoms it forms into its bodies are already conditioned by having been part of the body of an evolving entity in the solar system. They finish their work faster than the first two swarms do, but they can't move on until the swarm before them takes another step, so there they remain.

Any of my readers who have ever witnessed what happens in a room full of seven-year-olds who have nothing to do, or who remember how their own seven-year-old selves responded to such a situation, know what happens next. They start to play, and tolerably often, this means they get into trouble. That's what happens to the third swarm. They get rambunctious with one another and with the Planetary Spirit, and the result is what Fortune calls epigenesis.

That's a sufficiently important concept in *The Cosmic Doctrine* that it deserves a more complete description here. Epigenesis is what less careful philosophers call "free will." Consider the way that trainers in aquariums teach seals to perform tricks. They don't show them tricks and try to bully them into doing them; no, what they do is set things up so that the individual seals are rewarded randomly by a machine that spits out fish at unpredictable intervals. The seals, trying to figure this out, will repeat various things they were doing when the fish showed up. As the machine keeps reinforcing at random and the seals try harder and harder to make the thing cough up fish, they will work out various repetitive routines, many of which look cute to human beings. The trainer then starts deliberately reinforcing the cutest maneuvers, and the seals go on display, splashing about and balancing balls on their noses in the serene and largely accurate conviction that they've figured out how to get the humans to fork over the fish.

That's epigenesis. Any time a being capable of action ends up in a setting that provides random or quasi-random responses to action, you get epigenesis. Each individual being responds differently to it, and so epigenesis leads to differentiation, and to the beginnings of Personality. Over time, furthermore, as one layer of epigenesis overlays another, complex feedback loops form, so that this set of epigenetic behavior sets off that set, but only under conditions that don't put a third set into action. As individual complexity increases, linear cause and effect dissolve into the kind of strange loops Douglas Hofstadter explored so colorfully in his book *Gödel, Escher, Bach*, producing the unpredictable, reflective, innovative behavior we call thinking.

The third of the three primal swarms are therefore the Lords of Mind. They are the first of the swarms to become individual beings with their own distinct characters, because they are the first to go through epigenesis. The Lords of Flame lay down the basic patterns of existence, the Lords of Form provide the substance of existence, but the Lords of Mind elaborate, individualize, and create. In the metaphors of esoteric Masonry, where the Lords of Flame have the role of King Solomon, and the Lords of Form that of King Hiram, the Lords of Mind have the role of the third grand master, Hiram Abiff the widow's son, who was responsible for the ornamentation, the metalwork, and the day-to-day construction of the Temple.

There's a warning implied in that identification, though. As my brother Masons are well aware, and as other readers who know their way around Masonic symbolism have also learned, Masonic tradition has it that Hiram Abiff did not survive to see the Temple finished.

Epigenesis need not result in increased complexity and the awakening of mind. As the metaphor of seven-year-olds left to their own devices suggests, it can also result in chaos and disintegration.

Fortune makes a profound comment on this distinction. Epigenesis, she says, is what happens when energies that are trying to continue in one direction are stymied, so that they play among themselves and develop new aspects and relationships. The technical term for this process is "sublimation." If the blockage of the energies continues too long, however, the process reverses and the energies revert to a more primitive mode of functioning; the technical term for this retrograde process is "degradation."

In some of her other writings, Fortune uses the example of human sexuality to show the way that epigenesis starts with sublimation and ends with degradation. When children first reach puberty, they are in no way ready for the intricacies of sexual relationships, and so healthy societies prevent them from pursuing their urges to their natural fulfillment. The result is sublimation: the sexual energies, prevented from finding the usual outlet, flow instead into other pursuits, such as creativity, spirituality, and personal maturation. Once these other pursuits have become stable enough, the child is a child no longer, and is ready to enter into sexual life. Keep the barrier in place thereafter, though, and you get all the neurotic consequences of enforced celibacy, which can be described neatly enough (and were in fact so described, in ample detail, by Freud and his pupils) in terms of reversion to childhood stages that should have been long outgrown.

Degradation isn't a risk for the Lords of Mind. They come into being in a solar system that is still simple enough, and strongly enough pervaded by the patterns set out by the Solar Logos, that they complete their epigenesis on each plane in perfect harmony, laying down patterns that will awaken thought and Personality in the subsequent swarms. It is these subsequent swarms are the ones that run the risk of degradation if they remain too long in transitional stages, and also run the parallel risk of entering into modes of epigenesis that will take them out of balance with the rest of the solar system and send them spinning off on strange destinies of their own.

The second half of the building of the solar system, as the swarms reach the first plane and then begin the long ascent back to the Solar Logos, will be the subject of the next chapter, and of further chapters after that. The outward journey deserves close attention, though, because this is one of the places where Fortune's great metaphor can be applied most obviously to the details of human life. Most of my readers, for example, will have had the opportunity to interact with organizations at various points in their growth and development. The three primal swarms are, among other things, the stages in that process of growth.

Perhaps, dear reader, you have had the experience of helping to found a new organization. You already know in a small way the work of the Lords of Flame: how much effort it takes to establish brand new patterns of action and communication, encourage members to use those and not bring in other patterns from elsewhere, and learn to think of themselves as members of a group rather than individuals who happen to be drifting through a given set of interactions.

Or perhaps, dear reader, you have joined a group that has already been established but is hitting its growth curve. You know in a small way the work of the Lords of Form: what it takes to gather adequate human material together and bring it into harmony with the existing structures of the organization, and how often you have to go back to the beginning and repeat a familiar process before everything works smoothly at last.

Or finally, dear reader, perhaps you have had the experience of joining a well-established organization, and finding that the work that is open to you is a matter of elaborating an existing structure and working out the subtle variations that make the guiding principles a little better suited to each of the situations it encounters. You thus know in a small way the work of the Lords of Mind.

The same metaphor can be applied in other ways, of course. The thing that matters, as you study *The Cosmic Doctrine*, is that you learn to apply the metaphors of the work yourself, to use them as tools for thinking, and make sense of your world in the distinctive way Dion Fortune sketches out.

*CHAPTER SIXTEEN*

# The Influences of the Lords of Flame, Form, and Mind

## Reading

Revised Edition: Chapter 16, "The Influences of the Lords of Flame, Form, and Mind," pp. 76–79.

Millennium Edition: Chapter 17, "The Influences of the Regents upon the Globes," pp. 104–106, and Chapter 18, "The Goal of Evolution of a Life Swarm," p. 107 to the end of the fourth complete paragraph on p. 109 ("… through a general atmosphere.")

## Commentary

The commentary on the previous chapter discussed the journey of the three primal swarms—the Lords of Flame, Form, and Mind—from the Solar Logos through the seven planes of being to the material plane. This chapter explores the return journey, which is equally important. On the way down, the three swarms had the job of learning how to function on each of the seven planes, building bodies for themselves out of the substance of each plane, and in the process creating the planets and ensouling them with their Planetary Spirits.

113

On the way back up, they have a new task waiting for them, because there are other swarms of entities on the way down the planes in their wake. In place of the raw atomic matter they dealt with on the descent, they now have to cope with swarms of conscious beings, less developed than they are but of the same general type. That begins the moment the Lords of Flame finish their work on the seventh globe and return to the sixth globe, because the sixth globe at that point is still inhabited by the Lords of Form, who are just getting started on their own work on that plane.

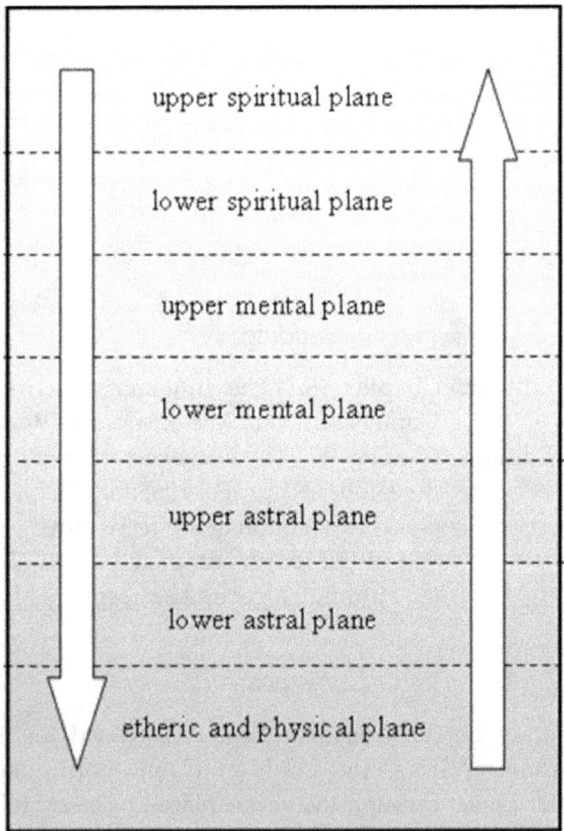

upper spiritual plane

lower spiritual plane

upper mental plane

lower mental plane

upper astral plane

lower astral plane

etheric and physical plane

Planes of Being 4

They're just getting started, in turn, because of the distinctive way they descend the planes. As noted in the previous chapter, the Lords of Form don't go down the planes in a single journey; they return to the

Solar Logos between their experiences on each of the worlds, and then have to work their way back down to the next world in order. So they're still traveling while the Lords of Flame are busy building the pattern of energetic stresses that forms the subtle body of the seventh globe, and they and the Lords of Flame thus end up inhabiting the sixth globe together.

The Lords of Flame, having already experienced the sixth globe, can perceive it as something separate from themselves—in the words of our text, they have objective consciousness, the state of which human waking consciousness is a first very rough draft—and so they can also perceive the Lords of Form at work on it. The Lords of Form don't yet have that capacity. They perceive only their own internal states—in the words of our text, they have subjective consciousness, like the consciousness human beings have while dreaming. So the Lords of Form don't perceive the higher evolution inhabiting the same world they do.

That lack of awareness, though, doesn't equal a lack of effect. Dion Fortune uses an awkward bit of phrasing—"the impactation of a cyclic rhythm inducing a vibration"—for a phenomenon that's utterly familiar to anyone who's ever given a push to a child's swing or set a cradle in motion. That gentle repeated push—the "cyclic rhythm"—sets the pushed object swinging. That's what the presence of the Lords of Flame does to the Lords of Form; the bodies the Lords of Form are building vibrate to the beat of the complex rhythm laid down by the Lords of Flame, and as a result the Lords of Form end up with capacities in that body that embody the experiences of the Lords of Flame as well as their own.

As the Lords of Form complete their evolution on the sixth globe, they become indirectly aware of the Lords of Flame. They haven't yet awakened into objective consciousness, but they can begin to notice that something's affecting the bodies they've just finished forming. Then the two swarms finish their work on the sixth globe; the Lords of Form go through the complex process described in the previous chapter, shedding their bodies to provide matter for the globe they've been on, and return to the Solar Logos to begin the journey down the planes one last time. The Lords of Flame, having finished their work on the sixth globe in the returning arc, move to the fifth globe—and the Lords of Mind, who have been waiting on the fifth globe, proceed at once to the now-vacant sixth globe.

Once they're on the fifth globe, the Lords of Flame busy themselves with the evolutionary work they need to do there. On the way out, they built bodies of the matter of each plane, and absorbed the rhythms and capacities of that plane; now, on the way back, they have achieved objective consciousness, and so they have to learn how to perceive and work with the other things and beings on each plane, using the body of that plane as a vehicle. They also interact with the swarm that's inhabiting that plane on the descending arc. The nature of that interaction varies from plane to plane and from swarm to swarm, but there's a generic term for that entire class of interactions, and that term is "initiation." We'll discuss that more a little further on.

It's important to remember here that the Lords of Flame, Form, and Mind are only the first three swarms—they're not the only swarms. The same process that set them in motion set other swarms following the same route after them, and each of those following swarms follows the same pattern on the descent as the Lords of Mind: advancing to a new planet once the previous swarm moves on, busying itself with the work of its own evolution, finishing that up, and then waiting until it's time to move further on. That waiting period is when epigenesis takes place—that's the process, remember, through which random movements give rise to new capacities in the evolving entities, giving each of them their own individual characters and possibilities. The Lords of Flame and Form don't engage in epigenesis, and so never become individuals. The Lords of Mind and those that come after them are individualized beings.

There's a crucial difference between the Lords of Mind and the swarms that come after them, though. In the course of their evolutionary journey, the Lords of Mind never encounter another swarm further along than themselves. When they leave the fifth globe for the sixth, the Lords of Flame leave the sixth globe for the fifth, so they miss each other. Similarly, when the Lords of Form vacate the seventh globe on the return arc, heading back up the planes to the sixth, the Lords of Mind go from the sixth globe to the seventh to complete their outward arc. Once the Lords of Mind start back up the planes, they find the globes fully tenanted, and the next chapter will describe the work they do there as initiators of individual beings.

The beings that follow the Lords of Mind down the planes, though, encounter the three primal swarms on the way down, and are transformed by the encounter, receiving capacities for action and perception they would not be able to attain so quickly on their own. Again, this is the basic pattern of all initiation. The initiations that humans confer on other humans in magical lodges have the effects they do, according to Fortune's metaphor, because they follow the "tracks in space" laid down by elder swarms as they interact with younger swarms.

The exact nature of these primal initiations, though, depends on which plane the younger swarm is on when it encounters each of the primal swarms. The process of descending the planes is, among other things, the process of building a body on each plane, and so whatever body your Divine Spark and seed-atom built while they interacted with the Lords of Flame is the body that resonates most closely with the primary forces of nature, because those forces were created and are commanded by the Lords of Flame. Similarly, whatever body your Individuality built while it interacted with the Lords of Form is the body that interacts most closely with the bodies of other entities, since the Lords of Form created and command all bodies.

The Lords of Mind can't be categorized so neatly. The first two primal swarms never individualize, and so they initiate the younger swarms collectively. The third swarm consists of individualized beings, and so its members seek out individuals of the younger swarms who are suited for whatever initiation each individual Lord of Mind has to pass on, and communicate that initiation to those individual beings and to them alone. The younger entities are still capable only of subjective consciousness; they become aware of their initiators only indirectly, and only at the point when they and the initiators are both ready to move on; but the initiations stay with the entities, and when they awaken into objective consciousness on the seventh globe, those initiations enable the younger entities to renew contact with the Lords of Mind in a fully conscious and intentional manner. (How that happens will be discussed in later chapters.)

For now, let's follow the three primal swarms back up the planes. On the way down, the task before them was to enter ever more completely into the planes of manifestation, to build bodies of each plane and to accept the limits of that plane in order to master its conditions and develop a corresponding set of capacities in themselves. They do all this in a state of subjective consciousness similar to the dream-state or, to use an even more appropriate metaphor, the state of consciousness of an unborn child in the womb.

Once they awaken to objective consciousness on the seventh globe, the task before the primal swarms—and every member of every subsequent swarm as well—is to let go of the limitations of each plane while retaining the capacities that those limits have developed. When this has been accomplished, the body corresponding to that plane falls away, but the capacity to form a temporary body of the matter of that plane remains. The Divine Spark and seed-atom then rise further and do the same thing on the next plane up. When the process completes itself on the upper spiritual plane, the plane of the first globe, the entity has become a fully individuated being, capable of ranging up and down the planes at will, and becoming embodied on any of them whenever this is convenient.

How that works, again, will be discussed later on. For now, it's useful to remember that the three primal swarms interact with the planets they dwell on in significantly different ways. The Lords of Flame, again, are the Creators and Masters of the forces of nature, and they interact with the members of each swarm collectively, giving an entire swarm certain capacities for mastering the forces of nature in their turn. The Lords of Form are the Creators and Masters of bodies, and they work on the substances of the planets rather than on the entities who dwell there. The Lords of Mind, finally, are individuals and work with individual entities, choosing those who can best respond to the initiations they have to offer, and thus contributing to the diversity and complexity of each of the later swarms.

Before we finish this chapter, it may be helpful to think about how you and I fit into this grand scheme. As human beings in the present cycle of our evolution, we are on the seventh globe, the globe of the etheric and physical plane, in the process of awakening from subjective to objective consciousness. (We're still in the middle of that process, which is why we have to spend some time out of every 24 hours or so in subjective consciousness—that's called "going to sleep"—and why so many of us have such a hard time thinking clearly about much of anything.)

All the entities currently tenanting this globe belong to the same swarm we do. Epigenesis being what it is, some of us are further ahead and some of us are further behind, which is why some souls became saints and Masters in the distant past and others are still doing time as blue-green algae. All of us will work our way through the lessons of the etheric/physical plane in due time. Right now, on the sixth globe, the globe of the lower astral plane, there are two more swarms, an older one getting ready to rise up to the fifth globe and a younger one waiting to take our place on the seventh once we finish our work here and rise up to the sixth, incalculably long ages from now.

You, dear reader, have received certain capacities for shaping the forces of nature from the Lords of Flame, but you share these capacities with every other member of our swarm. Your bodies—you have more than one of those, remember, because each globe has the substances of all the higher globes present in it—have been shaped by patterns impressed on the raw materials of this planet by the Lords of Form; these, too, you have in common with every other member of our swarm. Finally, long before you entered into a material body, you received certain initiations from one or more of the Lords of Mind, and you do not share these with every other member of our swarm; your individual mind, as it awakens from subjective to objective consciousness, has certain capacities it shares with certain other minds in our swarm but not with all, and the specific set of capacities you have—the specific initiations you have received, and then went on to develop through epigenesis on your own—is unique to you.

That's where you stand in Fortune's great metaphor. In the chapters to come, the focus will shift from where we are and how we got here to where we go next, and how.

# CHAPTER SEVENTEEN

# The Lords of Mind as Initiators

## Reading

Revised Edition: Chapter 17, "The Lords of Mind as Initiators," pp. 76–79.

Millennium Edition: Chapter 18, "The Goal of Evolution of a Life Swarm," from the fifth complete paragraph on p. 109 ("It is a peculiarity of all vibratory objects ...") to the end of the chapter.

## Commentary

Over the course of the last several chapters, we've covered the journey made by each of the three primal swarms from the upper spiritual plane all the way down to the plane of matter, where they awakened into objective consciousness and began the corresponding journey back up the planes. We've also talked about the swarms that follow the three primal swarms down the planes and then back up them again, and hinted at some of the ways that the primal swarms interact with the younger swarms that follow them down and then back up the planes.

Members of the primal swarms are able to interact with those of the younger swarms in certain ways. The Lords of Flame and Form, who are not individualized beings, interact with the following swarms collectively rather than individually. The Lords of Mind, on the other hand, are fully individualized, and they can select individual members of the following swarms to initiate. Both these means of interaction are of crucial importance as we proceed, because the influence of elder swarms on younger swarms plays an increasingly important role in evolution as the solar system's history unfolds.

To talk about this, Dion Fortune uses a metaphor that is precise but not always transparent to readers today. "It is a peculiarity of all vibratory objects," she says, "that they tend to tune with their own vibrations all objects of a slower rhythm than themselves." This is quite true, by the way—a vibrating object tends to make other objects vibrate in tune with it. Operatic sopranos used to use a trick based on this to show off the power and precision of their voices; they would sing at a note that made a wine glass vibrate so forcefully that the glass literally exploded.

Metaphorically speaking, the same effect is used in a more constructive way by entities on the way back up the planes as they interact with members of younger swarms on the way down. The elder being can communicate to the younger some of the capacities it has evolved on its journey, thus giving the younger being a substantial head start in the process of evolution. That's the nature and the purpose of initiation, and much of the rest of this chapter is among other things a discussion of how initiation works—veiled, of course, under the convenient concealment of the nearest approximate metaphor.

In Fortune's great Cosmic metaphor, there are three general classes of initiation. There are the initiations of the descending arc, which are discussed early on in this chapter. There are the initiations of the ascending arc, which are mentioned at in this chapter but not discussed in detail until later. Then there is the initiation of the Nadir, the point at which the direction of movement changes and descent gives way to ascent; this is also discussed later on.

The initiations of the descending arc are of importance here precisely because most of them are far in our past, long before the swarm of which we are part finished the long journey down the planes to the world of material incarnation. We all know on some level what it means to descend fully into matter, because we have all done exactly that at an earlier stage in the evolution of our individual souls. We all have some sense, however subconscious, of what is involved in descending through each of the planes above the material, adapting to the greater density and inertia of each new plane in turn, because that experience has left enduring traces in us. That helps us grasp the very different phenomena of the initiations of the Nadir and the ascending arc.

It's a classic bit of strategy that, having started talking about initiation, Fortune suddenly veers in what looks like a new direction and begins to talk instead about what happens when the first three swarms complete the ascending arc and return to the Solar Logos. She's not actually talking about something else, for what happens between the primal swarms and the Logos is a form of initiation. When the Lords of Flame set out from the seventh plane, they were little bundles of looping tracks in space vibrating feebly to the rhythm of the Logos. When they return, they are almost unimaginably more complex and powerful, having absorbed the vibrations of every plane and developed capacities of action and reaction on all of them.

The Lords of Flame have also picked up the capacity to form a group spirit, and developed that capacity through the hard labor of creating Planetary Spirits on each of the seven planes. This is crucial to what follows. As the Lords of Flame return to the seventh plane, the Solar Logos contemplates them, picks up the intricate rhythms of vibration they have learned from their long journey, and is conditioned by those rhythms, absorbing the lessons they have learned in the same way that they absorbed the influence of the Solar Logos itself as they set out; as the Logos initiated them, so they in turn initiate the Logos. In the process, the Solar Logos becomes the group spirit of the Lords of the Flame—or more precisely, the group spirit is absorbed by the Logoidal consciousness and becomes one of the modes or capacities through which the Logos can experience and act.

And the Lords of Flame? As noted in a previous commentary, they become those beings that occultists and ordinary religious believers alike call angels. More to the point, most of them do. Some of the Lords of Flame have reached the point of evolution at which they are capable of coming into conscious contact with the Cosmic atoms that created them, and these leave the solar system behind and begin the long journey of a traveling atom in the Cosmos, to become Great Entities and Solar Logoi themselves after a vast interval of time. The others settle down at the center of our solar system and carry out the will of the Solar Logos, moving up and down the planes at will to keep the solar system in harmony. As their journey down and then up the planes brought the basic pattern of natural forces into being, they work through those forces, maintaining the balance of nature when the epigenesis of younger swarms threatens to pull it out of balance.

The Lords of Form return in the same way and go through the same process. As mentioned in an earlier commentary, they become the beings known as devas by occultists. Those of the Lords of Form that don't make contact with their Cosmic atoms and begin life as traveling atoms in the Cosmos carry out the will of the Logos in the same way as the Lords of Flame, but their task is different. The Logos, as it mediates between its solar system and the Cosmic tides, is constantly evolving new archetypal concepts, and the Lords of Form take these and impress them on swarms of younger Divine Sparks who are still evolving.

Thus the swarms don't simply repeat the same sequence of bodies and states; they pass into new shapes and new experiences. Glance back over the history of life, on the one hand, or the history of human culture on the other, and it isn't hard to spot some of the archetypal ideas of the Logos as these arrive on the scene—for example, the way that mammals and birds, though belonging to distinct evolutionary lineages, both evolved warm blood around the same geological period, or the way that Greece, India, and China all invented philosophy in the same handful of centuries. In terms of Fortune's great metaphor, these are among the works of the Lords of Form.

The Lords of Mind, finally, pass through the same process as their two preceding swarms, and become intelligences, another set of spiritual beings that mediate between the Logos and its solar system. Like the other two primal swarms, their job is to range up and down the planes, bringing the solar system back into balance when it has been disordered by some vagary or other of epigenesis, but they can do so in a far subtler way than the others. The Lords of Flame work with the forces of nature, the Lords of Form work with the group souls of younger swarms, but the Lords of Mind are individualized, and so they work with individuals.

The Lords of Mind are thus responsible for initiation in the sense that occultists usually use that term: among their other deeds, they assist individual members of younger swarms who have completed the descent through the planes, and begun the return journey, to perceive planes higher than their own and bring down forces from those planes to assist the work of balance. These initiations of the ascending arc are by no means limited to occult lodges. Those churches and other religious bodies that preserve traditional sacramental rituals have their own set of initiations: for example, baptism and the ceremony of communion are initiations of this type, and so are holy orders when these are conferred by a bishop who has received apostolic succession.

Other initiations have survived in seemingly unlikely places. The initiations of Freemasonry, for example, are surprisingly potent even though most Masons have no notion of the real meaning of the rites they preserve and enact so carefully. It also happens, and not infrequently, that a Lord of Mind will guide an individual of a younger swarm through an initiatory process entirely outside of any organizational framework, or in the context of some organization or tradition with no initiatory tradition at all. When you encounter a case of spontaneous mystical experience, that's usually what has happened.

Nearly always, the Lords of Mind remain as disembodied (or differently embodied) presences, communicating with their initiates in subtle ways through the higher planes of being. Fortune has it, though, that now and again it becomes necessary for a Lord of Mind or some other entity of some more advanced evolution to take on a body on one of the planes of manifestation. This is done with the help of an initiate on that plane, who lends her reproductive system to the process. Yes, we're talking about virgin birth. Those of my readers who know their way around global mythology will recall how many important mythic figures are said to be born of a woman impregnated in one way or another by a deity—or, rather less often, of a goddess impregnated by a man. This is what Fortune has in mind here. When she described herself as a devout but unorthodox Christian, in other words, she wasn't joking.

Having dropped that tidbit to annoy the orthodox and give the rest of us something to think about, Fortune veers at once to a different theme. She reminds us that the Solar Logos has three primary aspects, reflecting the three great rings of the Cosmos, and goes on to envision the three primal swarms as representatives of these three primary aspects. While these three swarms evolved under the influence of the Logos alone, those that come after evolve under the influence of the Logos and its Regents, who are the Lords of Flame, Form, and Mind.

The subsequent swarms are assigned, not to the three primary aspects, but to the twelve Cosmic Rays that influence the Logos. Each swarm sets out from the seventh plane under the influence of one of these Rays, and takes on the imprint of that Ray. The group spirits of the later swarms, once they have finished their evolution, take on a special role in the evolving solar system. Only the three primal swarms have their group spirits absorbed by the Logos; the group spirits of the later swarms, once the Solar Logos has contemplated them and learned everything they have to teach, become the Star Logoi, exemplars of the influences of the twelve Rays in the solar system, subordinate to the Solar Logos but distinct from it. (Later editions of *The Cosmic Doctrine* renamed the Star Logoi the Ray Exemplars, but here again, I find the original term more exact.)

With the birth of the last of the Star Logoi, the solar system is complete. At its center is the Solar Logos, surrounded by its hosts of angels, devas, and intelligences; the seven planes radiate out from it, each with its planet and Planetary Spirit, each inhabited by Divine Sparks descending and ascending the planes; around the outer rim stand the twelve Star Logoi, each mediating the energies of one of the zodiacal signs, each surrounded by its own cloud of spirits who have completed the journey through the planes and now dwell rejoicing in realms of light.

Those readers who know their way around the Qabalah, and more particularly around the specific version of the Qabalah discussed in great detail by Dion Fortune in her classic book on the subject, will find much of this image familiar, but not all. Much more of it can be found in an equally ancient but far less heavily publicized tradition. In the writings of late Classical Neoplatonists such as Sallust and Proclus Diadochos, especially as interpreted by the great English Neoplatonist Thomas Taylor, Fortune's great Cosmic metaphor has its closest match. Read Sallust's *On the Gods and the World* or Proclus' *Elements of Theology*—again, Thomas Taylor's translations and commentaries are the most revealing in this context—and it's soon clear that you're in the same Cosmos Fortune has outlined in *The Cosmic Doctrine*.

This comes as no surprise. On the one hand, Fortune, her teacher Dr. Theodore Moriarty, and many of her close associates had a solid knowledge of occult philosophy, and at the time they lived, this normally included at least a nodding acquaintance with the writings of the old Neoplatonists. On the other, the entire Western occult tradition in modern times is a restatement of the Neoplatonic vision, as transmitted through the great Neoplatonic revival of the Renaissance. This is one of the things that makes *The Cosmic Doctrine* so important as a work of modern occult philosophy: it presents, in the form of the nearest approximate metaphor, the vision of reality that has been central to the tradition it represents since ancient times.

With this chapter, accordingly, Fortune's account of the genesis of the Cosmos and the solar system draws to a close. In the chapters ahead, we'll proceed to the third part of *The Cosmic Doctrine* and explore what it has to say about the process of initiation and spiritual development that awaits each of us, should we be willing to pursue it.

# PART III

## HUMAN EVOLUTION

CHAPTER EIGHTEEN

# Influences Acting on Human Evolution

## Reading

Revised Edition: Chapter 18, "Influences Acting on Human Evolution," pp. 84–88.

Millennium Edition: Chapter 19, "Tabulated Summary of Influences," pp. 114–115, and Chapter 20, "Cosmic Influences," pp. 116–120.

## Commentary

With this chapter, we begin the third part of our text. The first part dealt with the evolution of the Cosmos and the second dealt with the evolution of a Solar Logos and a solar system. Having drawn the outlines of the panorama of space and time within which we human beings have our very modest place, Fortune now proceeds to talk about human evolution—not as a process of the distant past, but as something going on right now in each of our lives.

It's very common in the Western world for people who are first trying to make sense of the concept of spiritual evolution to insist on thinking of it as something that individual souls do all

131

by themselves. Our culture teaches us to imagine ourselves as uniquely active beings doing things to a passive Cosmos. That way of thinking about human nature and destiny did not evolve by accident, and it has its role to play in the unfolding of human potential now and in the future, but it is a half-truth at best. There are certainly ways in which human individuals act on the Cosmos, but the Cosmos also acts on human individuals, and if we ignore these latter influences we are stumbling blindly in the dark.

As Fortune's convenient tabulation shows, there are three broad classes of influences that shape our consciousness and our evolution. The first of those classes comprises influences that come from or through the Solar Logos, the god of this solar system, who "hath set his tabernacle in the sun." As we saw in previous chapters, the Logos is influenced by the great cycles of the Cosmos: the rotation of the Ring-Cosmos in relation to the Ring-Chaos, which sets in motion immense tides of creation and destruction, and the twelve Rays, through which the Logos passes as he circles the Central Stillness in his orbit on the seventh Cosmic Plane. The Logos is also influenced by the gravitational attraction of other Great Entities on the other Cosmic Planes.

All these influences pass through the Logoidal consciousness to affect the solar system and every being in it. Their primary effect is on the activities of Planetary Spirits and group souls, but those affect individuals at second hand, sometimes in very powerful ways. As an example from the history of ideas, consider the concept of living an ethical life in the Age of Aries, when compassion was not even seen as a virtue and the goal of ethics was living a life of principled action independent of others, and compare it to the concept of living an ethical life in the Age of Pisces, when compassion was the central virtue and the goal of ethics was living a life of loving self-sacrifice in service to others!

The Solar Logos, meanwhile, is not a static being mired in perfection. Though he is vastly greater, more powerful, and more intelligent than any of the beings in his solar system, he too is growing, changing, and learning as his solar system grows, changes, and learns. Each swarm that ventures down the planes and then returns to the Logos brings back a rich harvest of experience that the Logos contemplates and incorporates into his own consciousness. The effects of this process also radiate outward to affect the Planetary Spirits of each planet and the group consciousness of the beings inhabiting each planet, and from there, shapes the lives of human (and other) individuals. Such changes move very slowly in terms of an individual human life, but sometimes, as noted above, it's possible to glimpse them by comparing past eras to the present.

Alongside the influences that flow outward from the Solar Logos, there are also influences shaping human life that derive from less exalted categories of being. We are currently incarnate on the physical plane, rather than one of the subtler planes through which we descended in past ages and through which we will ascend in ages to come, and that imposes certain very definite forms and limits on what we can accomplish as individuals and as a species.

There are also the Star Logoi (also called Ray Exemplars), the group consciousness of swarms of Divine Sparks that have completed their own journey down and then up the planes, and now serve the Solar Logos by mediating the twelve great Cosmic Rays. The Star Logoi are the entities behind the signs of the Zodiac as we experience them; each Star Logos picks up from the Solar Logos the particular influence of one of the Rays of the Cosmos, and radiates that into the solar system, influencing all things by the same process of resonance we discussed in earlier chapters. Their influences on human evolution are among the factors that astrologers track.

The Planetary Spirits are also among the sources of influence tracked by astrologers. As explained in previous chapters, the Planetary Spirits are "creations of the created," brought into being by the activities of the swarms of Divine Sparks as they travel up and down the planes. As each swarm completes its evolution on a planet, it resonates with the rhythms of the Solar Logos, and as a result the Planetary Spirits are attuned to the Logos. To make use of a word that C.S. Lewis borrowed from the medieval Neoplatonist Bernard Sylvester, the Planetary Spirits are the Oyarses of the planets, the Regents of the Logos in the turning worlds. The Planetary Spirit of the Earth, the earth goddess of so many ancient religions, is the being of this kind who influences human evolution most at this point in our species' history, but the spirits of the other planets are also active in our lives by way of other factors tracked by astrology.

The presence of other beings, more or less advanced than humanity, as an influence on human evolution is a complex matter, and will be dealt with at length in later chapters. So, too, are the laws of nature sketched out briefly in the tabulation, and they also will receive extensive discussion later on. Those readers who know their way around Rupert Sheldrake's writings, especially *A New Science of Life*, will find Fortune's take on natural law instantly familiar: the laws of nature, in her vision, are simply "tracks in space," patterns repeated so often that they keep repeating themselves whenever opportunity permits. That emphatically does not make them powerless! The laws Fortune presents here are, among other things, basic principles of magic, and careful attention to them will teach much.

The tabulation laid out at the beginning of this chapter (or, in the Millennium Edition, in the first of these two chapters) summarizes most of what will be discussed in the third part of *The Cosmic Doctrine*, and readers who familiarize themselves with the concepts listed here will be better able to navigate the complexities ahead. That becomes true as soon as we move from the tabulation to Fortune's analysis of the influences on human evolution that come from the Cosmos itself, which follows immediately afterwards.

Here Fortune plunges immediately into a branch of occult lore that was the subject of extensive and passionate discussion in her time, and for decades before and after. It was widely held in her time that the Piscean age, the period of 2160 years ruled by the zodiacal sign Pisces, had ended sometime in the last years of the nineteenth century or the first years of the twentieth, with very late 1887 or the beginning of 1888 as one commonly accepted date for the transition. For what it's worth, my take is that the occultists of that period were right. Compare the ruling ideas of the 21 centuries before 1888 with those of the period since that time, and correlate them to the differences between Pisces and its ruler Neptune on the one hand, and Aquarius and its ruler Uranus on the other, and it's not hard to watch the turning of the ages.

With the transition to the new Aquarian age, changes as drastic as those that followed the shift from Aries to Pisces are underway. Fortune's great metaphor provides, among many other things, a way to make sense of the process. Fortune refers to this branch of the study as sidereal astrology, and distinguishes it from planetary astrology. In some ways, "sidereal astrology" turned out to be an unfortunate choice of labels, because some astrologers have used the same label for a different kind of planetary astrology, in which the boundaries of the signs of the Zodiac are determined by the constellations rather than the solstices and equinoxes.

This is not what Fortune was talking about. Her "sidereal astrology" is the astrology of vast cycles of time marked out by the movements of the stars, and her "planetary astrology" is the standard system of Western astrology—tropical astrology, to give it its technical name—which sees the zodiacal signs as 30° wedges of the ecliptic, with the celestial point where the spring equinox takes place defined as 0° Aries. As the precession of the equinoxes moves different stars through these wedges, the influences of the zodiacal signs change subtly: that's Fortune's sidereal astrology as seen by a skywatcher on the physical plane. On the inner planes, the whole solar system moves through one after another of the twelve Cosmic Rays and is influenced by the immense cycle of the rotation of the Ring-Cosmos within the Ring-Chaos.

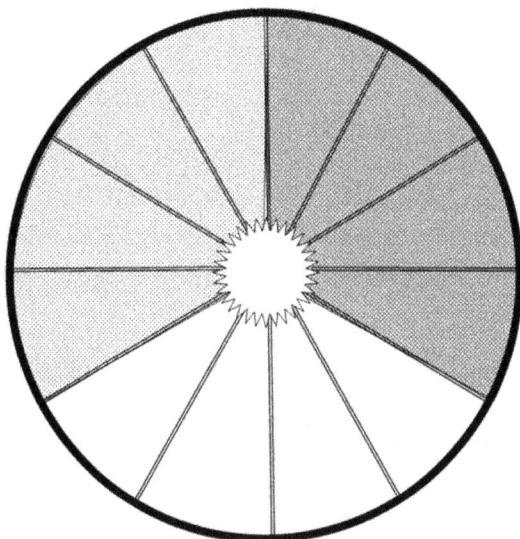

Rings and Rays

As so often, when she talks about occult teachings with significant practical implications, a certain evasiveness creeps into Fortune's writing. She explains that each phase of the rotation of the Ring-Cosmos is equal to four Ray phases. Thus the Ring phase remains positive through four astrological ages, and then switches to negative for four more—but which four? Only at the end of the chapter does she give the hint that's needed to bring clarity to the picture. The nineteenth century, she says, was a positive period; the first quarter of the twentieth—the only part of the twentieth that had passed by when she wrote *The Cosmic Doctrine*—was a negative period. Between these two, according to the occult teachings of her time, was the transition from the Piscean to the Aquarian age. So we know that from her perspective, the Geminian, Taurian, Arian, and Piscean ages took place under a positive Ring cycle, and the Aquarian, Capricornian, Sagittarian, and Scorpian ages to come will take place under a negative Ring cycle.

That doesn't mean, of course, that the four ages just past were "positive" in the simplistic modern sense, or that the four ages to come will be "negative" in that sense. It means that the four ages just past were typified by a movement toward the center, which then reversed, and the four ages ahead will be typified by a movement toward the periphery, which will then reverse. Each age under a positive Ring phase thus sees a gradual coalescence toward some standard, which then comes unraveled as the age ends. In the context of politics, think of the way the city-state became the fixed form of social organization in the Arian age, not only in the Mediterranean and the Middle East but in large parts of Africa, India, and the Americas as well, and how scriptural religions of salvation provided a similar fixed form in the Piscean age.

In the Aquarian age and the three ages that will follow it, if the hints of our text are anything to go by, an opposite procedure will be the rule. Instead of moving toward a common fixed form, the human societies of these ages will differentiate themselves more and more from each other, moving in their own unique directions over the course of each age, and then gradually blend and establish syntheses as the age draws to an end. One consequence is that the disintegrating and diversifying forces that came into play as the Piscean age entered its twilight period will continue to work for many centuries yet, and attempts to impose some kind of uniform vision on humanity during that time will simply generate resistance and accelerate the movement toward differentiation.

Across these broad (and broadly predictable) movements of time, as noted already, come a less regular set of influences that pass through the Logoidal consciousness into the solar system. These are the influences of other Great Entities on other planes of the Cosmos. The human mind isn't capable of grasping the calculations necessary to track when one of these comes into play, but we're fortunate in that there's a marker on the physical plane that can be used to track them: the appearance of comets. That makes sense even from a purely physical perspective: astronomers have suggested that what detaches comets from the Van Oort Cloud and sends them plunging into the inner solar system are the movements and gravitational forces of celestial bodies outside the solar system entirely. The occultist would simply add that these celestial bodies need not be composed of matter as we know it—that is, the substance of the seventh Cosmic Plane.

Fortune is quite correct that the astrology of comets still needs a great deal of development. As H.S. Green notes in *Mundane or National Astrology*: "There are many known comets that are permanent members of the solar system. These have not yet been examined astrologically or their influence determined." A great deal of very useful work could be done here, and Fortune's suggestion of using the spectrographic profile of comets as a way to tease out their influences is well worth following up on. One point worth keeping in mind in this research, though, is that in traditional astrology comets are always malefic influences—and *The Cosmic Doctrine* explains why.

Comets in *The Cosmic Doctrine* are the strange attractors of the solar system, reflecting the influence of Great Entities other than the Solar Logos. In a sense, they are similar to the Star Logoi, which mediate the influences of the twelve Cosmic Rays into the solar system. Two great differences divide the comets from the Star Logoi, however. First, the Star Logoi are group souls in harmony with the consciousness of the Solar Logos, and the influences they mediate have been assimilated to the solar system. Think of them as being like the electrical transformers that step down high-voltage current and make it safe for household use. The forces radiated by the comets, by contrast, have not been stepped down in this way, and are as dangerous to us as electricity straight from high-voltage transmission lines would be.

The second difference is that while the Star Logoi are group souls that have evolved into their current state and continue to evolve, the group souls of comets are incapable of evolution. They simply reflect the influence that created them in a repetitive, mindless way. This gives certain comets their second function in the solar system, that of scavengers.

Previous discussions of the influence of other Great Entities on the solar system have noted that these are the sources of positive evil—not the negative evil of the Ring-Chaos, the Cosmic thrust-block that enables creation to come into being, but the active evil of individual beings. The value of positive evil is that the entities who contend with it in themselves and in the world undergo a more intensive epigenesis: in human terms, they become wiser, stronger, and more richly individualized from the experience. Those entities who refuse to contend with the disruptive influence and assimilate themselves to it instead, not just once but in life after life, finally resonate with that influence so completely that they cease to incarnate on the same planet as the other souls of their swarm, and incarnate instead on a comet that embodies that influence.

The comet then proceeds on its way with its cargo of lost souls, sweeping out into unknown interstellar distances. In Fortune's metaphor, it does not stop there, but proceeds all the way to the Ring-Pass-Not at the boundary of the Cosmos itself. What happens there? Nobody knows. Fortune refers to it as the Unknown Death. When the comet returns to the solar system, perhaps after countless ages, the entities it carried with it are gone without a trace, and they and their karma never trouble the solar system again.

There's a curious parallel between this teaching and old Yuletide traditions surrounding St. Nicholas and his sinister partner, called Krampus in some parts of central Europe. St. Nicholas, as we all know, brings gifts for good children. Krampus, who is as hairy as a comet, carries birch switches to remind the others of their misdeeds, and a wicker basket on his back to take away those spoiled little horrors who fail completely to learn from such reminders. These latter are of course never seen again. Folklore is a funny thing; quite often it contains remarkably deep occult teachings in quaint symbolic form, and this is a good example.

All these Cosmic influences, the great tides of the Rings and Rays as well as the less predictable irruptions of cometary influence, have major roles to play in human evolution. On the broadest scale, a swarm leaves the upper spiritual plane to begin its evolutionary pilgrimage when the Ring phase of the Cosmos turns positive, and it finishes its outward journey on the physical plane as the Ring phases are changing, though how many phases will have gone by between those events is a complex matter. The same principle applies on a smaller scale; whenever an influence from the higher planes finishes its descent into matter and begins to rise back up the planes, this has to be done when the tides of the Cosmos are turning, and any working meant to influence humanity as a whole or any of its large collective groupings thus needs to pay close attention to the set of the Cosmic tides.

In this discussion, we also encounter for the first time the concept of the Left-Hand Path. That term was borrowed a long time ago from the Tantric occultism of India, and has been used in quite a range of senses in Western occult writings. Fortune uses it in an extremely specialized sense here and elsewhere. To her, as we will see, the Left-Hand Path is the path of retreat along the lines of our species' previous evolution, while the Right-Hand Path is the path of advance along the lines of our species' future evolution. The Left-Hand Path is thus not the same as the path that leads to the Unknown Death; the former responds to influences that are native to this solar system, while the latter reacts to influences from outside the solar system. The nature of the Left-Hand Path, and the reasons why the choice of a Path matters so greatly, will be covered in quite some detail in the chapters to come.

# CHAPTER NINETEEN

# The Logoidal Relationship to the Manifested Universe

## Reading

Revised Edition:     Chapter 19, "The Logoidal Relationship to the Manifested Universe," pp. 89–91.

Millennium Edition:     Chapter 21, "The Logoidal Relationship to the Manifested Universe," pp. 121 through the end of the second paragraph on p. 124, ending with "... the positive evil of the Manifested Universe."

## Commentary

As we proceed further into Fortune's discussion of human evolution, more and more of the concepts already discussed in *The Cosmic Doctrine* will be brought into play, because our evolution as individuals and as a species does not take place in a vacuum. We are able to be what we are, and to evolve in the way we do, because the Earth and the solar system have passed through long cycles of evolution before we came on the scene.

Our minds and their capacities were built by the labors of the Lords of Mind; the bodies we indwell and the planet we live on were shaped by the Lords of Form; the basic patterns of this solar system were laid down by the Lords of Flame; these first three swarms were able to become what they are, and to build the solar system as it is, because of the work of the Solar Logos—and behind the Logos, we can dimly glimpse its own vast evolutionary history as a Great Entity and a traveling atom, with the emergence of the Rings, Circles, and Rays of the Cosmos as the background to the Solar Logos itself.

To make sense of this short but intricate chapter, it's important to remember that the Solar Logos is the mediator between the Cosmos and the solar system it has created and conditioned. The Logos is fully conscious of its solar system and everything within it. It is not conscious, though, of the Cosmic background that works through it. In terms borrowed from human psychology, the Cosmos affects the Logoidal subconscious, and the Logos becomes conscious of the Cosmic influences affecting it only when those influences flow through it to affect its solar system.

This, as Fortune explains, is an important part of what the swarms of Divine Sparks do. As each swarm proceeds down the seven planes of the solar system, passing from world to world and accomplishing its subjective evolution on each world in turn, the swarm takes some factor in the Logoidal subconscious and embodies it in itself and the worlds it inhabits. On the way back up the planes, in turn, the swarm awakens into objective consciousness on each plane and becomes consciously aware of the factor that it has established—and when it returns to the Logos, the Logos becomes conscious of the same factor. The entire arc of evolution within a solar system is thus the process by which the Logos of that solar system becomes conscious of everything that it embodied unconsciously during its long journey up and down the Rays as a traveling atom.

There is a rhythm to this process, however, and it's one we have already encountered in other contexts in Fortune's grand metaphor. The Logos alternates between positive and negative periods, or to put things another way it spends some periods focused on objective awareness of its solar system and other periods in a subjective condition of absorption in Cosmic realities. Fortune compares this explicitly to the human process of reincarnation. The sending out of the swarms is equivalent to the process of incarnation; their return to the Logos is what we call death; and the period between one swarm and the next, when the Logos contemplates what it has learned and is withdrawn into its own consciousness, is equivalent to the state human beings enter into between lives.

It's a useful metaphor, worth close meditation as a way to help the student understand the relationship between the Individuality (the part of the self that endures from life to life) and the Personality (the part of the self that comes into being with each new body and dissolves at its death). Another metaphor is also worth considering, however, because the dance of the Logos and the swarms of Divine Sparks is also closely parallel to the human experience of waking and sleeping. We wake up each day and enter into objective consciousness, go out into the world, and encounter whatever we encounter; at day's end, when we go to sleep, we settle back into subjective consciousness, and our dreams are dim echoes of the processes by which we absorb the experiences of the day into our mental structure.

This kind of nesting of metaphors, by the way—in the present example, waking and sleep = life and death = the positive and negative phases of the Solar Logos = the positive and negative phases of the Cosmos—is very common in occult philosophy. To the occult teacher, having an abstract notion of some Cosmic process doesn't mean much; the goal of occult teaching is to enable students to understand such processes, and that inevitably means finding comparisons and metaphors for them in the realm of ordinary human experience. Of course, that makes the use of metaphor inevitable. You can replace each of the equals signs in the equation above with the words "is metaphorically equivalent to" and yield a more accurate result.

Of course, there's a reason why Fortune focuses on life and death as her core metaphor in this chapter, or more precisely several related reasons. First of all, very few people worry that when they go to sleep they won't wake up the next morning; in Western industrial societies, the same thing is not true of death, and getting past the mistaken notion that equates death with absolute extinction is an important step in occult education. (As she points out in one of her essays, the reality of reincarnation is something that should be taught far more widely than it is.) Second, if you understand reincarnation, you understand a great deal about the overall trajectory of the soul through time, and this makes it a good deal easier to assess your current life and figure out what to do with the challenges and opportunities that confront you.

On another, deeper level, understanding where you're going is useful if you're going to further the process of getting there, and that's what the next section of the text is meant to do. Here Fortune talks about the goal of all the backings and forthings of swarms and incarnations. For the Logos to awaken fully to its own potential, as already noted, it needs swarms of souls to act out in objective consciousness everything the Logos contains in its subjective consciousness, so it can experience its own internal content objectively, as though standing outside itself. Each time a swarm of Divine Sparks does this, in turn, the subjective content of the Logos that the swarm is sent out to make manifest becomes part of the objective solar system. In Fortune's terms, it becomes a new set of tracks in space, and so the solar system forever after mirrors that part of the Logoidal mind.

At the endpoint of this process, everything in the Logoidal consciousness is manifest throughout the seven planes of the solar system. The creation has become an exact copy of its Creator; more precisely, it has become the sevenfold body of its Creator, the perfect outward expression of the Solar Logos. In terms of Fortune's quirky but devout Christianity, this is the coming of the Kingdom of God. Before then—and in her view, we have a long way to go until that time arrives—the words of the teacher she liked to call the Master Jesus are relevant: "The Kingdom of God is within you." In Fortune's terms, the Divine Spark that guides the seed-atom at the center of your sevenfold body is in rapport with the Solar Logos, and expresses through you as much of the Logoidal nature as you have evolved the ability to work with. Until the process of unfolding the Logoidal nature is complete, that's as close to the Logos as you can come.

And after the process is complete? Having awakened to complete objective consciousness of its own nature, the Solar Logos directs its attention to the Cosmos, where it can now begin a new phase of activity, about which we can grasp absolutely nothing. All the tracks in space that formed the solar system have been synthesized into the Logoidal mind and exist as realities on the Cosmic level, and so they no longer function within the solar system. The solar system therefore dissolves back into formless atomic movement, which Fortune calls the "Night of Brahma" in the Millennium Edition and the "Night of God" in the Revised Edition. There will be a new day following that night—the entire logic of Fortune's system requires this—but here again, we cannot even begin to understand what it would be like when the Solar Logos, having absorbed another vast array of new experiences from another round of Cosmic experience, settles back down into the dream of the solar system to process those experiences and rebuild the solar system in their image.

Here again, though, as above, so below: the vast cycles of experience through which the Solar Logos grows and evolves are mirrored in the cycles we undergo as individuals and as souls. At the end of each life, we withdraw from material existence so that we can bring together the lessons of a life's worth of experiences, and prepare for a new cycle of experiences in a new incarnation. In the same way, at the end of each evolution, we withdraw from manifest existence entirely so that we can bring together the lessons of hundreds or thousands of lives in many different forms, and prepare for a new cycle of experiences in a new evolution.

Why is this necessary? In the last part of this chapter, Fortune explores some of the reasons behind the alternation of periods of manifestation and periods of dissolution, and in the process lays the foundations for crucial points discussed later on in the volume.

The pause between each swarm—the Lesser Night—is necessary because the Logos needs to synthesize the experiences the previous swarm has brought to it. This allows each new swarm to begin its journey with a richer set of reaction-capacities than those that went before it. Since each swarm has the task of bringing part of the Logoidal consciousness into manifestation in harmony with parts already manifested, its members need to begin their journey with all the experiences of the earlier swarms in their subjective consciousness. In the language of Fortune's metaphor, it takes time for the Divine Sparks to come into rapport with the rhythm of the Logos, and while that takes place, the solar system sleeps.

The substance of each of the seven planes, however, is not just sitting there waiting for the Divine Sparks to set it moving in new ways. One of the basic principles of Fortune's metaphor is that once set in motion, tracks in space keep moving, and so all the forms created by previous swarms are still in place, potentially or actually, waiting for souls of the next life-wave to inhabit them. This is problematic for two reasons—the first being that, as we've just seen, each new swarm of Divine Sparks begins its descent into matter at a greater level of complexity than the last, and problems ensue when the newcomers build bodies of matter that naturally moves in ways better suited to less complex souls. This is retrogressive, and forces a certain degree of deformity on the incarnated souls.

The second reason is even more serious. Part of what shapes the matter of each plane is the working out of the Logoidal ideas by previous swarms, but from the time of the Lords of Mind onward, part of it is epigenesis—the free play of Divine Sparks exploring their own possibilities and those of the plane they inhabit. The Logoidal ideas are profoundly simple, but the reaction-capacities of the souls who embody those ideas are immensely complex and by no means always appropriate either to the Logoidal ideas or to any given plane of manifestation.

This, as discussed earlier in these commentaries, is the origin of positive evil—not the negative evil that is the thrust-block of Cosmic inertia,
but evil in the ethical sense of the word. In a sufficiently complex consciousness, epigenesis becomes what in ordinary speech is called "free
will." It's easy to misunderstand this. Epigenesis happens any time you
have one process that produces random results and another process
that picks and chooses among the results, in terms of some set of preferences or goals. The result is one kind of freedom—movement toward a
desired set of ends via unpredictable paths.

Epigenesis develops into "free will" when the picking and choosing
process turns back on itself, and the preferences or goals are reinforced or
discarded depending on the results of actions guided by the first kind of
epigenesis. We all do this: "Now that I've tried this, I realize that it was a
bad idea all along." The result is a second kind of freedom—movement
toward unpredictable ends via unpredictable paths. That second kind
of freedom is the source of creativity and novelty in the world, but it is
also the source of positive evil, since epigenesis that becomes recursive
and changes its own goals can run off the rails into self-destructive and
self-defeating modes of thought and action.

All these vagaries are eventually synthesized by the Solar Logos,
but "eventually" takes its sweet time arriving. Meanwhile, positive
evil shapes the substance of the seven planes of the solar system, and
each swarm that makes its pilgrimage down the planes has to deal
with substance that has the habit of moving in directions shaped by
epigenesis—and by positive evil. The resulting wrestling match between
the Logoidal idea expressed by the Divine Spark and the various modes
of positive evil woven into the substance of the various bodies can be
observed in action in the ethical literature of every culture and era.

That is what the Greater Night clears away. When all the reaction-
capacities of the Cosmos are taken up into the Logos and synthesized, the
seven planes of the solar system dissolve into uncoordinated tangential
movement. It's as though the Solar Logos will hit the reset button for
the solar system and bring everything back to its original simplicity and
purity, so the new Day of God or Brahma can begin with a clean slate.
Until that happens—and in Fortune's view, at least, that time is still
long ages in the future—we have to contend with the legacies of the
swarms that came down the planes before us, for good or ill, and work
out our destinies and that of the solar system in that context.

CHAPTER TWENTY

# Influences of the Manifested Universe, Part 1

## Reading

Revised Edition: Chapter 20, "Influences of the Manifested Universe," p. 92 to the second to last paragraph on
p. 94, ending "... are produced in this way."

Millennium Edition: Chapter 21, "The Logoidal Relationship to the
Manifested Universe," from the third paragraph
on p. 124, beginning with "The teaching of the
last two lectures ..." to the end of the chapter on
p. 127.

## Commentary

This is an extremely dense chapter full of information relevant to
practical magic. In the Revised Edition, it's also twice as long as most
of the other chapters, and so we'll be spreading out our discussion over
two chapters. Pay close attention as we go—many of the details covered
here have direct practical application not only to magical practice but to
everyday life and to the wider realms of politics and society.

Fortune begins her discussion by talking about the influences from outside the solar system that were the subject of previous chapters. (She calls these influences "extra-universal," remember, because the word "universe" in her day was used as a label for the solar system rather than the entire Cosmos.) For the sake of clarity, she distinguishes two phases in this process: first, there are the Cosmic influences that act on the Logos, and then there are the influences of the Logos on the solar system that result from these Cosmic factors.

While the theological mainstream in her time and ours sees God as incapable of change and growth, Fortune's theology has no place for any form of static perfection. Everything in her great Cosmic metaphor is perpetually changing, reacting to changes in its environment, and growing into greater richness and complexity over time. Interestingly, this same point was made by the philosopher Alfred North Whitehead, whose process philosophy also rejected the idea of static divine perfection in favor of a vision of the Cosmos in which God and the Cosmos were both developing over time.

The possibility that Fortune read Whitehead's work is not a detail her biographers seem to have discussed, but the dates work. Whitehead's famous Tarner lectures of 1919, which set out the principles of process philosophy, were published in book form in 1920 as *The Concept of Nature* and saw some discussion in the literate end of the press and the general public, and the first version of *The Cosmic Doctrine* was written in 1923 and 1924. Whether or not Fortune was influenced by Whitehead directly, her ideas drew on the same trends in the intellectual life of the time as his, and one direction in which work with *The Cosmic Doctrine* might proceed in years to come would involve a close comparison of Fortune's ideas with Whitehead's.

The transformations of the Solar Logos, the god of this solar system, are of course not all caused by influences streaming in from the Cosmos. There are also the influences that come out of the evolution of the solar system, mediated by the swarms of Divine Sparks that journey down the planes and then return. Like the influences of the Cosmos, the influences of the solar system's evolution also shape the way the Logos acts on its solar system, and so both these sets of influences become part of the environment in which you and I, dear reader, lead our lives and pursue the work of spiritual evolution.

There are other influences that shape our evolutionary environment, and these other influences are the main subject of this chapter.

The concept of "tracks in space," which was introduced at the beginning of *The Cosmic Doctrine*, is essential to recall as a basis for what follows. Any repeated action or reaction inscribes a track in space, and so tends to become stereotyped. Seen from within Fortune's metaphor, the entire solar system—and indeed the entire Cosmos—is simply a pattern of tracks in space through which atoms and atomic composites move. That pattern, which Fortune calls an abstract mould, has been built up over time by the Solar Logos, using the swarms of Divine Sparks as its instrument. This abstract mould includes all the laws of nature studied by scientists, and a great many other laws of which scientists are completely ignorant at present.

These laws were not all laid down at the beginning of time. Some of them came into being by the evolution of the Lords of Flame, others by that of the Lords of Form, still others through the epigenetic play of the Lords of Mind, and we ourselves, as members of a swarm, are laying down tracks in space that will someday be laws of nature for the beings that come after us. Think of these tracks in space as being stacked like the levels of a building; the ground floor consists of the laws of physics and astronomy, which were laid down by the Lords of Flame; the first floor, which requires the support of the ground floor, consists of the laws of chemistry and biology, which were laid down by the Lords of Form; the second floor, which requires the support of the previous two floors, consists of the laws of ethology (animal behavior) and psychology, which were laid down by the Lords of Mind, and so on. Each depends on the ones before it.

Thus each kingdom of manifested existence in the solar system—radiant, mineral, vegetable, animal, and human—rises on a foundation consisting of tracks in space, which Fortune calls the elemental essence of the kingdom. Understand the laws that govern each kingdom and you have the capacity to work with those laws and make things happen in that kingdom. As Fortune points out, this is the basis of practical magic. Notice that magic as Fortune describes it is thus the opposite of supernatural, unless we take the "super" in "supernatural" to mean "extremely," as in "supercharged" or "supercooled;" magic is extremely, wholly, utterly natural, the use of natural patterns to bring about natural results in accordance with the natural human faculty of will.

Of course, the difficulty creeps in here because the established sciences of the modern Western world consider only the material world to be natural; everything else is supernatural, or unnatural, or simply nonexistent. As our text says, this is a strange fruit of epigenesis! To the occult philosopher, the material world is the lower three-sevenths of the densest and (metaphorically) lowest of the planes, the physical plane, which is one of seven subdivisions of the seventh and densest Cosmic Plane; the modern sciences are thus limiting themselves to 3/343rds of the whole Cosmos, or 3/49ths of this solar system—which seems a little restrictive.

An equal but opposite mistake is made by those religious philosophies that insist that the material world is pure illusion and that only the higher planes are real. Dion Fortune was raised in one of these—the Christian Science Church—and she encountered many others in her time, ranging from the more extreme end of New Thought to westernized versions of certain Asian spiritual traditions. To Fortune, these views are just as mistaken as those of scientific materialism. The material world has its own laws and principles, which have been studied intensively by modern science. When we are dealing with the behavior of matter and the denser sorts of energy, those laws need to be recognized and taken into account, but there are other modes and manifestations and planes of being which have their own laws, and which have powerful influences on human life.

Now comes a point of crucial importance. "The forces of each plane," our text explains, "are supreme upon their own plane, controllers of the plane below, and, when in contact with the plane above, are in their turn controlled."

Let's take this one step at a time. The planes are not simply arbitrary divisions of an unbroken continuum; each plane is a reality unto itself, and under at least some circumstances, the forces of each plane govern that plane. In the case of the physical plane, for example, the forces known to modern science generally rule what happens on their plane. The same is true of every other plane. Occultists have summed up this insight in a convenient phrase: "The planes are discrete and not continuous."

Under certain circumstances, however, the forces of one plane can spill over into a plane below it and control what happens in that lower plane. When that happens, the forces of one plane can control the activity of certain phenomena on the next lower plane. There's nothing supernatural or miraculous about this; it happens every time you decide to reach for something, and your hand moves: certain forces of the upper astral plane—those belonging to the Personality—control the activity of your material body, which is part of the physical plane.

Notice that this control is limited by the nature of the plane below—your hand remains a hand, and can only do those things that hands are capable of doing—and it is also limited by the nature of the connection between the planes—you can move your hand, but you can't move a coffee cup unless you use your hand or some other body part to do it. At the same time, the hand guided by the Personality can do things that the hand cannot do when the Personality is not guiding it—say, in a state of sleep or unconsciousness.

The same relationship can, finally, extend above the lower mind as well as below it. The Personality can reach upward to make contact with the Individuality and take direction from it. The Personality remains itself, and does not stop being a Personality; it continues to exercise all its usual functions on its own plane—but the influence of the Individuality guides its actions and makes it capable of doing things that a Personality cannot do by itself. Many people have had the experience of receiving a sudden flash of intuition that enables them to find their way through a difficult situation successfully; this is an example of the upward contact we're discussing.

The next paragraph of our text is just as complex, and requires equally careful unpacking. "For example, the laws of logic are supreme in the realm of mind. The images of mind control the forms of the emotions, but the images of mind are themselves controlled by the spiritual forces." Here again, let's take this a step at a time.

The laws of logic are the laws of that portion of the mental realm human beings can experience at this stage of our evolution; in Fortune's taxonomy, they belong to the lower mental plane, and on that plane they are absolute. Where they make contact with the planes below, they also have power—for example, the application of logic to the phenomena of the physical plane is the basis of modern science. At the same time, just as the control of the hand by the Personality only goes so far, so does the control of matter by logic. There have, after all, been plenty of perfectly logical deductions about the world by qualified scientists that have turned out to be dead wrong.

Less obvious but in many ways more significant is the role of the mind in controlling the emotions. As a trained psychotherapist, Dion Fortune had plenty of direct experience with the myriad ways that garbled ideas held in the mind can misshape the emotional life. Since her time, that linkage became the focus of several schools of psychotherapy, such as the Transactional Analysis of Dr. Eric Berne and the

Rational-Emotive Therapy of Dr. Albert Ellis; both these, and many other modes of therapy as well, focus on teaching patients to untangle counterproductive thought processes so that the corresponding tangles of the emotional life will unravel in turn.

The same process, again, works upwards as well as down, and back before psychotherapy was taken over by the pharmaceutical industry, some of the most innovative and promising ventures in the field focused on finding ways to make that connection between the Personality and the Individuality, so that inner guidance from the spiritual plane can sort out the tangles of the mental plane and allow the emotional life to right itself. That was also a central theme of Fortune's own work with healing, as described in books such as *The Circuit of Force* and, on another plane, her *Rites of Isis and of Pan*.

That act of reaching upward is of critical importance, and not just when the emotional life is a mess. The next four paragraphs of our text explains why. Chapter 18 of *The Cosmic Doctrine* discusses the Left-Hand Path in an abstract manner; here, Fortune begins a more detailed analysis of that Path. (The term "Left-Hand Path" has been used in many different ways over the last two centuries or so; in Fortune's terminology, remember, the Left-Hand Path is the path of regression, of falling back into an earlier phase of evolution.)

To understand what follows, it's necessary to remember that to Fortune every act of creation descends through the planes of being to the physical plane, the plane of effects, and then cycles back up the planes to its source. When all goes as it should, the impetus that sets the act of creation in motion begins on the first or upper spiritual plane and descends all the way to the seventh or physical plane, and then rises all the way back up.

At our present stage of evolution, the proper completion of the circuit depends on the actions of the Personality, which functions on the upper astral and lower mental planes. If the Personality reaches upwards to connect with the descending influence from the Individuality, the result is a complete circuit, and the Personality is energized and empowered with the forces of the higher planes. If the Personality closes itself against the contact with the Individuality, on the other hand, the higher planes never come into play. In the absence of occult training or certain other influences, the result is the starved, empty state of the psyche so often encountered today, which leads so many people to try to fill the void at the center of their beings with the chatter of the mass media or the false certainties of ideology.

Bring occult training into play, however, and things become considerably more serious. The disciplines of any form of occult training link up the levels of the self from the Personality on down. If this is done by someone who has turned away from the Individuality, the result is a half-circuit in which force flows down from the lower mental or upper astral plane to the physical plane and back up to where it started. Inevitably a short circuit occurs, and the force flows across at the level of the lower mental or upper astral planes, as shown in the diagram below. The force is guided, not by the higher planes, but by the patterns laid down in the subjective mind during our species' descent through the planes; it is therefore subconscious rather than conscious.

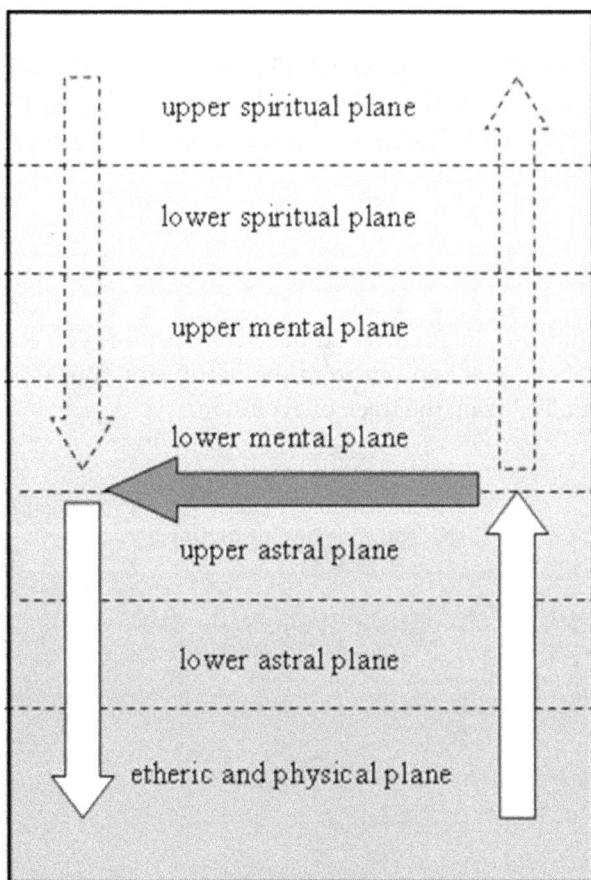

The Broken Circuit

Thus the forces that come through to the conscious mind are shaped by subconscious drives and automatisms rather than the expanded awareness of the upper mental and spiritual planes. The result is a debasement of the Personality, in which complex mental abilities end up being used for crude and unthinking ends. I suspect many of us have met people like this, who display a surface patina of intellectual brilliance or personal charisma that conceals a complete inability to think reflectively and an equally complete unwillingness to take responsibility for their actions.

If Fortune is correct—and her comments here are supported by those of many other occult authors—those who follow this path are not simply left to their own karma. Because their actions can affect the broader life-wave of which we are all parts, those greater beings who have responsibility for overseeing human evolution can intervene and send the corrupted soul back down the ladder of evolution to try again. Notes Fortune, "Certain types of mischievous malicious idiots are produced in this way"—and "idiot" was in Fortune's time a specific medical diagnosis, equivalent to profound mental retardation.

The moral to this story is that there's a point to the habit, enjoined in the teachings of many traditional occult schools, to begin every working with an invocation of the Higher. Reach up the planes through prayer, contemplation, and meditation, so that what inspires you comes from the planes above you and not from the detritus of your evolutionary past, and you'll stay on the track of evolution.

## CHAPTER TWENTY ONE

# Influences of the Manifested Universe, Part 2

### Reading

Revised Edition: Chapter 21, "Influences of the Manifested Universe," from the last paragraph on p. 94, beginning "The doctrine of the planes ..." to the end of the chapter.

Millennium Edition: Chapter 22, "Influences of the Manifested Universe," pp. 128–134.

### Commentary

With the subject of this section of *The Cosmic Doctrine*—teachings concerning the Planetary Spirits (or Planetary Beings), Star Logoi (or Ray Exemplars), and spiritual evolution—we again come into territory that has much to do with practical magic. Fortune's writing here is extremely careful, since as always she was concerned about not handing out practical teachings to those who were not equipped to deal with them. In order to make sense of what she has to say, it will be necessary to jump back and forward a bit as we proceed.

Let's begin with the Planetary Spirits. In Chapter 14, Fortune explained that Planetary Spirits are "creations of the created," patterns of enduring movement in space laid down by the three primal swarms in their journey down and back up the planes. They are kindled into being by the Lords of Flame, given bodies of the substance of each plane by the Lords of Form, and elaborated by the epigenetic play of the Lords of Mind. They do not have Divine Sparks of their own, and so their evolution depends on the evolution of the beings who are incarnated on them in the course of those beings' descent and ascent through the planes.

As we have seen in previous chapters, too, the planets did not come into being all at once. The primal swarms made them one at a time as they descended through the planes. In those chapters, the genesis of the planets was presented in a simplified form, as though the swarms moved step by step away from the Sun as they descended. That was useful for the sake of instruction, but the actual order—an important key to the practical dimensions of *The Cosmic Doctrine*—is rather different, and is shown in the diagram below.

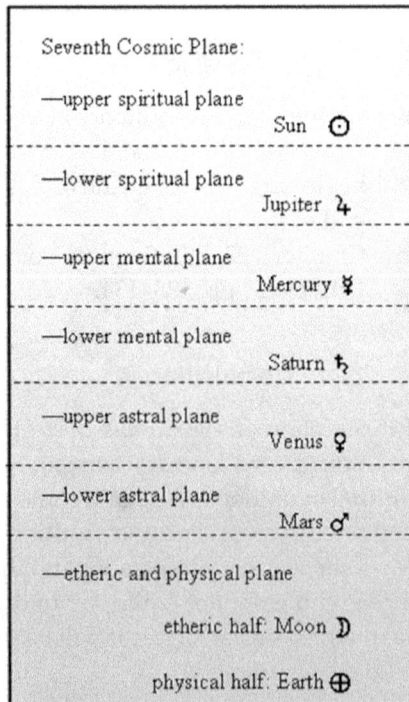

Seventh Cosmic Plane:

—upper spiritual plane
                    Sun   ☉

—lower spiritual plane
                    Jupiter   ♃

—upper mental plane
                    Mercury   ☿

—lower mental plane
                    Saturn   ♄

—upper astral plane
                    Venus   ♀

—lower astral plane
                    Mars   ♂

—etheric and physical plane

                    etheric half: Moon   ☽

                    physical half: Earth   ⊕

Planes of Being 5

As noted in that earlier chapter, the Earth was the last planet formed, and is thus the planet of the physical plane; the Moon represents to us the upper half of the physical plane, the realm of etheric forces. Mars corresponds to the lower astral plane, the plane of instincts and passions, and Venus to the upper astral plane, the realm of the higher and more abstract emotions. Saturn is the planet of the lower mental plane, the realm of concrete mind, and Mercury the planet of the upper mental plane and the abstract mind. Jupiter, the first planet formed, is the planet of the lower spiritual plane, and the Sun itself represents the forces of the upper spiritual plane.

To what extent this order reflects the actual events of the solar system's formation is a question I propose to leave to the cosmologists. As metaphor, it works well, because the planetary forces as understood in astrology and invoked in magic do in fact correspond very precisely to the planes assigned to them here: the cycles of Mars match the passions and instincts, those of Venus, those of emotion and creativity, and so on. From now on, when you think of the swarms moving down the planes in their great journey, imagine them moving from planet to planet in the order given, dwelling on each world in bodies formed of the substance of the corresponding plane—bodies of the upper mental plane on Mercury, in other words, and the lower astral plane on Mars. This reflects, and in a certain sense might explain, the fact that of all the planets in our solar system, the Earth appears to be the only one that has physically incarnate life on it.

No doubt many readers will have noted by now that this scheme assigns no role in the process of spiritual evolution to the planets Uranus and Neptune, for minor planets such as Ceres and Pluto, or for any of the smaller bodies that make up the solar system (other than comets, which we discussed earlier). There is a good practical reason for this. The seven planets Fortune includes in her scheme are also the ones that have extensive bodies of magical lore built up around them. Any mage with a grasp of the traditional lore knows how to invoke the energies of Venus or Saturn, for example, while the same is not true of Ceres or Neptune. Centuries of hard work will have to go into reworking the existing lore of planetary magic to fit a ninefold rather than a sevenfold system, and in the meantime, mages have other duties to attend to. It may also turn out that, in the magical systems of the far future, the other planets, minor planets, moons, asteroids, and Kuiper belt bodies will have roles unrelated to providing homes to incarnate beings.

The Planetary Spirits of the seven planets Fortune discusses here are responsible for that last task, and they are the great conditioning influences for the evolution of each swarm as it passes from world to world. As explained back in Chapter 14, each Planetary Spirit acquires bodies corresponding to all seven planes, so that eventually swarms of Divine Sparks will be able to undergo the full evolutionary cycle on a single planet. Eventually is not yet, though, and the Planetary Spirit with which we are most concerned—the Planetary Spirit of the Earth—is the youngest of the Planetary Spirits, and since she is the planet of the physical plane, her highest and subtlest aspect is on the higher etheric sub-planes of the physical plane.

Each of the Planetary Spirits, however, also has a Lord of Flame as its guide and guardian. In the language of ceremonial magic, these Lords of Flame are the archangels of the planets; other traditions have their own names for them. Each of these beings has other spiritual beings working under their direction to further the evolution of the Planetary Spirit and the swarms who work out a stage of their evolution on the planet. Fortune refers to these helping spirits as "Initiates who know the consonants of the Names," which is a subtle bit of Cabalistic word-play: originally, written Hebrew included the consonants of words but not the vowels, which had to be learned from a teacher in the days before the current system of vowel points came into use. In the same sense, the spirits who serve the archangels of the planets are furthering their own evolution by doing so; having mastered the obvious aspects of the plane on which they operate, they are learning the subtle inner aspects of the plane through their labors.

The Star Logoi are similar to the Planetary Spirits in certain important senses. As explained in Chapter 17, the Star Logoi originated as the group souls of the swarms that followed the three primal swarms, and they now mediate the forces of the Zodiac. Each of the Star Logoi has a Lord of Mind assigned to it as its guide and guardian; in ceremonial magic, these are described as the angels of the twelve signs of the Zodiac. Each new swarm receives particular guidance from the Star Logos corresponding to whichever one of the twelve Cosmic Rays was affecting the solar system at the time the swarm set out down the planes, but all twelve of the Star Logoi influence each swarm and establish twelve basic types of soul in each swarm.

Our Earth is in the midst of all this. It has a Planetary Spirit who is the youngest of her kind and still has long ages of evolution ahead of her.

It has a Lord of the Flame, called the archangel Sandalphon in Cabalistic literature and other names in other traditions, who is the regent of the Solar Logos on this world. It has many other spiritual beings inhabiting it, including Lords of Form and Lords of Mind; and it also has beings of our swarm who have completed the work of this plane and, having been initiated by the Lords of Mind, assist the evolution of other souls.

As Fortune points out, this involves work with the other Planetary Spirits and their Regents, and also with the Star Logoi, because the Planetary Spirit of the Earth reaches only as far as the etheric sub-planes, and humanity has almost completed its evolution on those sub-planes. To awaken the capacities of the higher aspects of the self—those that correspond to the planes above the physical—the Planetary Spirits and Star Logoi and their guiding archangels and angels must be brought into the picture, because they possess contacts with the higher planes that our Planetary Spirit has not yet evolved. This has important implications for human evolution.

As incarnate human beings, we have already received the initiations of the Earth and the Moon. We have awakened to objective consciousness on the physical plane, and the next great step for us will take us from Earth to Mars, where we will begin the process of awakening to full objective consciousness on the lower astral plane. That journey will not be made with spacecraft, however, since the densest bodies we will have then will be made of the substance of the lower astral, and the transition will be a movement of souls rather than of bodies. As Cosmic time is reckoned, Fortune says, that transition is not far off. What does that work out to in human terms? Our text doesn't say—nor, of course, does it say how literally or metaphorically this statement is to be taken.

There's a practical lesson to be learned from this point, however. At this stage of our species' collective evolution, for a great many of us, a fixation on the purely material aspects of life—on what Fortune calls "the supreme humanity of the animal aspect"—is a form of retrogression that leads to the Left-Hand Path. Remember that Fortune gives a very specific meaning to that term, one that differs from some of the uses it's been given since her time. The diagram shown below offers a useful mnemonic; for Fortune, the Left-Hand Path is the path of retreating back along the line of evolution already accomplished, while the Right-Hand Path is the path of forward motion toward modes of evolutionary experience we haven't had yet. Both rise up the planes—but one involves gaining abilities we haven't developed yet, while the other involves shedding abilities we've gained and reverting to older forms.

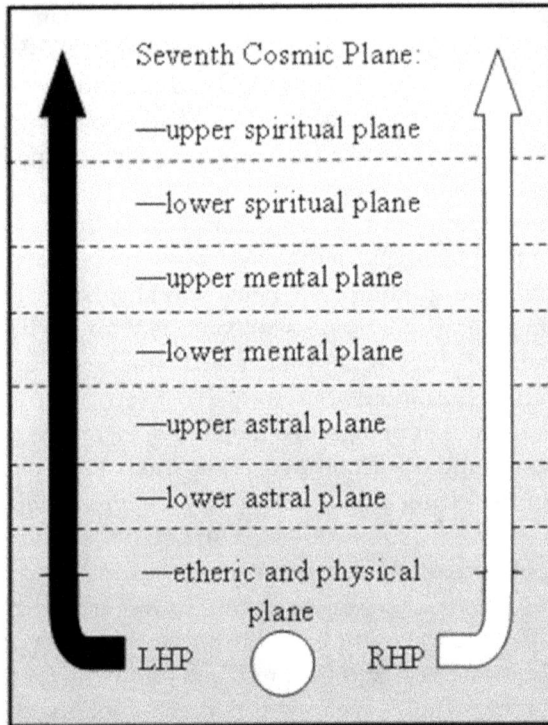

Planes of Being 6

The rest of this chapter needs to be understood with some care, as Fortune here brings in her own personal religious beliefs. At the time she penned *The Cosmic Doctrine*, she believed, as many Christians in her time believed, that the polytheist faiths of the past were appropriate at an earlier stage of evolution, but that they had passed their time and the strict monotheism of the Abrahamic faiths was appropriate now. She also believed, as many people influenced by the Theosophical movement believed, that monotheism was also a transitional phase, and that it would be supplanted in turn by reverence for the Masters and the hierarchies responsible for spiritual evolution, with Christ as the Master of Masters off beyond the hierarchies.

These beliefs were very common in Fortune's time, but not many people hold them these days, even in the occult community. Fortune herself, later on in her career, reevaluated her dismissal of the gods and goddesses of traditional Paganism, and ended up using her considerable abilities as a novelist and ritualist to attempt to reestablish reverence for Isis and Pan in the modern world. If you happen to be a Theosophically influenced Christian, in other words, by all means take what she says at face value; if not, take it as the way a broader pattern of ideas looks from within the worldview of a Theosophically influenced Christian.

That pattern of ideas can be outlined readily enough. On each plane except for the physical plane, there are always two swarms moving through—one in a subjective state descending through the planes, the other in an objective state rising back up. The swarm on the descending arc receives its initiation from the swarm on the ascending arc. So far, so good—but here on Earth, at the Nadir of the arc where involution ends and evolution begins, there is only one swarm present; there ain't nobody here but us chickens. Furthermore, in Fortune's scheme, the most important initiation of all—the initiation of the Nadir, the point at which the individual soul wakes to objective consciousness and begins to make use of the potentialities it has picked up on its long journey down the planes—can only be given and received on the physical plane.

This initiation is therefore conferred straight down the planes, as Fortune says, "by those who have attained perfection on the seventh plane"—that is, the upper spiritual plane, which has the sun for its planet. This is the initiation of the Logos, which Fortune identifies with the initiatory aspect of the Christian faith. That identification works well enough so long as it is not treated as an exclusive matter, since the logic of Fortune's great metaphor requires that all the souls in our swarm (or nearly all, since the comets take some few) receive that initiation, and this includes people who completed that part of their journey long before Christianity came into existence. One way to understand this part of the metaphor is to see the initiation of the Logos as something that every religion can provide to its believers.

There are subtleties to this scheme that deserve close attention. While our swarm was still completing its descent into matter, having arrived on this planet but not yet fully awakened to objective consciousness on the material plane, we still interacted to some extent with the beings of earlier evolutions, whom we called spirits, gods, and many other terms of the same kind. This corresponds precisely to the worldview of traditional societies, full of spirits and half-glimpsed beings of all kinds—the "demon-haunted world" Carl Sagan denounced so angrily, if you will, as well as the world full of gods that the Greek philosopher Thales described in reverent terms. At the Nadir, the point of deepest descent into matter, that is no longer the case, and the only beings who can reach us at that point are the perfected entities of the upper spiritual plane.

Fortune suggests, though, that this is a temporary state. On the far side of the initiation of the Nadir, the terrible silence of a Cosmos of empty space and dead matter gives way to a living world again. We again come into contact with other spiritual beings, but our relationship with them has changed. We have awakened into objective consciousness, and can begin to perceive the planes above matter; we can, once that point has passed, begin to take part in the greater processes of the Cosmos, and prepare ourselves to help later evolutions as we have been helped. To make use of a homely metaphor, we will cease to be clients and will be hired as members of the staff—in entry-level positions, to be sure, but with very nearly limitless possibilities for advancement.

Within the structure of Fortune's great metaphor and the broader context of occult tradition generally, it is not unreasonable to speculate about whether other groups of human souls made the same transition before us, either in civilizations known to history or in those more distant ages that occult literature and Fortune's own writing discusses—the Atlantean era, the Lemurian era, and so on. Whether or not this is the case, the entire structure of *The Cosmic Doctrine* requires that all other created beings in our solar system, from the Lords of Flame downward, have been through some equivalent of the same experience we are undergoing now: the temporary descent into a world made only of matter and void, the collective equivalent of the mystic's Dark Night of the Soul, followed by a return to life and light.

# CHAPTER TWENTY TWO

# The Lords of the First Three Swarms and Natural Laws

## Reading

Revised Edition: Chapter 21, "The Lords of the First Three Swarms and Natural Laws," pp. 100–103.

Millennium Edition: Chapter 23, "Teaching Concerning Other Evolutions Inhabiting A Planet Simultaneously," pp. 135–140.

## Commentary

In this chapter, we are still tabulating all the various influences that bear on human evolution; if you page back to Chapter 18 of the Revised Edition or Chapter 19 of the Millennium Edition, we've gotten to 2 (d), "Influences of other evolutions sharing the same planet." At this stage in Fortune's great metaphor, the laws of nature as we normally experience them come into play, and so do the beings behind those laws—on the one hand, the Lords of the first three swarms; on the other, the elementals.

Here, of course, we run headfirst into one of the great differences between the occult and scientific worldviews. One of the central (though usually unmentioned) principles underlying the entire mind-set of modern science is the quest to abolish personality from the universe. From the earliest days of the Scientific Revolution, it's reliably been the case that a theory only counts as properly scientific if it reduces phenomena to the mechanical level and excludes every trace of person-hood from it.

It was in that spirit that the scientists of Port-Royal in eighteenth-century France insisted that animals didn't actually feel pain—no, of course not; they were simply clever mechanisms contrived by God to make sounds that resembled cries of pain if you cut them apart while they were still alive. That same depersonalizing agenda explains much of the rapture with which Newton's theory of gravity was greeted by the scientifically minded public when it was first published. By reducing the Cosmos to a great machine, Newton made it possible to pretend that the Planetary Spirits and intelligences had been abolished once and for all.

As we saw in the previous chapter, this is a phase that every being has to pass through, and the fact that so many people have passed through it over the last few centuries suggests that a great many souls in our swarm have been going through the initiation of the Nadir at this time. Occultism, however, is intended for those who have passed through that initiation and are beginning to reawaken to a world full of life and light, and so the occult tradition rejects the depersonalized Cosmos of science root and branch. To the occultist, every energy is an entity, and the Cosmos is not a machine but a vast community of living, conscious, intelligent beings of many different kinds and levels, whose interactions create the phenomena that we experience. Fortune places herself solidly in this tradition throughout *The Cosmic Doctrine*, and the present chapter is one of the places where this becomes most obvious.

She has already pointed out that on any planet there are two great classes of beings, one on the descending, involutionary arc, and the other on the ascending, evolutionary arc. On the physical plane, the plane we currently inhabit, those classes belong to the same swarm of Divine Sparks: those who have not yet finished the descent into matter form the involutionary class, while those who have completed the descent and begun to awaken into objective consciousness form the evo-lutionary class. As we've already seen, however, there are beings who are not of our swarm also inhabiting this planet. The most important of these are the elementals, and Fortune devotes much of this chapter to a discussion of them, their origin, and their destiny.

She assumes, of course, that her readers already know what elementals are and how they are classified, and that's no longer a safe assumption to make. Elementals, then, are spiritual beings who inhabit the material substances of the natural world. They have been classified in various ways, but the taxonomy almost everyone in the occult scene has used for the last four centuries was the work of that astonishing force of nature, Philippus Aureolus Theophrastus Bombastus Paracelsus von Hohenheim, whose fourth name is responsible for the English word "bombastic" and who most people know these days as Paracelsus.

According to Paracelsus, the elementals are divided among the four traditional elements: gnomes for earth, undines for water, sylphs for air, and salamanders for fire. (The word "salamander" originally meant a fire spirit, and only later on became another word for a newt.) If for some reason you dislike the traditional names of the elements, you can call them solid matter, liquid matter, gaseous matter, and energy, and be equally accurate. The elementals are embodied in these elements, and guide and govern them; they are, as Fortune points out, the personal side of those repeating patterns that scientists call the laws of nature.

The Lords of Flame, Form, and Mind are responsible for the creation of the elementals, and create them by the same process we've observed in so many other contexts already. A Lord of Flame, let's say, expresses the will of the Logos by setting up a particular pattern of movement in space. Through repetition, that movement becomes an enduring pattern, and the Lord of Flame can then do something else, while the pattern of movement repeats itself endlessly and gradually draws other patterns of movement into harmony with it. This is the same process by which every kind of being comes into existence, but there's a difference—we and the elementals start the process at opposite ends of the ladder of the planes.

We have seen in earlier chapters how each of us begins on the seventh plane, the upper spiritual plane, as an Individuality which gradually clothes itself in a body of seventh-plane atoms, and descend the planes from there. Elementals, by contrast, begin on the first plane, the physical plane, and gradually build upwards from there. We start by becoming Individualities and then develop Personalities to learn the lessons of the planes of manifestation; they start by becoming Personalities and then, in some cases, develop Individualities to learn the lessons of the Unmanifest.

Since we and they inhabit the same planet, humans and elementals come into contact constantly. Most of these contacts are casual and harmless. When you light a fire, climb into a full bathtub, breathe in fresh air, or stand on the earth, you're interacting with elementals. So long as you do so in this purely material way, you run no risks.

Once you set foot on the path of occult training, on the other hand, you begin to develop the skills that can bring you into contact with the inner side of the elemental world: your Personality and the Personalities of the elementals can interact. This is where problems can creep in, because the human etheric body (or, as Fortune calls it, the etheric double) has more than one function. It is the vehicle by which we can interact with the elemental realm; it is also the vehicle of the passions. To come into contact with elementals on a personal level thus tends to shift the passions into overdrive. If you can control yourself under those conditions, you're fine—but if you can't, it's possible to land in serious trouble.

There used to be an immense occult literature about sexual relationships between humans and elemental spirits, some of it serious, some of it less so, and Fortune was writing when that subject was routinely discussed in occult circles. Nowadays, the occult scene is less well-educated about that, among many other things, so a few basic points have to be covered so that readers can figure out what she's talking about. The crucial point to keep in mind is that sex is not just a matter of the dense physical plane. The involvement of the etheric and astral bodies is what makes sex different from other kinds of friction. Elementals don't have physical bodies of the kind we do—their bodies on the dense physical consist of processes within the world of "inanimate" matter—but they have etheric and astral bodies, and yes, sexual intimacies can take place on the subtle planes. (If you've had sex in a dream, you've had an experience of this kind.)

That's what Fortune is talking about when she explains that it is possible for a human being to be mated with an elemental. Does this happen? Certainly, that's what the traditional lore claims, and there are enough accounts of the type that it seems unwise to dismiss it out of hand. Such relationships are addictive and obsessive for the human partner, since the elemental partner stimulates the etheric body to overwhelming states of passion that no amount of ordinary sexual activity will satisfy. There are various ways this can end up, none of them particularly good for the human partner.

There is also, as Fortune points out, the risk that the elemental Personality will absorb the human Personality or simply replace it, linking up with the human's Individuality for the rest of that incarnation.

(This doesn't require sexual interactions, though those can foster it). This is one of the ways that a nonhuman soul can end up in a human body. Such individuals are a distinct type, one that was once well-recognized, and not just in occult circles; they tend to be highly attractive and charismatic, especially in a sexual context, and completely heartless—not malicious, but simply incapable of understanding that they ought to care about what happens to the human playthings they so easily break and cast aside.

Does all this mean that elementals are too dangerous to deal with? Not at all. It simply means that you have to deal with them the right way, and this starts by mastering the elemental passions in yourself. (Please note that "mastering" does not mean "getting rid of"!) The advice of the Golden Dawn Theoricus degree remains sound: "Be thou therefore prompt and active as the sylphs, but avoid frivolity and caprice. Be energetic and strong as the salamanders, but avoid irritability and ferocity. Be flexible and attentive to images as the undines, but avoid idleness and changeability. Be laborious and patient as the gnomes, but avoid grossness and avarice." Develop the elemental powers within yourself in a balanced fashion, and you gain the ability to interact with the elementals themselves in an equally balanced fashion.

Some occult schools make a point of working with elementals from this condition of balance—the Rosicrucian lineages are particularly well known for this, and Fortune's own Fraternity (now Society) of the Inner Light worked extensively with elementals in her time. Other schools are less interested in elemental magic. *The Cosmic Doctrine* doesn't deal with the fine details of magical practice, of course; the reason Fortune included information about the elementals in this chapter is that she was going through the whole range of occult factors that influence human life, and the elementals are part of the Cosmos we inhabit and affect us directly and indirectly at every moment of our existence.

On the last page or so of the chapter (in the Revised Edition) or the first and last pages (in the Millennium Edition), however, Fortune veers onto two other subjects in a way familiar from previous chapters. One of these is the relation between the Lords of Flame and the Lords of Form. These two primal swarms form a polarity of influences—force and form, potentiality and actuality, life and death. What is the role of the Lords of Mind in all this? Fortune leaves that unanswered. The answer, of course, is that the first two swarms establish the basic polarity of being, and the third resolves it into a ternary: between force and form, consciousness; between potentiality and actuality, the act of manifestation; between life and death, that broad middle ground we brush against in dreaming and see clearly in the great transformations of the soul.

That's one of the two subjects. The other is an assignment of the primal swarms to specific sets of laws of nature, which raises far more questions than it answers. The Lords of Flame, Fortune tells us, are behind the laws of physics. The Lords of Form are behind the laws of chemistry, and the Lords of Mind are behind the laws of biology. Finally comes a fourth swarm—the Lords of Humanity, which is what we will be when we finish our long pilgrimage back up the planes of being—to whom are assigned the laws of sociology.

What makes this neat tabulation difficult to square with the rest of *The Cosmic Doctrine* is that the explanations of previous chapters either imply or state outright that the three primal swarms completed their journey up and down the planes long before we set out on our pilgrimage, and that other swarms have gone before ours—enough other swarms, for example, to provide the twelve Rays with their Star Logoi. Here, by contrast, the sequence is laid out in a way that makes it look as though we're following right behind the Lords of Mind. Are there classes of laws of nature that come between biology and sociology, which will be ruled by the swarms ahead of us when they get back to the seventh plane? Or is something else going on? As so often happens, this is left for the student to contemplate.

# CHAPTER TWENTY THREE

# Influences Which Humanity Exerts Upon Itself

## Reading

Revised Edition: Chapter 22, "Influences Which Humanity Exerts Upon Itself," pp. 104–107.

Millennium Edition: Chapter 24, "Influences Which Humanity Exerts Upon Itself," pp. 141–147.

## Commentary

In this chapter, we're in the final stage of wrapping up the explication of the list of influences on human evolution that was given in Chapter 18 of the Revised Edition and Chapter 19 of the Millennium Edition. That list doesn't include a specific heading for the influences laid down by past generations of humanity, which may simply have been a typo; perhaps a new edition might include the following: 2 (e) Influences Humanity Exerts on Itself.

In the next chapter, we'll be going on to start exploring the second half of the tabulation, in which Fortune lists some of the fundamental laws of magic. The chapters that follow are as instructive as they are evasive, and the chapter we are considering here shares in that character, as the influences of humanity on itself that Fortune wants to talk about have to do with the religious and magical traditions of the past.

She begins with a crucial distinction that is too often overlooked. Under ordinary circumstances, human beings at our present state of evolution are conditioned and guided by the influences of the Planetary Spirit of the Earth, the great elemental consciousness that has been established by past evolutions on this planet, and will pass on the results of our experiences to the evolutions that come after us. Those who have raised their basic level of consciousness above the physical plane, however, are conditioned and guided instead by the Planetary Spirits of the planet that corresponds to their level of consciousness, as set out in Chapter 20 of the Revised Edition and Chapter 22 of the Millennial Edition: for example, those whose consciousness has risen to the lower astral plane are guided and conditioned by the Planetary Spirit of Mars, those who have risen to the upper mental plane by the Planetary Spirit of Mercury, and so on.

This is important because this shift of conditioning influences is one of the things that initiation is intended to do. Initiation is the process of establishing a connection of consciousness to one of the higher planes; it can take place either through a ceremony conferred by others, followed by intensive personal work, or through sustained solitary effort; when it "takes"—which does not always happen—the soul of the initiate is no longer entirely under the sway of the Planetary Spirit of the Earth, and can proceed with evolution at a faster pace than humanity in the mass.

For humanity in the mass, by contrast, the Planetary Spirit that matters is that of the Earth, the Great Mother of countless ancient theologies. This is necessary, but it's also challenging, because the Planetary Spirit of the Earth embodies all those modes of consciousness that have been built up in the past. As Fortune comments, it's dangerous for souls at one point along the arc of evolution to turn back toward the conditions of an earlier point along that same arc. It can be necessary to do this, if the lessons of that earlier point have been forgotten or distorted, but it's always risky, because it can lead to retrogression and devolution, the process that Fortune describes as the Left-Hand Path.

The aftermath of Dion Fortune's own career offers an opportunity to see both the positive and negative aspects of this kind of work in action. Later in her life, she became convinced that too much influence from an excessively narrow mode of Christianity had caused the lessons of the older Pagan dispensations to be forgotten or distorted, leaving a great

INFLUENCES WHICH HUMANITY EXERTS UPON ITSELF

many people unable to experience healthy sexuality or even inhabit their own bodies fully. Some of the major magical workings she performed in the 1930s—her Rites of Isis and of Pan, on the one hand, and her magically themed novels, on the other—were intended to overcome this imbalance by exposing overcivilized English men and women to doses of old-fashioned Pagan nature spirituality.

The sexual revolution and the revival of a robustly sexual Paganism duly followed, and in due time, significant parts of both these movements veered off into a variety of abusive and destructive dead ends. To some extent, this is simply another example of the way that the opposite of one bad idea reliably turns out to be another bad idea—excessive sexual repression, as it turned out, was no worse than excessive sexual expression—but it also shows how easily what starts as a helpful corrective to existing imbalances can lead to imbalances of its own.

The conditioning influence of the Planetary Spirit of Earth is also called the "Earth-pull," and this is a useful turn of phrase because it expresses one of the core features of that influence. To feel the Earth-pull is to be drawn more deeply into material embodiment, to attend to the body, its passions, and its material surroundings. When a swarm of Divine Sparks is first descending to this planet, the Earth-pull is a wholly beneficial force, because it helps the members of that swarm attune themselves to the realities of material existence and learn the lessons of incarnation in dense matter. Once individual members of the swarm finish that process, awaken to objective consciousness on the material plane, and begin taking the first tentative steps on the Path of Return, the Earth-pull becomes an obstacle.

Three factors help these awakening souls overcome that obstacle. The first, as already noted, is the influence of initiation, which enables those souls who receive an initiation to balance the Earth-pull with the very different influences of one or more of the other Planetary Spirits in the solar system.

The second is what Fortune describes, in the Theosophical language of her day, as "the work of the Great White Lodge." Elsewhere in her writings, she describes this as the way of the mystics, those people who live lives of renunciation and devotion, not to seek their own redemption but to help redeem others. Their labor plays a crucial role in the collective karma of our species, and it also makes the struggle against the Earth-pull easier: the mystic who renounces every ordinary human desire is counterbalancing the Earth-pull, and laying down a track in space that makes it less difficult for others to lift their consciousness away from the purely material level.

The third of these counterbalancing factors is the planetary entity or archangel of the planet, the advanced spiritual being who has taken on the role of guardian of the Planetary Spirit. In Cabalistic terms, the angelic being who guides the Planetary Spirit of the Earth is the Archangel Sandalphon; other traditions have their own names for this mighty being. His work includes that of modulating the Earth-pull, so that individual souls who are ready to begin the Path of Return are not challenged beyond their strength—though they are always challenged, of course. As with anything else worthwhile, access to the Path of Return must be earned.

The influence of the Planetary Spirit has its complexities, though, and it's worth taking some time to understand those. We can start with the individual human being. As Fortune comments, the whole range of evolutionary possibilities available to us as human beings can be sorted out into three categories. The first category comprises those that we have experienced in past lives, which have done their work and are now latent in us. The second comprises those that we are exploring in our lives right now, which are doing their work and are active presences to us. The third comprises those which have been reserved for future lives, which exist for us now only as untapped potentials.

The Planetary Spirit embodies those possibilities that, for most of humanity, belong to the first category alone. The evolution of a swarm is a slow process, to be sure, and there are human souls who are still exploring aspects of being human that most others internalized long ago, just as there are human souls who have proceeded far beyond the level most of us have reached. Fortune suggests, however, that, on average, our present humanity is about two-thirds of the way through the work it has to perform on the physical plane. Most of us, in other words, are past the stage at which the Earth-pull is drawing us in the direction of our further evolution, and into the stage at which the Earth-pull becomes a challenge to be confronted and overcome.

One of the things that makes the challenge so serious is an intriguing detail of the way that the Planetary Spirit influences human souls. Inevitably, Fortune explains this through a metaphor. She imagines the human possibilities we've just discussed as forming a vertical sequence—think of a stack of schoolbooks, with kindergarten primers at the very bottom and college textbooks up at the very top. This stack or sequence is then reflected in the Planetary Spirit, and like any reflection it's reversed, so that the first thing you encounter when you contact the Planetary Spirit is the most basic and primitive possibilities that humanity explored in its earliest days—the kindergarten primers of our image. Only by going further and deeper is it possible to reach the more complex and more nuanced possibilities explored later in humanity's evolutionary journey.

It's for this reason, Fortune points out, that when dealing with the influences of the Planetary Spirit, it's important to be able to do this from the standpoint of full objective consciousness. Approach them in a state where objective consciousness has been dispersed or eclipsed—in dissociative states such as trance, for example—and the mind is swamped by them, unable to think clearly or to shake off the domination of the atavistic influence that has seized it.

From a magical perspective, that was the trap into which a large group of German occultists had fallen by the time *The Cosmic Doctrine* was written, and all of Germany would fall over the decade thereafter. The primeval patterns in the Germanic group-soul that ultimately gave rise to Nazism could have been tapped in a state of full objective consciousness, using techniques such as individual meditation, and become a creative ferment in a society afflicted with too much rigidity and rationality. Instead, the occultists of the Germanenorden, the Thule-Gesellschaft, and other proto-Nazi occult groups used the first drafts of the ritual methods that saw their ultimate expression in the Nuremberg rallies, and they and the German nation ended up overwhelmed by the upsurge from the deeps, swept away in a flood of archaic contents that led them straight to genocide and catastrophe.

Fortune pauses at this point in her argument to insert two apparently irrelevant discussions that have a great deal to do with practical magic involving the Planetary Spirit and its influences: one relating to time and the other to space. She notes that the phases of the physical plane—the lunar cycle and the seasons of the Earth—are not given the importance they deserve in considering horoscopes. This is true in general, but it's especially true when dealing with the magical influences of the Planetary Spirit. There are times and phases, and seasons in which certain primal influences rise to their fullest strength.

Most people know, for example, that werewolves are supposed to show up at the time of the Full Moon. Very few remember that this bit of traditional lore reaches back to primeval shamanic warrior traditions across the northern reaches of Eurasia, whose initiates used possession by animal spirits and rituals enacted at the Full Moon to whip themselves up into states of superhuman strength and cruelty so that they could overwhelm their enemies in battle. Nowadays, we'd call such states "acute homicidal psychosis," and even in modern warfare there's no place for them, but the influences remain and may explain some otherwise incomprehensible crimes.

As with time, so with place. The holy place of an ancient religious cult or magical initiation will retain the power to awaken corresponding energies in people who spend time there in a receptive state, for good or ill. That can be extremely useful for people in whom such energies are underdeveloped—your typical modern intellectual, for example, who lives a life too detached from earthy influences and the power of the blood, can gain a good deal by spending time in the holy precincts of some robust old Pagan faith—but they can be extremely destructive to those who already have such energies well-developed. Human nature being what it is, the latter are the ones most likely to seek out such places.

Here Fortune inserts a note that deserves close attention. Each religious and magical tradition of the past, she suggests, came into being to develop some specific set of human possibilities, and continues so long as there are still people who need help developing those possibilities. What makes an old religion or an old magical tradition fade out is that it has succeeded in its work: it has made the characteristics it set out to develop part of ordinary human consciousness. The school of Pythagoras, for example, had for its work the development of certain contacts on the mental plane; its initiates treated number theory and geometry as profound mysteries, as indeed they were at that time. Centuries passed, the initiates succeeded in laying down tracks in space that any human mind could follow, geometry became an ordinary school subject rather than a religious mystery, and the capacity for abstract mentation that geometrical training was meant to develop became a normal human capacity.

Does that mean that there's no point in "picking up the contacts," as occultists in Fortune's time liked to describe the process, of initiatory traditions and religious cults of the past? Not at all—but it has to be done carefully, using methods that raise the archaic contents to the level of objective conscious awareness rather than those that submerge the mind in a flood of atavistic force. Done the right way, such work has robust possibilities. On the one hand, as already noted, it's a fine way to clear up imbalances in the Personality—a theme Fortune develops at great length in her novels, especially *The Goat Foot God* and *The Sea Priestess*.

On the other—well, here Fortune is being coy. The levels of the Planetary Being contacted by the old cults have close connections with the elementals, she says, and therefore "the contacts of an atavistic cult may be far-reaching." Contacts with elementals are not particularly far-reaching, but each such cult, according to material that Fortune herself has covered in earlier chapters, was brought into being by a Lord of Mind, and contacts with such a being can be far-reaching indeed.

It's worth noting that when ancient religious traditions are successfully revived, the new version of the tradition very often involves practices and traditions distinct from the old, though clearly linked to them by common threads of meaning and purpose. In this case, from within the perspectives of Fortune's great metaphor, what has happened is that people working with the symbols of the old cult have made contact with the Lord of Mind who created it, and have been guided by the latter to reframe the tradition in forms better suited to the current phase of human evolution. The Druid Revival of the eighteenth century, the Classical Greek Pagan revival of the nineteenth century, and the rebirth of Norse and Germanic Heathen spirituality in the twentieth century are among the examples of this process at work. It's a valid form of magical work, and one that will doubtless see plenty of new (or rather old) ground broken in the centuries ahead.

CHAPTER TWENTY FOUR

# The Law of Action and Reaction

## Reading

Revised Edition:   Chapter 23, "The Law of Action and Reaction," pp. 108–111.
Millennium Edition:   Chapter 24, "The Law of Action and Reaction," pp. 145–151.

## Commentary

We have now finished our exploration of the forces bearing on human evolution, and are about to launch into Dion Fortune's tabulation of some of the core laws of magic. If you have the Millennium Edition, unfortunately, that tabulation is made a little more difficult by some really bad formatting—I get the impression that somebody forgot to proofread this far into the book, because in my copy, at least, the table of planes is a complete mess. I've attached a corrected version below to help readers sort out what Fortune is saying.

**Cosmic Planes:**

1st

2nd

3rd

4th

5th

6th                          **Our Universe:**

7th    Sun             7th    Upper Spiritual

       Jupiter         6th    Lower Spiritual

       Mercury         5th    Upper Mental

       Saturn          4th    Lower Mental

       Venus           3rd    Upper Astral       **Sub-Planes of the**

       Mars            2nd    Lower Astral       **Physical Plane:**

       Earth           1st    Physical           7th    Etheric

                                                 6th    "

                                                 5th    "

                                                 4th    "

                                                 3rd    Gaseous

                                                 2nd    Liquid

                                                 1st    Chemical


                                                 1 Latency = 2 Potencies

Table of the Planes


It may come as a bit of a surprise to the more scientifically minded of my readers to find Newton's law of motion listed as a law of magic, but there it is: in magic as in physics, every action has an equal and opposite reaction. That rule is the basis for a great deal of traditional occult thought. It has certain complexities not dealt with in physics, however, for physics by definition deals solely with the physical plane—the lowest of the seven planes in our solar system, one-seventh of the world we as human beings inhabit, and 1/49th of the greater Cosmos in which we are placed.

According to Fortune, action and reaction are equal and opposite when measured on the same sub-plane: for example, the sub-plane Fortune calls the chemical sub-plane of the physical plane, the world of solid matter as we know it. If the action is on one sub-plane and the reaction is on another one step higher and lower, however, the potency of the one on the higher sub-plane is the square of the potency of the one on the lower. If the action is on one sub-plane and the reaction is two sub-planes removed, the potency of the higher is the square of the square, i.e., the fourth power, and so on.

Even on the physical plane, this works tolerably well. Think of the amount of moving water in a stream that it takes to move a rock along the streambed, or the far greater masses of wind that it takes to fill a sail and set a sailing vessel in motion. (Our standard measurements, sensibly enough, are all calibrated with reference to solid matter to make the calculation easier.) What Fortune intends to discuss here, though, is what happens when you move forces up and down the planes above matter—a process that plays a central role in practical magic.

Imagine, Fortune suggests, that you could take one of the primal atoms discussed in the early chapters of *The Cosmic Doctrine* and split it apart. Each atom consists of two currents of movement in space locked into a vortex, so that the result seems static from outside. Break the bond that unites them, and you have two independent currents which have between them far more force than the atom itself could exert. There's an additional wrinkle here, though, because the liberated forces are on a higher sub-plane than the atom was.

Two of Fortune's technical terms are necessary for what follows: sublimation and degradation. To sublimate a force is to raise it to a higher sub-plane or plane. To degrade a force is to sink it to a lower sub-plane or plane. When you sublimate a force one sub-plane, you square it; when you degrade a force one sub-plane, you reduce it to its square root. Each atom of solid matter is therefore the static form of an immense amount of force, and if all the force in a single ounce of clay could be liberated at once—as Fortune points out—the resulting explosion would wreck the planet. (Remember that she was writing this long before the first nuclear weapon tests.)

The same principle applies to the subtler planes of being, and this is the core theme of this chapter. As a human being, your consciousness normally functions on what Fortune terms the lower astral, upper astral, or lower mental planes: the lower astral if your life is guided by passions and collective norms, the upper astral if your life is guided by imagination and feeling, and the lower mental if your life is guided by personal ideals and reflective thought. Each of these planes contains seven sub-planes. Even on the lower astral plane, there is plenty of difference between the nearly animal consciousness of the lowest sub-plane and the shrewd folk-wisdom of the highest sub-plane, just as there is plenty of difference on the lower mental plane between the mind just waking to the life of ideas and the mind that has reflected deeply and begun to catch whispers of the next plane up.

To move from one sub-plane to a higher sub-plane is to unravel a static vortex and free a great deal of force of the type found on the plane under discussion. If this is done too suddenly, especially when the leap in question covers more than one sub-plane, the resulting explosion can be disastrous; these are the spiritual crises that leave people gibbering in corners, or worse. In the ordinary way of things, the movement up the sub-planes takes place much more slowly, a little of the vortex being unraveled at a time; this is the ordinary way of spiritual evolution, and Fortune uses a mathematical metaphor here to make sense of it. If the sudden unraveling of the vortex is raising something to its square, she suggests, the ordinary process of evolution is like addition. You can get to $7^7$ (seven to the seventh power) by adding 7 plus 7 plus 7 … It's going to take you a long time, though.

There is a middle ground between the sudden shattering revelation and the slow slogging process of ordinary evolution, however. That middle ground is initiation, which Fortune compares to multiplication: 7 times 7 times 7… gets you there a lot more quickly than addition, but without the sudden shock of squaring. This is the central work of a magical lodge like Fortune's Fraternity (now Society) of the Inner Light, and it's also something that can be pursued by the individual. This latter is not something Fortune discusses here, since *The Cosmic Doctrine* was written for members of the Fraternity of the Inner Light, but it should be remembered through the discussion that follows.

The process of initiation as Fortune sets it out is straightforward. The initiating group constructs, through ritual and the use of the trained imagination, a structure in the groupmind to receive the energy released from the initiate's awareness and give it a useful form. (This structure is made up of imagery, narrative, and the other features of effective initiatory ritual.) In the ritual of initiation, the candidate is brought into contact with that structure after having been placed in a receptive psychological state. When the initiation works, the candidate's consciousness rises to a higher level, and the force released by that upward movement— like the flash of an old-fashioned photographer's flashbulb—imprints the structure on the candidate's consciousness, giving the candidate a form that can be used to understand and work with the new capacities of awareness.

(Notice that Fortune is remarkably evasive in her terminology here. At one point, she says that the movement from sub-plane to sub-plane is like squaring, and initiation is like multiplication; a few paragraphs down, she seems to be implying that each grade of initiation results in the attainment not of a sub-plane but of an entirely new plane. My working guess is that this bit of obfuscation was deliberate, so that those who didn't read carefully and meditate on what they read would get confused.)

So sublimation, in one of its forms, is the result of initiation. Degradation is another thing entirely. When you degrade a force, you take its two opposing polarities on one sub-plane and lock them together into a vortex, so that you create a much weaker force one sub-plane further down. This can be risky, because whatever structure of consciousness or substance the original force used to fill is left empty, and other things can fill it—including things that you really, truly don't want filling it.

Here Fortune gives some extremely useful pointers about obsession. That's a technical term for the condition in which a spirit has effectively supplanted the Individuality in an incarnate person, so that instead of being guided by the Individuality, the Personality is guided by the spirit. (It differs from possession, which is the condition in which a spirit has supplanted the Personality itself.) Obsession happens when the Personality has undergone degradation in the technical sense used above, and is functioning on a lower sub-plane than it previously occupied. That leaves the open space through which the spirit enters.

That happens when the human will, the will of the Personality, becomes inhibited—when the person stops willing and regresses to a passive, will-less state of awareness in some aspects of life. There are spiritual and pseudospiritual practices that do this, as Fortune was well aware, and it can also happen as a result of deliberate contact with demonic entities—the "lower types of evolution" she mentions in passing. The basic rule here is that in every aspect of life, the mage acts intentionally; if she chooses to be receptive to astral influences, say, it's a willed receptivity, wholly under her control; if she seeks to surrender herself to a deity, as you see so often among religious mages, it's a willed surrender, done freely and through perfect control of the self.

In any magical action, equilibrium must be maintained. That has another dimension, for when you sublimate a force—raising it to a higher sub-plane and unraveling it into its component forces—that leaves an empty space on its original plane. The same thing happens if you degrade a force—bringing it down to a lower sub-plane and locking its component forces into a stable vortex. The trick to maintaining equilibrium, of course, is that you balance these two actions against each other. If you set out to bring a force down into manifestation on the physical plane, you need to sublimate a comparable force up out of the physical plane, to maintain equilibrium.

This is why, among other things, traditional occult training balances workings of spiritual development against workings of practical magic. By practicing the former, you sublimate yourself, unraveling vortices of fixed energy and expressing the freed forces on higher sub-planes; by practicing the latter, you further the descent of energies that are already in the process of flowing into manifestation and help with the process of creation.

There are advanced forms of this kind of work, suitable for very skilled practitioners only. "The Sephiroth when reversed are the Qlippoth," Fortune comments in passing; you have to know your way around magical literature to know that the Sephiroth are the ten primary realities that form the Tree of Life, and the Qlippoth are demonic beings who originated in the universe before ours. One potent way to manifest the power of the Sephiroth is to degrade the Qlippoth—to lock their polarized forces into a stable vortex, forcing them down a subplane and weakening their power. Old legends about binding demons are metaphors for this process.

To do this with the Qlippoth themselves, as already noted, is a very advanced form of magic. Each of the Qlippoth, however, has a reflection in the human soul, and one way to make use of Fortune's formula is to use it on these reflections. Take any habit of passion, imagination, or thinking that is automatic, mindless, and destructive—these are the classic markers of demonic influence—and meditate on it until you can pick it apart into its two component forces, which alternate in your psyche. Then you pit the two component forces against each other until they lock into a stable vortex, and their ability to influence you is reduced to the square root of its previous potency. The two forces will differ from person to person—one person may balance anger with shame, another may balance anger with fear, or what have you—but by figuring out the balance and bringing the two forces into contact, degradation happens; a demon is bound.

A different kind of advanced magic is the subject of the last section of this chapter, and it's a kind that very few people do these days. It used to be standard practice in late nineteenth- and early twentieth-century occultism, as a result of the influence of Spiritualism, for advanced practitioners to engage in mediumship, seeking to contact the beings known as "the Masters" in Theosophical literature. Some occult schools still teach this, but many do not, as the practice turned out to have a range of downsides, including the one Fortune hints at in the last sentence of this chapter.

Too much power brought into the Personality inevitably tries to earth itself out, and it normally chooses the earthiest possible way to do that. This is why ministers in those branches of Christianity that like to whip up emotions to a fever pitch, seeking to raise enough energy in this way to perform healings and other remarkable events, so often end up being caught in sexual embarrassments of one sort or another. It's why sexual scandals are so reliable a part of the history of alternative spiritual groups, and why "the all too frequent overweighting of the lower aspects of the occultist" gave magical practitioners a reputation as sex fiends in Fortune's time.

There are, fortunately, other ways to commune with benevolent nonhuman intelligences that don't have this same downside. If you belong to an occult school that teaches the practice of mediumship with the Masters, and can learn how to do it safely from people who have enough experience to matter, that's one thing, and close study of (and meditation on) the last three paragraphs of this chapter will be helpful. Otherwise, it's probably best to leave that practice strictly alone.

# CHAPTER TWENTY FIVE

# The Law of Limitation, Part 1

## Reading

Revised Edition:    Chapter 24, "The Law of Limitation, Part One,"
pp. 112–114.
Millennium Edition:    Chapter 26, "The Law of Limitation," p. 152 to
the end of the first paragraph on p. 255.

## Commentary

All through the chapters, we've already covered, without drawing unnecessary attention to that fact, Dion Fortune has been laying the foundations for detailed, practical instruction on the art of magic. To some extent, that long slow buildup is a matter of camouflage, of a kind very familiar to any of my readers who know their way around the occult literature of an earlier time: you've got to have the patience to work through the earlier chapters, and understand the terminology they present, in order to make sense of the exposition of practical methods when that arrives. Yet it's also true that the more you understand about the magical vision of the universe, the more effectively you can use the technical details when you finally get to those.

In this chapter, we've gotten to some of the technical details. Hang onto your hats. What follows, though it's deliberately broken up into brief glimpses and comments, is among the clearest expositions of the mechanics of magical practice you'll ever find in print.

Let's start with the very first sentence of the chapter: "Limitation is the first law of manifestation; therefore it is the first law of power." Yes, I know, that statement flies in the face of some of the most deeply rooted habits of contemporary popular culture. To the modern mind, rules are made to be broken, and limits exist solely as things to overcome; pop-culture spirituality prattles on endlessly about limitless this and infinite that. Tell most people these days that willingly accepted self-limitation is a source of personal power—in fact, the *only* source of personal power—and they'll look at you as though you suddenly sprouted an extra head.

Fortune is quite correct, though, and the rejection of limits in today's popular culture is among the main reasons that so many people just now lead lives of failure and frustration. There are reasons why the idea of limitlessness has been spread so enthusiastically and systematically in recent years, and we'll get to those in the next chapter.

Power without limitation is power wasted. If you spill some gasoline and light it, all you'll get are flames, smoke, and a little waste heat. Put the same gasoline into an engine, where it will be imprisoned in the hard limits of a steel cylinder when it's ignited, and it can send your car zooming down the road. This is the same principle Fortune introduced back in Chapter 2 under the label of "negative evil"—the thrust-block that provides the resistance necessary to put energy into motion—but in this chapter, she takes that concept much, much further.

Even the Solar Logos, Fortune suggests, had to accept limits in order to act in the world. She's on solid traditional ground there. In the writings of Isaac Luria, one of the greatest Jewish Cabalists, the process of creation begins with an act of self-limitation on the part of God: the first thing an infinite deity has to do, in order to create a universe, is to make it possible for there to be something that isn't God. This withdrawal of the divine presence, *Tzimtzum* in Hebrew, set the creation of the universe in motion. Fortune may well have been familiar with the Lurianic teachings; she was certainly familiar with Christian teaching about the tremendous self-limitation that God had to accept in being born as a human being, so that his death could accomplish the redemption of humanity. Here again, limitation is the key to power.

Now consider the second paragraph. Better yet, read the second paragraph three times slowly, paying attention to every word. (If you've got the Millennium Edition, where the text is divided into paragraphs differently, do this with the first four sentences of the second paragraph.) What's being described here is the basic template for magical operations. If you want to bring any energy into manifestation on any plane, you have to create a form for that manifestation on the plane immediately above the plane where you want the energy to take action. The diagram below shows Fortune's taxonomy of the planes again, for reference. (This is not the same taxonomy I use in my own writing, so be warned.)

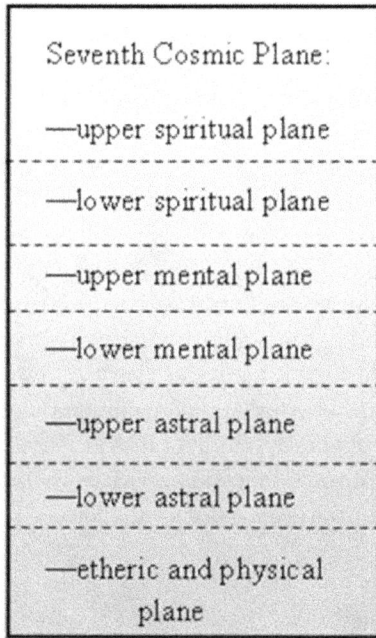

```
Seventh Cosmic Plane:

—upper spiritual plane
- - - - - - - - - - - - - - - - - - - - -
—lower spiritual plane
- - - - - - - - - - - - - - - - - - - - -
—upper mental plane
- - - - - - - - - - - - - - - - - - - - -
—lower mental plane
- - - - - - - - - - - - - - - - - - - - -
—upper astral plane
- - - - - - - - - - - - - - - - - - - - -
—lower astral plane
- - - - - - - - - - - - - - - - - - - - -
—etheric and physical
        plane
```

Planes of Being 2

If you want something to happen on the physical/etheric plane, you build the form for it on the lower astral plane, the realm of the passions; if you want something to happen in the realm of the passions, you build the form for it on the upper astral plane, the plane of imagination, and so on. You build the form on the next plane up, and then call down forces from the planes further up and fill the form with them; the union of force and form then precipitates down onto the plane below the form, and takes effect. Ignorance of this principle is responsible for a great deal of failed magic.

For example, a lot of pop-culture magical practices try to affect attitudes and habits of thought (which belong to the lower mental plane in Fortune's system) using emotional energies from the lower astral plane. If you want to affect attitudes and habits, you have to build your form on the upper mental plane instead, the plane of meanings and insights; all you can do on the lower astral is shape the etheric and physical plane—whence the frequency with which ideologies that use such methods end up trying to control people rather than convincing them.

Next comes the most important rule of magic you will ever learn. If you retain nothing else from this book, retain these words: "In order to achieve an end you must outline that end and limit yourself to it, rejecting all that is irrelevant." There. You've just learned the secret of magical attainment. It really is that simple—but "simple," of course, is not the same thing as "easy."

You can attain anything that's possible for you to attain if you follow Fortune's rule. Let's say you want to have a million dollars. Nothing could be simpler. All you have to do is focus your entire life on making that million dollars. When you get out of bed each morning, assess every hour of the day before you and figure out how you can use that hour as a stepping stone to your million dollars. Consider every activity you might engage in, and if it doesn't further your goal of making money, skip it. Treat every penny that comes your way as a tool for making more money—one of the secrets of wealth, of course, is that you get rich by making your money earn money for you. Have your eyes constantly open for opportunities to earn money, and pay just as much attention to saving the money you earn and putting it to work for you. Do this, and you'll have your million dollars much sooner than you think.

Note, please, that there are things you cannot achieve this way. "In all undertakings the prime requisite for success is to know what you cannot do:" Fortune's words offer a useful warning. Not everything is possible for a human being. Not everything is possible for *you*. If you don't have certain kinds of inborn talent, for example, you will never become a great mathematician. (Mathematics is one of the fields in which experienced teachers can tell very promptly which of their students has what it takes and which, no matter how hard they work at it, will never do any original work of value.) If you're tone-deaf, please don't decide to become an opera singer—the world has already had its Florence Foster Jenkins. Here again, the Law of Limitation is important: if you recognize your own personal limits, you can use them as thrust blocks to put yourself in motion in some other direction.

What if you want to achieve more than one thing in your life? Fortune's already waiting there for you. To the extent that you can, you do one thing at a time. Earn your million dollars; then, once you've got that magic figure in your bank account, take a break, relax, recover from the effort, and then choose the next thing on your list—climbing Mount Everest, say—and do that. Then take another break. The breaks are important; too much focus, too much intensity of will and singleness of purpose, will unbalance you and lead to various unhelpful states, such as fanaticism or mental illness. The traditional habit of setting aside a couple of days a week and a couple of weeks a year to rest from labor is a good one, and should be applied as well to the work we're discussing.

Fortune makes a useful distinction in this context. The terms she uses for the two sides of the distinction are "limited consciousness" and "limitation of consciousness," which is perhaps a little more confusing than it has to be. By the first, Fortune means a consciousness that focuses on a narrow range of things because it's never encountered anything else. By the second, she means a consciousness that has encountered many things and chooses to focus on a narrow range of them for its own purposes. (The great mistake of every form of puritanism is that it confuses these two very different things.) The alternation between concentration and relaxation is a good way to avoid that trap; each period of relaxation, in Fortune's words, provides "broadened consciousness and developed character," which then become the basis for future acts of deliberate and temporary limitation of consciousness.

Another useful point follows. Everyone who's gone through the process of taking up magical practice for the first time knows just how difficult it is to get any results early on. That experience, Fortune points out, is the result of simple inertia, and it doesn't work to try to overcome that by the unaided will. That's where the force of habit becomes an ally of the neophyte. By doing a set of practices by rote, even when they don't seem to be accomplishing anything, a new momentum is established, and this balances out the existing inertia and gives the individual will the deciding vote. The same principle can be used in many other forms of magical working: if you want to overcome the inertia of a habit, don't try to white-knuckle it. Instead, establish a countervailing habit and let that build its own momentum.

The next point Fortune makes has to be understood in the context of her time. In the early twentieth century, Theosophy was the template on which most occult teachings were based. One of the ideas central to Theosophy was a belief in the existence of a spiritual Hierarchy of ascended Masters, who accepted good Theosophists as students and servants. Another was an insistence that good Theosophists should stay away from magic, and limit themselves to meditation and occult study. Fortune here is simply reassuring her more Theosophically inclined readers that there's nothing wicked or forbidden about magical practice, so long as it's done in an ethical and appropriate manner. Here again, she's quite correct; ceremonial magic is not for everyone, but it's a valid option as part of a spiritually oriented life, and the principles Fortune sets out in this chapter can also be put to work in less obviously magical ways.

Let's go on. One of the major challenges faced by those who want to make a change in the world, whether or not they use the specific technical toolkit of the ceremonial magician, is the awkward but inescapable detail that the individual human being counts for very little in the context of the Cosmos as a whole. Scale matters in magic. If you set out to change the world, or a nation, or a community, or even a family all at once, the inertia of your target's existing habits will overwhelm any energy you can bring to bear, and you will fail. As Fortune points out, though, this doesn't mean that you can only achieve small things. It means that if you want to achieve great things, you have to take them one step at a time, focusing on one small change that will further your intention, working on that until it happens, and then moving on to the next small change. The strategy of magic on a large scale is the strategy of drops of water falling on a stone and wearing it away.

Two principles of magical tactics should always be applied while using this strategy, and Fortune gives them both. First, no matter how tightly you focus on a specific detail of the broader problem, always keep the whole context in mind, and see what you're doing in terms of the movements of the Cosmos as a whole. This is one of the reasons that occultists who know what they're doing use astrology and other forms of divination to guide their work. By checking the ebb and flow of the Cosmic tides, either directly through the positions of the planets or indirectly through the divinatory oracle of their choice, they stay in touch with what the Cosmos is doing. Less obviously magical ways of doing the same thing are of course also important.

The second principle is to find and make use of the natural divisions within the whole system you intend to affect. Nothing in the universe is an undifferentiated whole. There are always lines of fracture, points at which one part of the problem can be separated from other parts. Here Fortune's advice is extraordinarily canny. Most people, in and out of occult circles, try to find the natural divisions on what she calls the mental plane, the plane of concepts and ideas, but this often doesn't work well: things that seem very distinct conceptually very often have close connections in practice, while a single concept can cover several distinct phenomena.

What Fortune recommends instead is to pay attention to the emotions involved in the situation you are trying to affect. Look for differences in emotional reactions among the people who are involved. Notice what they want most, and what they want first. Since human beings are complex, figure out what appeals to one side of their nature and what appeals to another side. Then choose a part of the problem that's linked to a specific, distinct emotional pattern, focus on it with laser intensity, and achieve the change you want.

One last detail of magical technique rounds off this short but extremely important chapter. The advice given earlier to alternate between periods of intensive one-pointed focus and periods of relaxation and broadened consciousness has another reason behind it, and Fortune gives it here. Your capacity for focus enables you to bring power to bear and accomplish work with it, but the power is generated in the periods of relaxation. It's the latter, the periods when consciousness broadens and relates to the widest possible range of experience, that provides the broad and solid base for the pyramid of your power; only on that base can you rise to the apex of perfect, deliberate, willed focus, and accomplish wonders.

Whew! That's a lot of ground for a single short chapter. Spend the next month contemplating it line by line. If you practice magic, see how you can apply the insights offered here to your own practices. If you don't practice magic, consider applying the same insights to your own life. They work equally well either way.

# CHAPTER TWENTY SIX

# The Law of Limitation, Part 2

## Reading

Revised Edition: Chapter 25, "The Law of Limitation, Part Two," pp. 115–118.

Millennium Edition: Chapter 26, "The Law of Limitation," from the second paragraph on p. 155 to the end of the chapter on p. 159.

## Commentary

The section of *The Cosmic Doctrine* we reviewed in the previous chapter covered some of the core principles of magical practice. This next serving from Dion Fortune's buffet goes even further into the practical details of operative magic, covering material that to the best of my knowledge appears nowhere else in print. In the process of this exposition, our text veers in some odd directions, using terminology that appears nowhere else in *The Cosmic Doctrine* and taking on a noticeably different tone—different enough that it's at least possible that Fortune has quietly incorporated into her text material from another source, perhaps a document she received from her own teacher.

One aspect of that difference in tone is a certain ruthless pragmatism, and the first paragraph puts it on full display. To understand what's being said here, it helps to know that some of the commonplaces of today's New Age spirituality have a long pedigree. In Fortune's time, as in ours, a great many spiritual schools taught pupils to think of themselves as infinite, limitless, radiant beings, one with vast Cosmic reservoirs of light and life, and to imagine light and life flowing through them in unfailing abundance. That's a very pleasant thing to do, and it can be very helpful in the early stages of spiritual training, especially for people who have been raised to think of themselves as weak, wretched, and sinful—but it comes with a price tag. As our text says, "This enabled the power to use them, not them to use the power."

In a well-managed occult school, that's not necessarily a problem. Students begin by meditating on limitless light and life and love, and in the process they pay part of their dues by contributing their energy and intention to the egregor—the group mind—of the school. Later on, as they advance, they learn other ways of doing things, and can begin drawing on the stored energy in the school's egregor. Unfortunately, the idea of meditating on limitless light and life and love didn't stay the property of well-managed occult schools; it became a common practice in the pop spirituality circuit, where there were no senior initiates to take the students aside one by one and tell them, "Okay, now you can learn what this is *really* about."

The Law of Limitation is the secret of magical power, and as our text says, it was withheld from those on the probationary path—those, in other words, who were not yet finished readying themselves for initiation. Notice the past tense: "was withheld." An approach had been tried, and turned out to have unexpected downsides, so a more complete explanation was provided to Fortune and her students, so they and others could avoid those downsides.

The more complete explanation unfolds from points made in our previous discussion. The previous chapter discussed how magic worked on one plane begins on the next higher plane: the operative mage builds a form on the higher plane, and it then "condenses" onto the lower plane as a structure of forces that has magical effects on the lower plane. That's crucial to understand, but it's incomplete, because it doesn't explain how you build the form on the higher plane. Now Fortune puts it into context by giving "the knowledge of the method of making forms."

The secret is quite simple, and if you know your way around old magical rituals and have thought about their structure, you know it already. Every magical working starts on the highest plane the operative mage can reach and descends from there, plane by plane, until it reaches the plane which is intended to affect. Fortune describes three stages in that process. On the lower mental plane, the mage sets up a repeating pattern of thought, which moves from abstract principles to specific details and then works its way back up to abstract principles. In most rituals this pattern of thought is spoken aloud as an invocation, beginning and ending with a prayer to a deity and including the specific intention of the working in the middle.

Once this has been formulated, the next form to be established is on the upper astral plane, which is among other things the plane of emotions. Here each stage in the circular pattern of thought is linked to feelings (and also, though Fortune does not mention this, to vivid imagery, another aspect of the upper astral plane). Thus the operative mage doesn't read the invocation as though he was reciting the contents of a laundry list. When he addresses the deity at the beginning, he feels a sense of veneration and awe appropriate for entering into the divine presence; when he addresses the deity at the end, he feels gratitude, knowing that the working will succeed, and so on.

The third form to be established is on the lower astral plane, and the energies to be brought into play here are those our text primly describes as "the driving force of the nature." The lower astral is the plane of the passions. In Fortune's own system of magic, the driving force put to work at this stage was sexual energy pure and simple. That doesn't mean that ritual sex or any other kind of sexual activity is involved; it means that Fortune and the other members of her magical order knew and practiced various disciplines that would temporarily divert sexual energies to magical purposes. (This isn't particularly difficult, and she gives instructions for a simple version of the exercise in her book *The Problem of Purity*.) Once the form has been established on the lower astral, in turn, it condenses into the etheric/physical plane, and magical results follow in due time.

In terms of the symbolism of *The Cosmic Doctrine*, the pattern of thought on the lower mental plane corresponds to the Ring-Cosmos, the pattern of feeling on the upper astral plane corresponds to the Ring-Pass-Not, and the pattern of passionate energy on the lower astral plane corresponds to the Ring-Chaos. This may seem counterintuitive at first glance, since in the first chapters of our text, the Ring-Chaos comes into being immediately after the Ring-Cosmos, and the Ring-Pass-Not comes third. Still, one of the essential rules for understanding occult philosophy can be phrased simply enough: when you find something that doesn't make instant sense, study it carefully, because it's trying to teach you something.

What Fortune has outlined here is the magical theory of asceticism. All ascetic practices—fasting, celibacy, you name it—use the passions of the lower astral as a thrust-block, a Ring-Chaos against which the Ring-Cosmos of a concept held on the lower mental plane can push. As always in such workings, the risk taken by the ascetic is that of having the forces reverse their polarity—in this case, that happens when the passion becomes the active force and the intention to resist it becomes static, a thrust-block against which the passion can build its force. This is what gives rise to the failed ascetic—the celibate who loses control of his lust, the public vegan who slips away to the next town once a month to visit a steak house, and so on.

The older approach, which is also that of occult tradition, is to alternate periods of asceticism with periods of normal healthy expression of the physical passions. The teachings that lead orthodox Jews to keep the Sabbath, and devout Christians to fast during Lent, are expressions of the same wisdom that had priests and priestesses in ancient Egypt spend one week out of every month in temple service, subject to a galaxy of taboos and purifications, and the rest of the month in the community living a much more ordinary lifestyle.

Just as the Ring-Cosmos rotates with respect to the Ring-Chaos, now aligned with it, now at right angles to it, so the operative mage alternates periods of ascetic practice with periods of a more ordinary lifestyle; just as the Ring-Pass-Not traces out the boundary between Cosmos and chaos, in turn, the operative mage accepts certain simple restrictions that are meant, to borrow a phrase from Freemasonry, to keep the passions within due bounds. To turn to another metaphor from our text, the pendulum swings one way and then another, tracing out an arc of a circle.

All this, as Fortune points out, has to do with the involutionary arc— that is to say, the process by which spirit becomes matter. In the broadest sense, these paragraphs can be studied to understand the eons-long process by which our swarm of souls descended from the seventh plane to the plane we now inhabit, the plane of matter. In a more limited sense, they can be studied to understand the process by which each of us entered into incarnation in our present bodies, and the way in which the karma we bring from previous lives. In a more limited sense still—the sense that we have been exploring here—they can be used to understand the process by which magical workings have their effects. They do not explain the phenomena of the evolutionary arc—the process by which matter returns to spirit. That is subject to a different law, the Law of the Seven Deaths, which we'll study in the next installment of this commentary.

Two other points need to be made here. The first has to do with the relationship between the Personality and the Individuality—between the identity you've constructed out of memory and habit over the course of this incarnation, and the identity you had before your mother and father were born. (This is one of the places where unfamiliar terminology slips in. In one part of this chapter, Fortune suddenly refers to the Individuality as the Oversoul, and in another she refers to it as the Essential Self.) The Individuality is the whole of which each Personality is a precisely limited part, and the descent into incarnation follows the same downward trajectory we've been tracing in this chapter. This is why, as Fortune points out, magical workings intended to deal with karma are best framed as invocations of the Individuality.

The second point is more complex, and like most of the material in *The Cosmic Doctrine*, is approached through a metaphor. The Law of Limitation applies only when considering a single plane. In Fortune's handy metaphor, it is like a two-dimensional figure—say, a geometrical drawing on a sheet of paper. You transcend the limits by introducing the third dimension. What this means is that limits that are necessary and immovable on one plane can be put into a broader context and made less restrictive by bringing in the influence of another plane.

We explored one way this works in an earlier chapter, when we discussed the sublimation and degradation of forces from plane to plane. Two forces that are locked together on one plane can be sublimated by raising them to a higher plane, at which point they are no longer locked together; the upward movement releases the energy that binds them together. Two forces that are locked together on one plane can also be degraded by taking them down to a lower plane, at which point you no longer have two forces but a single thing that can move freely.

There is another way to use the third dimension, however, and this is the one that Fortune stresses in this chapter. So long as your awareness remains focused on the plane where the two forces are in conflict, you are caught up in the conflict and limited to the range of options—usually a narrow one—that the conflict leaves open. If you can raise your awareness to a higher plane and perceive the conflict as a subset of the Cosmos, one process among many, governed by Cosmic laws and working out the purposes of the Solar Logos, you are no longer caught up in it. The conflict simply becomes one part of a broader field of action, and you can recognize its limitations, let it proceed toward balance, and go do something else while the conflict works itself out. Metaphorically—or not so metaphorically—you die to the conflict and rise above it.

The rest of this chapter is devoted to unfolding that metaphor, and laying the ground for the following chapter and its discussion of the Law of the Seven Deaths. Central to this discussion is a conceptual reversal that's been central to the Western occult tradition since the days when seekers after wisdom sailed from the newborn city-states of Greece to sit at the feet of priests in the ancient temples of Egypt. In the jargon of the Greek mysteries, *soma* equals *sema*: the body, *soma* in Greek, is a tomb, *sema* in the same language.

To be alive in a material body, from the perspective of spiritual existence, is to be dead and buried. To be released from the material body through the process we call death is to be born into light and life. Initiation, the work of the Mysteries, is the process of awakening to light and life while still incarnate in the body. As Fortune points out, this is why any sequence of initiation rituals at least once, and often more than once, uses the symbolism of death and burial. The goal of the work of initiation was set out as exactly as one could wish by J.R.R. Tolkien in a vivid passage in *The Fellowship of the Ring*: "those who have dwelt in the Blessed Realm live at once in both worlds, and against both the Seen and the Unseen they have great power." (This is one of quite a few places in Tolkien's fiction where he used specific turns of phrase standard in the occult scene of the early twentieth century. While he was a devout and highly orthodox Catholic in later life, I've long suspected that he dabbled, or more than dabbled, in occultism during his youth.)

There are seven rungs on the ladder of initiation, as Fortune says in one passage, and three degrees, as she says in another. These sayings are not as contradictory as they appear. The three degrees are the stages of the Lesser Mysteries, which involve, respectively, the mastery of desire, the mastery of fear, and the experience of death and resurrection.

There are seven rungs on the ladder of initiation; these are the seven stages of the Greater Mysteries, which relate to the Seven Deaths discussed in the next chapter. Those of my readers who are Freemasons, or know their way around the symbolism of Freemasonry, may find it useful in this regard to reflect on the three Craft degrees and the mysterious ladder of Kadosh; there are close equivalents in other systems of initiation, the one established by Fortune herself among them.

The last paragraph of our text sets all these matters in their broader context. In an earlier chapter, we explored Fortune's concept of the Initiation of the Nadir, the experience at the point of the deepest descent into matter in which the soul comes into contact with the Solar Logos directly. That is what is being discussed here. The task you have set yourself is the incarnation you are currently in. You circumscribe that task by becoming aware that the situation you're in, the karma you bear, and the strengths and weaknesses you have at your disposal, define the work that you have in front of you in this life. You see that task in relation to the Cosmos by placing this life, if only in imagination, in the context of many lives, and of the great process of involution and evolution in which this life is so brief an episode. You see the Cosmic archetype by contemplating the divine, under whatever form and name you find most appropriate; you see the circumscribed form by contemplating yourself and your life—and through those two contemplations, you draw in creative force and focus it upon the events and circumstances of your life. How this is done will be explored in the most difficult chapters of this book, which we will examine shortly.

# CHAPTER TWENTY SEVEN

# The Law of the Seven Deaths

## Reading

Revised Edition: Chapter 26, "The Law of the Seven Deaths,"
pp. 119–123.
Millennium Edition: Chapter 27, "The Law of the Seven Deaths,"
pp. 160–166.

## Commentary

In the chapters of *The Cosmic Doctrine* we've studied over the last few chapters, Dion Fortune has passed on an extraordinary body of practical occult instruction—more of that relatively rare commodity, as noted earlier, than you'll find in many entire books on magic. In this chapter, she goes even further into the deep places of occult philosophy and practice. The last two chapters covered the work of the involutionary path, the process by which each of us descended into the world of matter, which is also the process by which each of us began our current incarnation, and the process by which any of us can learn to wield magical powers. The material she covered in those chapters is essential to understand how we got here and how we can work with the world that surrounds us. The material in this chapter is even more crucial, because it deals with where we go from here—and how.

It's worth taking a moment in this context to recall the scheme of spiritual evolution Fortune has sketched out for us in previous chapters. Each of us began as a Cosmic atom, born of tangential movements in the Central Sun, where the twelve Rays intersect and set vortices spinning, and then drifted out to whichever Cosmic Plane corresponded to our basic structure. Each of us was caught up and swept along in the movement of the Great Organism, who became our Solar Logos as it moved out to the seventh Cosmic Plane, and each of us then became part of the great cloud of Cosmic atoms surrounding the Logos in the early days of the solar system. Each of us, caught up in the rhythms of the Solar Logos, became a three-part organism—a Cosmic atom, a seed-atom created by the movements of the Cosmic atom, and a Divine Spark that reflected the Logoidal influence.

In that threefold form, each of us swirled around the Logos for long ages while the Lords of Flame, Form, and Mind brought the worlds into being. Each of us then began our own long pilgrimage down the planes, existing in the dream-state of subjective consciousness, evolving on each plane the capacity to build a body of that plane, conditioned on each plane by the rhythms of the Planetary Spirit active on that plane, and guided by the Lords of Mind. Each of us descended all the way to the lowest plane of the solar system, the plane of dense and etheric matter, where we worked our way through a long series of incarnations on that plane. Each of us finally awakened to objective consciousness and took our first steps on the long road back up the planes to the throne of the Logos—and here we are.

The Seven Deaths are the seven steps that lead to the way of ascent. Let's take them, as Fortune does, one at a time.

The First Death has already been discussed in these commentaries at great length. Take two forces in motion and bring them together so that they intersect, and a vortex is born, which absorbs the movement of both and spins in place. The moving forces die to themselves, and a stable pattern in space is born. Everything enduring in the Cosmos, from the three great Rings to the least grain of dust in our solar system, comes into being by some form of that process. Notice the core principle here: the death of one thing is the birth of another.

The Second Death has also been explored in various ways in these pages. (Please note that this isn't the "Second Death" talked about in writings about the afterlife.) In the First Death, the moving forces and the vortex exist on the same plane. In the Second Death, there's a change of planes. Two forces come together on one plane, and the vortex they create comes into being on the next plane down. This is death from the perspective of the higher plane—two forces die—and birth from the perspective of the lower plane—a vortex is born.

Your birth into this life happened that way: a soul ready to descend into matter and the energies set in motion by an act of reproductive sex flowed together and formed a vortex, which brought your body into being. From the perspective of the higher planes, as Fortune discusses further on, you died and were buried in a body. From the perspective of the lowest plane, the one you experience with your ordinary senses, you were born. Yet the same equation can work the other way around. The vortex can and, indeed, must finally unravel and release the forces that created it. From the perspective of the lowest plane, each of us will die; from the perspective of the higher planes, each of us will be born out of matter. Your birth was an example of the Second Death. Your death, the death of your present body, is an example of the Third.

The Third Death is death as we usually mean that term. Each soul alternates between periods of being alive (in the conventional, material sense of that word) and being dead (also in the usual material sense of that word). As Fortune points out—and she's in line with a great deal of Western esoteric tradition in doing so—we gather up experiences in what we call life, and absorb and benefit from those experiences in what we call death. In Fortune's precise if amusing bovine metaphor, "we graze in the fields of Earth, and lie down to chew the cud in the fields of Heaven." We plunge into the maelstrom of life, to borrow a different metaphor from a Marvel comic-book character, and then rest on the shores of death to catch our breath and make sense of what we've experienced.

Does this imply that death is nothing to be afraid of? That's exactly what it implies. The prophetic religions of the last two and a half millennia or so have a lot to answer for, but one of their most disastrous missteps was the effort so many of them put into making death as terrifying as possible, in an attempt to scare people into being good. Of course, it didn't work, and it turned the normal, natural, healthy process of ripening toward death into a nightmare for countless millions of people. Nor have the materialists and atheists who came after them improved matters any by insisting, in the teeth of considerable evidence, that when you die, you stop existing. A considerable share of the follies and brutalities of the modern world are caused by the inability of so many people to think of death as anything but the worst outcome they can imagine.

Fortune's advice here is excellent. Spend some time, not just once but regularly, imagining yourself leaving your physical body at death, and still existing. Read books on occult teachings about the afterlife— Fortune's own short book *Through the Gates of Death* is a good place to start—and use those as a guide to reflection. Imagine yourself between lives, a conscious being still embodied in some of the subtle bodies you presently have, interacting with other dead people and with spiritual beings who have never had bodies, or last had them ages ago. Get used to the idea of being dead, so that you no longer fear it. The prophetic religions made death terrifying by convincing people to imagine themselves frying in Hell. The same work of the imagination can be turned around and used in reverse. Get comfortable with the reality of death and you'll find it much easier to live fully and joyously.

What makes this easier than it might be is that we all undergo an experience very closely related to death at regular intervals—for most of us, every night. Yes, that would be sleep, which is the Fourth Death. Sleep is far more important, and far more complex, than the conventional wisdom would have you believe. When you sleep, your Individuality—the real you, the you that existed before your mother and father were born—detaches itself from its masks and bodies to the extent that it is able. Those Individualities that still have a lot of work ahead of them on the human level rise only to the astral planes, the planes of desire, and contemplate in subjective consciousness the images of human desires. That is appropriate for them, since they need to pass through the experiences generated by those desires

Those that have gone further may rise to the mental planes and contemplate abstract ideas. This is the source of those dreams that offer answers to problems, provide guidance in life, and now and then foresee the future. Genuinely creative people, those who don't simply recycle the contents of an existing stock of tropes but develop their own creative language, gather the material for their work in dreams that are consciously forgotten but subconsciously recalled. Finally, those who are in the process of outgrowing the human level of existence rise to the spiritual planes and wake to objective consciousness on those planes. The Personality usually does not remember such awakenings, but the

Individuality does, and it can make adjustments in itself and its current Personality to correct its course.

The same differentiation according to evolutionary levels happens after death. Souls that have completed only a small part of their journey on the human level spend most of their time between lives on the astral planes. In some cases, all their time is spent there, and the newborn child ends up with substantial traces of the Personality of the last life. Most often, though, and more and more often as the soul gains experience, it rises through the planes to whichever sub-plane was the highest it reached in life. This is where the Fifth Death happens. The soul awakens into objective consciousness, recognizes itself as the Individuality, and knows its Personality as one of its expressions rather than its true self. The Christian language ("beholding the face of the Father") that Fortune uses here may or may not appeal to you; if it doesn't, try to see through it to what it symbolizes.

One of my teachers, many years ago, liked to suggest that we are like people who were stuffed into gorilla suits in early childhood, so early we don't remember it. The suits are very cleverly made; they stretched with you as you grew, and allow you to eat and drink and excrete and move and do all the other activities of life—but you're still stuck in a gorilla suit. Then one day, by chance, you notice a little glint of metal down low on your belly, and on examination discover that it's a zipper pull. You pull it open, and discover two things. The first is that a lot of what you thought was true about yourself is only true of the gorilla suit. The second is that you can take the gorilla suit off, look at yourself in a mirror, and say, "So this is what I actually am." The gorilla suit is your Personality, the person under the gorilla suit is your Individuality, and the process of taking off the gorilla suit is a fair metaphor for what happens in the Fifth Death.

At the end of this section of the chapter, Fortune includes a comment that really doesn't communicate much unless you know a once-famous comment by Helena Blavatsky: "What you desire, that you become." I imagine the old Russian mystic saying that with a cold little twinkle in her eye, because she's quite correct—just not in any sense that her listeners were likely to understand. Fortune's comment is thus meant to help her students avoid making smoking craters of their lives. If you desire power, you will indeed obtain vanity; vanity, in turn, will slam you face-first into one miserable experience after another; eventually, as a result, you will learn strength, foresight, and wisdom—and thus gain power. Blavatsky and Fortune are both right: your desires will give you the results of what you have permitted yourself to desire, and those results eventually will give you your desire. It's just that the road there may not be to your liking. Be careful about what you let yourself desire!

Trance, the Sixth Death, used to be a great deal more important in occultism than it is today. What Fortune calls "normal psychism"—the use of the trained imagination ("picture consciousness" in her terms) as a replacement for trance states—has long since become standard, as its dangers are considerably less. Fortune summarizes the dangers neatly here. When you enter trance, the sub-plane of being with which you are in contact will depend precisely on your own inner state, and the risk of being drawn into negative magic by unfulfilled desires is not small. There are ways to avoid this, and the specific measures she gives here are among them; if you happen to have a talent for trance states and choose to develop that talent, Fortune's advice is good. Otherwise, you're better off working with ordinary imagination, where your conscious mind remains in control of the situation, and it's easier to keep the passions in check.

The Seventh Death, finally, is illumination, the state that Eastern spiritual practices call enlightenment. In this experience, the Individuality awakens to full objective consciousness while the physical body is still alive and wide awake. The Personality is seen for what it is, a temporary mask that the real you uses to interact with the physical plane and the other beings incarnated there, and the Individuality can experience the reality of all the planes at once. It's an overwhelming experience, even when it happens only for an instant—which is usually the way things work out at first. To exist in this state permanently is to step beyond the human level of existence while still in a human body.

Fortune uses a neat play on words here to communicate the total reversal of perspectives that happens when illumination arrives or, on a smaller scale, when consciousness begins to glimpse the reality of the Individuality through the mask of the Personality. "A living death"—back in the day, that was a convenient shorthand for a life so miserable and restricted that it was, in the imaginations of those using the phrase, indistinguishable from death. Look at death from another perspective—the perspective that Fortune offers in this chapter—and the concept proceeds to stand on its head. To be dead is to be free of the limitations of matter and capable of rising up into consciousness of the Individuality. To pass through illumination is to achieve that state while still incarnate in a physical body. The quote from Tolkien's *The Lord of the Rings* cited in the previous chapter is a good description of the result.

To become an initiate in the full, rich sense of the word—the sense that Fortune is using here—is "to live at once in both worlds," to dwell simultaneously on the physical plane and the inner planes, to be in full possession of the powers of a spiritual being while still in full possession of a physical body and all its functions. This is not an easy state to attain. In one of her other books, Fortune mentions that it takes a minimum of three lifetimes devoted to occult study and practice to achieve that condition—and it takes enormous perseverance and discipline to accomplish all the necessary work in just three lifetimes! Keep in mind, however, that this is a very advanced stage on the Path; there are plenty of worthwhile achievements to accomplish on the way there, and even the first steps have their benefits.

# CHAPTER TWENTY EIGHT

# The Law of Impactation

## Reading

Revised Edition: Chapter 27, "The Law of Impactation," pp. 124.

Millennium Edition: Chapter 27, "The Law of Impactation, or the Transmission of Action from One Plane to Another," pp. 167–170.

## Commentary

Most of the material we've covered so far in this commentary can be found in equally detailed form in both the standard editions of our text. This chapter and the following one are exceptions to that rule. Both these chapters in the Millennium Edition are nearly three times as long as the corresponding chapters in the Revised Edition, and include diagrams left out at the time of revision. There's a reason why the Revised Edition was published with these things left out. Like the last several chapters we've examined, this one deals with the techniques of practical magic—specifically, in this case, the techniques of practical polarity magic, the central magical method of Dion Fortune's teaching.

Fortune isn't the only writer of her period, or most of a century before her time, to be evasive about this. Eliphas Lévi, in his *Doctrine and Ritual of High Magic*, is equally evasive about what he calls the Grand Arcanum, the secret of bringing magical forces into manifestation. That's what Fortune is talking about here, too, and Lévi's symbolism echoes Fortune's closely enough that it's pretty clear that they're presenting a shared tradition.

Let's start by considering the general theory of impactation, which is covered in the four paragraphs of this chapter from the Revised Edition. (This is all of p. 167 and the last paragraph on p. 170 in the Millennium Edition.)

We can begin with some definitions. The basic pattern of movement on the planes of being, as we have discussed in previous chapters, is involution followed by evolution: a soul, an energy, or an influence descends the planes from the upper spiritual plane to the physical plane, and then returns up the planes from the physical plane to the upper spiritual plane. (The diagram below is a reminder of how this works.) Any action that furthers one or the other of those movements is natural and beneficial—when an energy, say, is descending the plane, magical work that helps it on its way down is a good idea, but trying to make it go back up the planes before it has finished its descent is not.

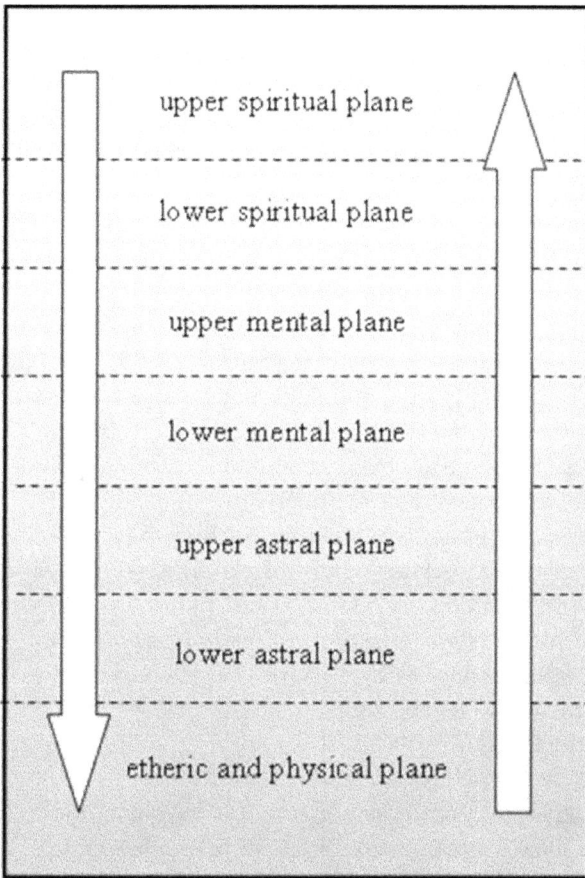

| upper spiritual plane |
| lower spiritual plane |
| upper mental plane |
| lower mental plane |
| upper astral plane |
| lower astral plane |
| etheric and physical plane |

Planes of Being 4

There are specific terms for upward and downward motion on the planes depending on whether what you're trying to affect is on the descending or the ascending arc of its journey. If it's descending into manifestation, further descent is called impactation, while turning around and going backward is called disintegration. If it's rising back up out of manifestation, upward movement is called sublimation, while turning around and going back down into matter again is called degradation. Those aren't value-neutral terms, and they're not intended to be—disintegration and degradation have exactly the effects those words suggest.

This follows from the nature of the process we're discussing. As Fortune explains, currents of unformed force descend the planes into matter because material objects provide the structure that allows them to organize themselves into form. Once the force has settled into its proper form, it can rise up out of matter while still maintaining the form it has received without the scaffolding of material substance. To go back up the planes before descending all the way into form is to fail to coalesce into a stable form, and disintegration follows. To go back down into matter when the material form is no longer necessary is to fall back into the confusions and complexities of matter, and degradation follows.

So the wise occultist acts by impacting forces that are descending into manifestation in matter, and sublimating forces that have already earthed out on the physical plane. That isn't as restrictive as it might seem, because there are always a great many currents of force descending at any given time and a great many more seeking to rise up out of manifestation, and it's purely a matter of choosing which one to work with at any given time. Astrology is the classic way to figure out which currents are descending, by the way, and natural magic—the knowledge of which currents of energy are already in manifestation in herbs, stones, and other natural things—is the classic way to figure out which currents are ready to rise back up.

Sublimation, as our text says, is the art of separating the subtle from the dense. ("Thou shalt separate the earth from the fire, the subtle from the dense, gently and with great ingenuity," says the Emerald Tablet of Hermes Trismegistus.) Impactation is quite another matter. To bring a descending energy further down the planes, the process is identical to the one we have examined several times in this commentary already, especially in the formation of the Cosmic atoms: two tangential forces encounter each other, form a vortex, and descend to the next plane down, where they become a stable node that can enter into interaction with other things on that plane.

So far and no farther the Revised Edition takes us. It's in the Millennium Edition, which is based on the privately printed 1949 version, that the text goes further—in a guarded and allusive way, to be sure, but clearly enough that the meaning can be extracted.

Imagine, our text proposes, that you want to express an abstract concept in a concrete form—that is to say, you want to take something on the lower mental plane, the plane of abstract thinking, and give it a form on the upper astral plane, the plane of concrete imagery. (The same principles apply to the transition from each plane above the physical to

the one below it, but this set of planes makes for a good clear example.)
As it stands, the concept remains a concept, not a concrete image, and it
cannot make the descent on its own.

It can only crystallize into an image when it is combined with something else—"an entity of a different type to your own," in Fortune's
evasive phrase. The "type" in question is either involutionary or evolutionary. What is being said here is that you need to bring the concept
that is descending into form together with something else that is rising
up out of form, and link the two in a particular manner. For the involutionary pattern—the concept you want to transform into an image—
the parts of the image that can be expressed in astral form are moving
toward impactation, and the parts that cannot are moving toward disintegration. For the evolutionary pattern—the influence rising up out
of form—the parts that can be expressed as a mental concept are moving toward sublimation, and the parts that cannot are moving toward
degradation. The diagram below expresses this: 1 and 2 are the two
things to be combined, 1 the descending concept, 2 the rising form; +
and – indicate descent and ascent, respectively. The leftward half of the
diagram shows the halves of 1 and 2 that are moving with the flow of
nature, and the rightward half the halves that are moving toward disintegration and degradation, respectively.

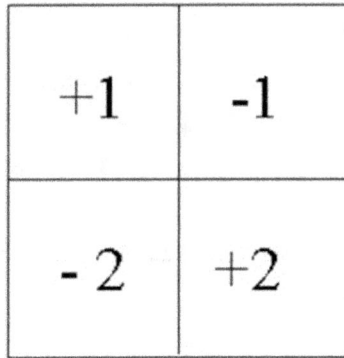

| $+1$ | $-1$ |
|---|---|
| $-2$ | $+2$ |

Impactation 1

What happens when you join the two—"gently and with great
ingenuity"—is that you create a symbol. Suppose the concept you
want to express is that of the natural unfolding of the human spirit,
and suppose the influence rising up out of form is the image of a rose.
The image becomes a vehicle for the concept, so that the concept can

take a step further down into manifestation. The concept becomes a vehicle for the image, so the image can take a step further away from manifestation. That's the art of impactation: you impact something and sublimate something at the same moment. The same thing happens, and of course Fortune is broadly hinting at this all through the chapter, when a man and a woman have sex and conceive a child.

Something curious happens in the aftermath of the act of impactation, though. The two things that join together do so, in a certain sense, horizontally—no doubt Fortune chose that turn of phrase quite deliberately, and she and her students chuckled about it. The concept becoming an image and the image becoming a concept are on the same level, the boundary between the lower mental and upper astral planes, and they unite on that boundary. The diagram below shows what happens next: the halves of both that are moving downward unite, as do the halves that are rising upwards. The conceptual dimensions of the idea and the image sublimate together into higher levels of being, while their imaginal dimensions descend together into manifestation: meditating on the rose as a symbol of unfolding spirit leads to intuitions of meaning, that is, while the same interaction has encouraged quite a few people who've contemplated the rose as a symbol to plant rose-gardens! Horizontal union leads to vertical separation: that's the key to the process, and it opens up some of the deeper dimensions of what Fortune is discussing.

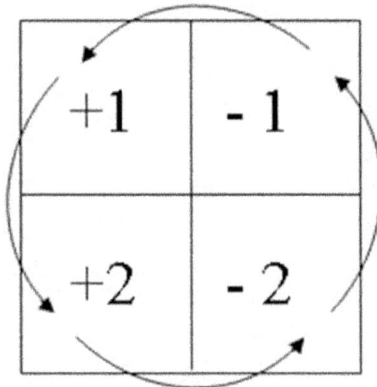

Impactation 2

One of Fortune's essays included in the anthology *Applied Magic,* "The Circuit of Force," helps clarify how this works.

In order that any thing or factor shall be brought down from a higher to a lower plane, it is necessary to analyze it into the contradictory factors that are held in equilibrium in its nature. To do this, one imagines the opposite extremes of which it is capable and expresses them separately while retaining in consciousness their essential unity when in equilibrium.

In practice, you become aware of the highest and lowest aspects of whatever it is you want to bring down to a lower plane, and work with each of these as already described.

Yet the two aspects of the concept, and the two aspects of the rose, are never entirely separate. Rather, each recombines with its partner, and sets up a rhythm in consciousness, like two couples in a dance who are constantly changing partners. This is what gives symbols their magical force, and also their elusiveness. You can never pin them down, because the symbol and its meaning are constantly trading places and exchanging aspects of themselves. Analysis fails because it relies on dividing things into their components, and what makes a symbol powerful is not a component but a constantly changing set of relationships among all the components. The diagram Fortune uses for this is a hexagram, as shown below; the positive and negative aspects of each of the two forces interlock and interchange to produce a stable pattern that unites force and form, impactation and sublimation.

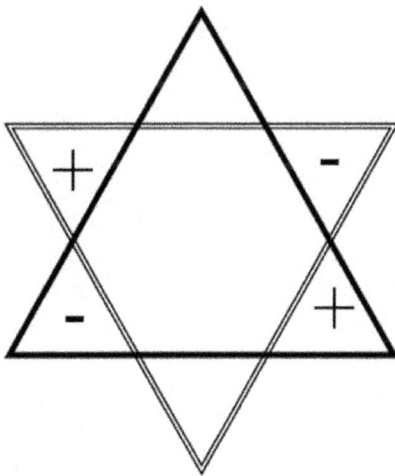

Impactation 3

That far, Fortune's example proceeds. Anyone who has read the published accounts of workings by Fortune's students, such as Alan Richardson's *Dancers to the Gods*, or studied Fortune's Rites of Isis and Pan in the recent edition capably edited by Gareth Knight, can take it a step further. That being the case, it seems unnecessary to be mealy-mouthed here.

This same process is at the heart of certain classes of polarity workings which are performed by properly trained operative occultists. These workings are not sex magic in the usual sense of that phrase, but it would be wholly inaccurate to say that sex has nothing to do with them. In this form of working, the force that is descending into manifestation is sexual energy, and the form that is rising up out of manifestation is the human soul—either an individual soul or the collective soul of a group or a nation. The participants should be sexually attracted to each other but should not have sex with each other, to keep the energies from earthing out in the time-honored fashion. The exact methods used vary from one type of polarity work to another, but in all cases sexual energy is raised by one participant or group of participants, and gathered up and directed into a form established and maintained by the other participant or group of participants.

That's the horizontal dimension. The vertical dimension is also present, of course, and it can be best understood by tracing out the whole process in an actual example. The Rites of Isis and Pan mentioned above are well suited to this as they have been published in their entirety. The participants in the working were the audience, who provided the sexual energy, and the people performing the ritual, who provided the form into which the energy flowed. The pattern of ideas the rites were meant to help bring down into manifestation was one that Dion Fortune wrote about at great length in her essays and novels—the need for a saner attitude toward sexuality in the Western world. That was the downward movement. The upward movement? That took the form of the spiritual exaltation of the participants.

*This was the method of the ancient Mysteries.* The rites performed at Eleusis, Samothrace, and the other centers of the old Mystery cults didn't make use of sexual desire as their motive force, so far as we know, but the culture in which they existed had to cope with different emotional and psychological burdens than the one in which Dion Fortune lived and worked. The principle was, however, the same: a horizontal energy flow between two participants or groups of participants, one providing the energy, the other providing the form, brought certain ideas into concrete manifestation and simultaneously furthered the spiritual development of all the participants. Consider the ceremony of Communion in a sacramental Christian church and you can see exactly the same process at work, with adoration as the motive force, the congregation providing the energy, the priest and his assistants providing the form, the ideals of the Christian faith descending into manifestation and the participants being exalted spiritually by the working.

That which is impacted, Fortune points out, is a reflection of the combined nature of the impactors. No one can bring down an influence into manifestation in a clearer form than they themselves can experience and embody it, and those who participate in a working of this kind always remain in some sense connected to it. It's possible to weaken that connection by establishing what Fortune calls the bar of impactation—a firm distinction between the higher plane on which the working is done and the lower plane on which its effects manifest. Think of an inverted letter A, like the one below. The two diagonal lines represent the descending influences from the two elements of the operation, and the crossbar is the bar of impactation. When the bar of impactation is solidly in place, the participants can leave the working behind, and others can take up the work and continue it without disrupting the basic structure.

$$\forall$$

Upside Down A

This chapter is full of hints as to how such operations may be done, combined with the calm suggestion that the student will need to meditate on the text repeatedly to figure out what exactly is being suggested. As the Revised Edition puts it, "more has been said here than you may realize." This is true enough, but the interested student can go much further by combining meditations on our text with a close study of the rituals already cited and Dion Fortune's novels, along with the useful commentary on the novels in Penny Billington and Ian Rees' book *The Keys to the Temple*. It's not at all impossible, through that course of study and practice, to get a very clear sense of exactly what Fortune is sketching out in this chapter, and will outline in even more detail in the final chapters of our text.

# CHAPTER TWENTY NINE

# The Law of Polarity

## Reading

Revised Edition:      Chapter 28, "The Law of Polarity," pp. 125.
Millennium Edition:   Chapter 29, "The Law of the Aspects of Force or
                      Polarity," pp. 171–175.

## Commentary

As mentioned in the previous chapter of this book, most of the text in
the two editions of *The Cosmic Doctrine* covers the same ground in much
the same way, but two chapters have significant differences—the two
covered in the previous chapter of this commentary, and in this one. In
both cases, the difference is that some material in the original, privately
published edition was left out of the Revised Edition, and then put back
into the Millennium Edition. In both these chapters, the material that
was left out has to do with polarity magic, the central secret of Dion
Fortune's magical teaching. The previous chapter covered the technical
methods; this chapter covers certain details of theory that allow those
technical methods to be put to work in a remarkable diversity of ways.

The single page of material that got into the Revised Edition includes the beginning and the end of the wider discussion, so we can begin with the first two paragraphs included there, which are identical to the first two paragraphs of this chapter in the Millennium Edition. The first point made here is that just as the Law of Impactation we discussed earlier depends on the Law of Polarity for its function, the Law of Polarity depends on two more laws, the Law of the Attraction of the Center and the Law of the Attraction of the Circumference, which we have not yet studied. Notice here the difference between the occult approach to instruction and the standard approach: instead of covering the theory first and then proceeding to the practice, the occult approach is to present the method of practice, make sure that it has been learned, and then provide the theoretical perspectives that make the practice work.

The attraction of the center and the attraction of outer space have already been discussed repeatedly in our text, of course. Back in Chapter 3, we saw that the Cosmic Days and Nights set the rhythm of the Cosmos: during a Cosmic Day, the influence of the Ring-Chaos puts in motion a new cycle of manifestation, while during a Cosmic Night, the influence of the Ring-Cosmos causes the cycle to end. Later we saw that currents of motion in space stream out from the Central Sun, go as far as they can before reaching the boundary of the Ring-Pass-Not, and then turn and stream back in toward the Central Sun, whence they flow out again. That same dynamic sent the traveling atoms on their way, and later still, once the traveling atom that became the Logos of our solar system reached the seventh Cosmic Plane and began to dream a dream of worlds, that same dynamic sent the seed-atoms that became conscious beings like you and me down the planes to the realm of dense matter and then back up again to the Logos.

In making sense of this passage, it's important to remember that to Fortune, the words "positive" and "negative" are not moral labels. "Positive" is the pressure that moves things down toward manifestation. "Negative" is the pressure that moves things up toward abstraction. Those two pressures—the downward motion from the Logos into manifestation, and the upward motion from manifestation back to the Logos—are the prime polarity in every working. Both are always present. Whenever something moves down the planes into manifestation, something else moves back up the planes in response, and vice versa. Whichever of these is the intention of your working, the other must always be taken into account.

For the moment, think of the flow of energies into and then out of manifestation as a rope that runs through a pulley overhead. If you pull down on one side of the rope, the other will go upwards. If you want to lift something, you connect it to one side and then pull it down on the other. If you want to lower something, you connect it to one side and then let the other rise up in a controlled fashion. This is what Fortune called the circuit of force, and it is an essential principle in magical workings. When you want something to descend into manifestation, what will you send up out of manifestation to balance it? When you want to lift yourself up to higher levels of awareness, what will you bring down into manifestation to balance it?

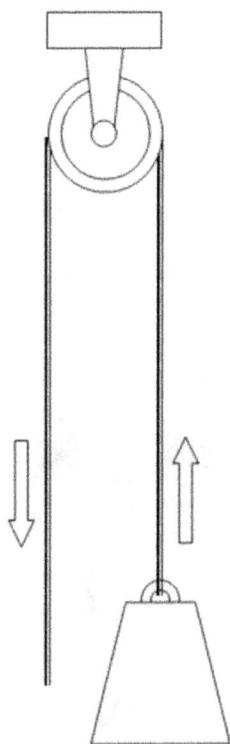

Pulley

The pulley makes a good first approximation of the process, but as Fortune points out, things are not so linear as that, because of the way that each plane relates to the planes above and below it. This is where the caduceus, the rod of Mercury, comes into the picture. The caduceus is central enough to the symbolism of Fortune's grand metaphor that the first published edition of *The Cosmic Doctrine* had a caduceus printed on the cover. If the rod at the center of the caduceus is the straight line of ascent and descent, the two serpents that twine about it are the interchanging currents that move from plane to plane.

At this point, we leave behind the material printed in the Revised Edition and begin to explore the text found only in the Millennium Edition. To make sense of this, it's necessary to know something of the symbolism Fortune assigned to the planes. Each of the seven planes of being has an exemplar from mythology who represents its influences in a vivid and magically effective form. Hermes or Mercury, the bearer of the caduceus, is the exemplar of the lower mental plane; Orpheus, the demigod of music and master of the elementals, is the exemplar of the upper astral plane. Fortune's explanatory diagram takes the caduceus of Mercury and places it on the lyre of Orpheus, whose seven strings are the seven planes of our solar system, as shown here. (Yes, I know that this is not what Greek lyres actually looked like. Fortune was writing a manual of occult philosophy, not a treatise on historical musicology, and some degree of artistic license has to be expected from her.)

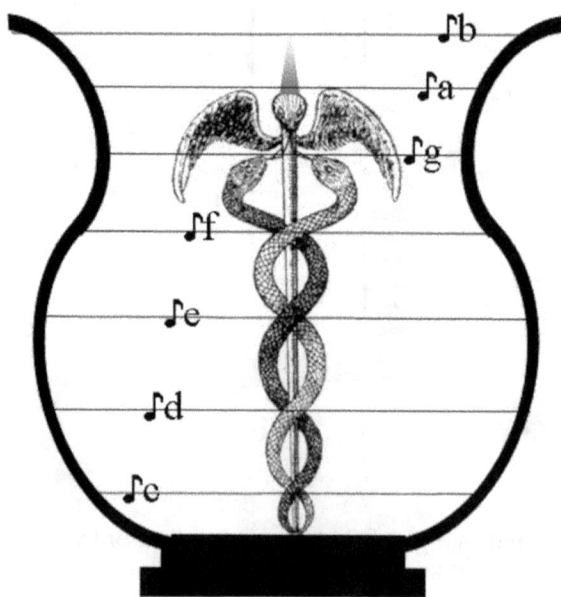

Caduceus and Lyre

Notice that on each plane, the black and white serpents exchange sides. This is crucial for the metaphor, because under most conditions the planes sort themselves out into alternating polarities—thus, for example, if the physical/etheric plane is negative, the lower astral will be positive, the upper astral negative, and so on. This is why Fortune's workings normally involved two or more people who had opposing polarities. Imagine two people doing magic together. On the etheric sub-planes of the physical plane, one of them is positive, and one is negative—that is, one is projecting force and the other is receiving it and giving it form. On the lower astral, though, the flow goes in the opposite direction, and so on up the planes. This allows power to come down the planes all the way from the upper spiritual plane, passing back and forth from one participant to the other so that it is always flowing through a body of positive polarization. Then the force flows back up the planes the same way, passing back and forth so that it is always flowing through a body of negative polarization. That back-and-forth process creates the symbolic caduceus, and the power flows.

Here Fortune gets very technical. Remember that to create anything on a lower plane it's necessary to take two things on a higher plane and bring them into relationship, creating a vortex that manifests itself on the next plane down. To balance that process with an upward motion, you take two equivalent things on the next plane down and bring them into relationship, then establish a unity on the higher plane that expresses itself in the form of those two things. Thus you're balancing the descending triangle with an ascending triangle.

All this can be understood more easily through an example, and the one I have in mind is one we discussed in the last chapter, the communion ceremony practiced by sacramental Christian churches. In this working, the horizontal polarity is provided by the congregation, the positive pole that provides the energy, and the priest, the negative pole that draws forth that energy and gives it form. The vertical polarity is provided by Christ and the world. The method of the pulley is in evidence here: through the communion ceremony, the ideals of Christianity descend into manifestation in the Christian community, and the consciousness of each participant is raised to an extent determined by their individual readiness to accept such an ascent.

But there's more going on here than a simple pulley-dynamic, of course. To begin with, while the priest is receiving the energies of the congregation on certain planes—the physical, the upper astral, and (if he and they can reach this high) the upper mental planes—he is simultaneously giving energies to the congregation on the lower astral, the lower mental, and (if he and they can reach this high) the lower spiritual planes. This allows a current of force to descend, shuttling back and forth between them, all the way from the upper spiritual plane to the physical plane, and to rise back up again. The more effectively this is done, the more potent the effect of the rite.

The ritual is also designed to work with the relation between two polarized concepts on the lower mental plane—sin and redemption are the usual set. Those concepts have exact equivalents on the upper astral plane of emotion—contrition for one's sins on the one side, and the exaltation that comes from deliverance on the other. So we have the descending triangle in which the concepts of sin and redemption guide the manifestation of Christian ideals in the world, and the ascending triangle in which the emotional reactions of the congregation and the priest assist the birth of higher modes of consciousness in all the participants.

This is of course only one example, though it is one that most people in the contemporary Western world know well enough to follow. Others can be found detailed in *Dion Fortune's Rites of Isis and of Pan*, edited by Gareth Knight; in *The Magical Battle of Britain*, also edited by Knight; and in Fortune's occult novels. Go through a few of these examples with the framework just above in mind, and you will have no problem figuring out how polarity magic works in practice.

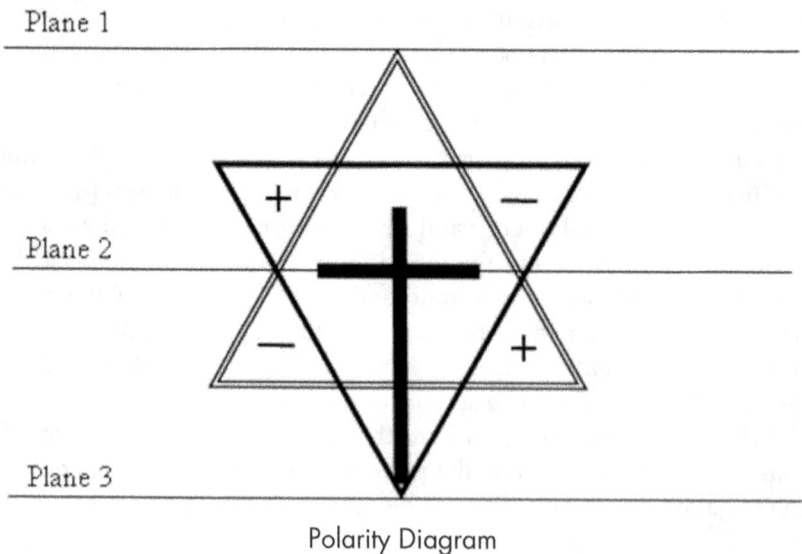

Plane 1

Plane 2

Plane 3

Polarity Diagram

This is only one application of the theory of polarity, however. Another has to do with ordinary relationships among human beings—sexual and otherwise. If a relationship only functions on one plane, it will be temporary, because no circuit of force is formed: one participant has a surplus, the other has a lack, and once the surplus flows away and the lack is filled, the relationship dissolves. A stable relationship requires the involvement of at least two planes, so that the flow one way can be balanced by a flow the other way on another plane. Fortune's book *The Esoteric Philosophy of Love and Marriage* expands on this in detail.

Another broader application has to do with understanding phenomena of every kind, and will be found especially useful in meditation. If you take any phenomenon and explore it in detail, you will find that it can be understood as the result of two polarized phenomena on the next higher plane. If you understand this, and trace out the hidden duality on the subtler plane that lies behind the outward unity on the denser plane, you can understand aspects of the thing's behavior that a less nuanced analysis will miss.

Still another, far more focused application has to do with the potential for polarity between the Personality and the Individuality—between the Lower Self of a given incarnation and the Higher Self. If the Lower Self systematically neutralizes all its characteristic activities on all the planes on which it is normally active, the Higher Self will sometimes manifest. This is the key to certain kinds of religious and mystical practice, but it also has another application to which Fortune alludes only in the most cryptic style: "You will perceive that here you have certain important clues to the practice of that which induces that which is not in that which thinks it is, but is not." For reasons I don't propose to discuss, I'm going to leave that just as obscure as Fortune did; those who want to understand it have the necessary tools in discursive meditation, and the necessary data in this and the previous chapters of this book.

Finally—and here we return to the material that was preserved in the Revised Edition—the workings of an occult lodge, or any other spiritually oriented group, are subject to certain applications of the same principle. Under normal circumstances, such a group will gather around a teacher or leader who has achieved an insight, or a group of insights, on a plane above that on which the members of the group normally operate. The principles discussed in this and the previous chapters set out what happens next—the horizontal polarity between the teacher and the students, the vertical polarity between higher and lower planes, the force that descends the planes through teacher and students alternately and rises back up again the same way, the paired concepts on one plane and the paired emotions on the other, all these play their usual roles.

In a group of this kind, however, the flow cannot be sustained indefinitely. Sooner or later, the members of the group will have absorbed everything they can from the teacher, and the teacher will have given everything he or she has to offer to the group. A Cosmic Day in miniature has ended, and a Cosmic Night begins, in which the patterns thus established can stereotype themselves so that a further wave of evolution can build on the foundation thus laid. The familiar rhythm of spiritual groups, in which they alternate periods of intensity with periods of relative quiescence, comes from this process.

At the very end of the chapter, Fortune gives two sentences that are worth a month of meditation all by themselves. Here they are: "You will observe that throughout all manifested life the co-operation of two factors is essential for all 'form' building. Force, however, works as a unit because its polarity is in the Logos." At the very beginning of *The Cosmic Doctrine*, Fortune set out a prime duality between space and movement, and here we encounter it again, reworked to fit the distinctive characteristics of this little corner of the Cosmos. As the background for all existence in this solar system, conditioning everything else, the Solar Logos corresponds to space, and the currents of force that flow out from the Logos are forms of movement. The relation between them is one of polarity, and every point made in this chapter about the practice of polarity can therefore be applied to the creation of the solar system— and, indeed, of the Cosmos itself. The working out of the details of that application is left as an exercise for students.

CHAPTER THIRTY

# The Law of the Attraction of Outer Space

## Reading

Revised Edition: Chapter 29, "The Law of the Attraction of Outer Space," pp. 126–128.

Millennium Edition: Chapter 30, "The Law of the Attraction of Outer Space," pp. 176–179.

## Commentary

We are approaching the end of *The Cosmic Doctrine*, and this and the next chapter neatly sum up the implications of the philosophy that Dion Fortune has been expounding in the pages of her book. Those readers who have been following along closely will doubtless already suspect that she did not carry out that summation in any simple or straightforward way, and they are of course quite correct. This chapter in particular is deliberately deceptive in certain ways. For reasons that will become clear as we proceed, Fortune tried to trick her readers into a particular reaction, and then used that reaction to make a point of immense importance. She also drops an unexpected hint that invites readers to go all the way back to the beginning of the book and reinterpret the entire project of *The Cosmic Doctrine*.

The chapter begins by recapitulating one of the core themes of the book. The Solar Logos, we are reminded, sets the ongoing process of creation into motion after a period of indrawn meditation by propounding to itself a new conception of existence, which then takes shape as an evolutionary impulse and cascades down the planes. That impulse is carried on its way by a swarm of entities, each of which starts out the journey as a seed-atom united with a Divine Spark and provided with a simple body of seventh-plane atoms. Down the planes it goes, embodying itself in ever more complex forms, until it finally reaches the first or physical plane, the one you and I perceive in our current incarnate forms.

When the Lords of Flame made that descent, near the beginning of the life cycle of the solar system, there was nothing waiting for them on each plane but a cloud of unformed atoms, ready to be gathered up into planetary spheres. Each subsequent swarm must cope not with a cloud of possibilities but with a structured planet with its own existing processes and patterns already established in place. In terms of the basic metaphor of our text, the Lords of Flame have to work with only such random tracks in space as have been laid down by the uncoordinated movements of the atoms on that plane, but the Lords of Form have to work with a coordinated system of tracks in space laid down by the Lords of Flame, and each subsequent swarm in turn has to deal with the tracks in space laid down by all the preceding swarms.

Previous chapters have discussed this, of course, but not in the terms Fortune uses here. In this chapter, we are told to envision this situation in terms of a conflict of "will" and "form"—the quotation marks are Fortune's. The idea of form has appeared repeatedly in these pages already, but will (or, as she further defines it in later paragraphs, the will-to-live of the Logos itself) has not. We have seen some discussion of epigenesis, which Fortune equates with the free will of individual entities, and a very few times in our text references appear to the will of the Solar Logos—a "Cosmic will," defined as the momentum of the Logos implanted in it by its experience in the Cosmos before the birth of the solar system. We have not seen any previous discussion of a Logoidal will-to-live—but every reader of *The Cosmic Doctrine* among Fortune's own students, or in Fortune's own time, will have seen that phrase, stopped cold, and said some variant of, "Oh, so *that's* what she's been talking about."

The German philosopher Arthur Schopenhauer gets very little attention these days. During Dion Fortune's lifetime, by contrast, his main work, *The World as Will and Representation*, was widely read and discussed, not by philosophers—Schopenhauer despised the professional philosophers of his day, and their successors have by and large returned the favor—but by artists, writers, scientists, and occultists. (To cite only one example, from Schopenhauer's world as will and representation to the world as will and imagination in Eliphas Lévi's *Doctrine and Ritual of High Magic* is the smallest of steps.) A detailed discussion of Schopenhauer's philosophy would take us far from our subject, but the core concepts of his analysis are relevant here. To Schopenhauer, the world of our experience consists of representations: we do not know a sun and an earth, as he phrases it, but an eye that sees a sun, and a hand that feels an earth. With one exception, everything we encounter and everything we can encounter is a representation, not a reality.

That one exception is will. If you consider your hand as an object, you can see it and touch it, and it behaves like any other representation. At the same time, your hand has another dimension. Obviously, you can move it; less obviously, you can attend to it, perceiving it from within. These are expressions of will. Schopenhauer starts from simple manifestations of will like these and reasons step by step to a conclusion that runs like a subterranean current all through the work of Dion Fortune and a great many other occultists of the nineteenth and early twentieth centuries: the reality behind all these representations is will, the Cosmic will-to-live, of which our human consciousness is one grade or expression, and which surges outward continually through all beings and things. Fortune sums up Schopenhauer's vision more concisely than he ever did with a vivid metaphor that appears in several of her works: "God is pressure."

To speak of the Logoidal will-to-live and its interaction with forms would have instantly evoked Schopenhauer's ideas in the mind of any educated person at the time *The Cosmic Doctrine* was written. Fortune didn't stop there, however, because the relationship between will and form she presents is not a comfortable one. The will-to-live always seeks to express itself freely, while form always seeks to confine the will-to-live within its existing patterns, and so the will, in Fortune's phrase, is irked by forms it cannot escape. This is the source of the warfare between spirit and flesh that religious thinkers have discussed at such length over the years, and to which Schopenhauer devoted much of the fourth part of *The World as Will and Representation*.

Thus the Logoidal will-to-live, embodied in each of the swarms of souls, streams down the planes, descending ever deeper into worlds of established form, until it finally reaches the physical plane, the furthest extent of the creative process and the realm in which form is most rigid and resistant. There each of the souls that has made the descent faces the challenge of the initiation of the Nadir; it stands alone, in the terrible silence of a world that for the moment seems to be reduced to empty space and dead matter, and its task is to turn toward the illuminated beings of the seventh plane to receive the initiation that will complete its descent into matter and begin its ascent into spirit.

This is not the only option for a soul at this stage, however. The momentum of the Logoidal will-to-live, striving to overcome the irksome burden of form, pushes it in the other direction, away from the seventh plane and toward the abysses of outer space. So does the pressure of the forces of a Manifested Universe, which naturally seek equilibrium with the emptiness of the void. So, finally, does a factor Fortune has mentioned in a very different context: the Penumbra.

Back in Chapter 18 of this commentary, we discussed the role that comets play in the economy of the universe, as the scavengers that gather up those few souls who systematically turn their backs on evolution and take them to the Unknown Death. The Penumbra is where that happens. All these failed projects of evolution remain visible just beyond the Ring-Pass-Not of the solar system. There is a difference of some importance here between our two editions; in the Millennium Edition, which reprints the original privately printed version, we read that these are the forms "which having been disintegrated against the inner shell of the Ring-Pass-Not remain as an image" while in the Revised Edition the same passage reads "which having not been disintegrated against the inner shell of the Ring-Pass-Not remain as an image." I suspect the Millennium Edition is correct here, and the images of the Penumbra are phantoms, the last echo of those beings and forces that have undergone the Unknown Death.

That's not what it looks like to souls who face the temptation of the Nadir, and Fortune is at some pains to phrase things so that we feel the temptation ourselves. This is the point at which each soul gazes out into the void and imagines what it would be like to break out of the solar system entirely, to shake off every limitation, "to leap that gulf," as our text says, "into the freedom of Outer Space where there is no law, and men are as gods."

Those readers who remember the laws already tabulated in *The Cosmic Doctrine* will instantly sense the trap here. "Limitation is the first law of manifestation; therefore it is the first law of power." That was the opening sentence of Chapter 24 (Chapter 26 in the Millennium Edition), and it is arguably the most important law taught in our text. The freedom of outer space is a fictitious freedom, for where there is no law and no limitation, there is no power and no manifestation—only dissolution into the void. Freedom is found not by overturning law and limitation but by accepting them, internalizing them, mastering them, and thus becoming free to use them and work with them. To recognize this is to overcome the temptation of the Nadir, receive the initiation of the Nadir, and begin the journey to genuine freedom.

It's worth taking some time to understand this, since the mental habits of today's popular culture make the temptation of the Nadir considerably easier to fall into and the initiation of the Nadir considerably less easy to receive. Think back to the first chapters of our text, where Fortune explored the role of negative evil as a thrust-block for action. The laws and limitations experienced by incarnate beings in the planes of manifestation function exactly the same way. Each of us is conditioned by the forms of the physical plane, and through that conditioning, we are able to bring our own energies into perfect equilibrium. Then, having overcome the conditions of the physical plane by internalizing them, we rise to less restrictive planes, where we have the capacities we developed on the physical plane and can use them more freely.

To put all this in terms of a concrete metaphor, the laws and limitations of the physical plane are to souls what the barbells, dumbbells, and kettlebells of a weight room are to bodybuilders. It's certainly possible to put down the irksome burden of, say, a couple of hundred pounds of cast iron disks on a steel bar, rather than doing three sets of difficult lifts with them. The consequence of putting it down, however, is that you don't get the gains. The material plane may be an unusually heavy and clumsy weight to lift, but those awkward features simply make it a better instrument for exercise!

All this, finally, relates back to the philosophy of Arthur Schopenhauer in ways that Fortune's own students would again have realized at once. One of the central themes of *The World as Will and Representation* is precisely the process by which the will-to-live overcomes itself or, to use Fortune's metaphor, overcomes its own outward momentum in order to turn back on itself. In Schopenhauer's view, this self-overcoming is the source of music, literature, and the arts, on the one hand, and holiness and the salvation of the soul on the other. *The Cosmic Doctrine* does not discuss the arts, and Fortune's conception of holiness and salvation is both more complex and more subtle than Schopenhauer's, but the connection is clear.

I suspect Fortune put the reference to Schopenhauer's philosophy so late in our text precisely because the connection is so clear. *The Cosmic Doctrine* is not a book to be read once and then set aside, having been mastered. Getting out of it all that has been put into it requires repeated readings and a great deal of thought and meditation. The first time through, most readers will have missed the quiet hints that show the underlying presence of Schopenhauer's ideas here, as in so many other occult writings of the late nineteenth and early twentieth centuries. On the second reading, those hints will stand out, and help the reader penetrate to a second level of understanding of the text. On the third reading, and those that follow, other elements will be more visible. That's the way any classic of occult literature is meant to work.

For those readers who are on their first journey through *The Cosmic Doctrine*, however, the point that matters most in this chapter is the temptation of the Penumbra. This is a serious matter, and Fortune wants us to feel it: to wallow at least briefly in fantasies of tumbling out into the void and fulfilling all those empty images of impossible desires. She leaves us deliberately in that state at the end of this chapter. In the next—the final chapter of this book—she brings everything back together in a final synthesis.

CHAPTER THIRTY ONE

# The Law of the Attraction of the Centre

## Reading

Revised Edition: Chapter 30, "The Law of the Attraction of the Centre," pp. 129–133.

Millennium Edition: Chapter 31, "The Law of the Attraction of the Centre," pp. 180–185.

## Commentary

We have arrived at last at the final chapter of *The Cosmic Doctrine*. Each of the two editions of our text has a collection of assorted material appended after the last chapter, labeled "Part II" in the Revised Edition and "Afterthoughts" in the Millennium Edition, but these are more or less random notes on the material we've covered. Those who want to make a thorough study of *The Cosmic Doctrine* should certainly study those final notes and meditate on them, but there is little I can say about them that will be useful.

As for this final chapter, any of my readers who are unwary enough to expect Dion Fortune to finish things up with a nice straightforward exposition of the points she wants to make are going to be disappointed.

True to form, this chapter is intricate and richly ironic, a bravura perfor-
mance of multilayered metaphors to wind up this extraordinary work.
It deserves—and requires!—many readings in order to unpack what it
has to say.

The concept that frames this chapter's discussion is one that we've
encountered repeatedly over the previous chapters. Once the Cosmos
or a solar system or an individual being has finished the process of
coming into existence, every new influence starts from its center, which
is also its highest plane, and proceeds outward and downward to the
periphery, which is also its lowest plane. There, once it has finished
coming into manifestation, it returns inward and upward to the center.
On the way down, it evolves the capacity to take on a body of each
plane through which it passes; on the way back up, it is conditioned
by the body it indwells on each plane, and then sheds that body once
it has taken into itself the capacities of that body—or, to use a different
metaphor, once it has learned the lessons of that plane.

We followed that same process many chapters ago, as we tracked the
original traveling atoms of the Cosmos on their journeys up and down
the twelve Cosmic Rays. We followed it again with the Lords of Flame,
Form, and Mind, and again, in more detail, as we talked about the path
that each of our souls has followed from the upper spiritual plane down
to the plane of dense matter, where we are now embodied for the time
being. In several previous chapters, we examined the turn from the outward to the inward arc in which each of us, and our species as a whole,
are now engaged. Now our text turns to the same theme one more time,
with an eye toward the path back up the planes—the path of return to
the center.

There are three ways to follow that path. Two of them reach their
destination, and the other fails to do so. Our text explores them one at
a time.

The first, the one that has occupied most of our attention all along, is
the way of evolution. In a certain sense, this is the easy way; it requires
no particular effort on your part. All you have to do is let yourself be
carried along with all the other souls in the swarm to which you belong.
Now of course if you choose this route you can count on being tossed
about like a twig in a torrent, flung this way and that, driven up against
one obstacle after another, and then again left to circle aimlessly for a
while until the current picks you up again and carries you on, but in due
time you'll reach the destination toward which the waters are flowing.

On the physical plane, the way of evolution follows a familiar pattern. Each participant in the current descends into matter, and there works out its own evolution for a time, until it has gone as deep into matter as it can—reaching, as our text says, the utmost complexity of material organization. Once it has reached that point, it begins to synthesize that complexity into a unity, and that synthesis happens on the etheric sub-planes, not the sub-planes of dense matter. As that takes place, the physical expression begins to break down.

This is not just true of individual souls, by the way. As our text points out, it also describes the way that ideas descend into manifestation and take on conceptual form. Before a thought has taken on solidity in the realm of matter, it is what Fortune calls an inceptive idea—"vague intuition" might be a good translation of this technical term. Only after it has taken material form does it become a concept. Writers experience this process all the time: a scene in a story or an explanation in an essay is a blurred half-formed pattern of possibilities until the material effort of fingertips on a keyboard turns it into something solid and definite, which can then be refined further by the labor of revision. Once the idea has entered the realm of concepts, in turn, it can detach itself from the specific words that brought it to that point; this release from verbal form corresponds to the breaking down of the physical form.

Each of us, in this novelist's metaphor, exists as a vague pattern of inceptive possibilities until the events of our lives write us down in black and white. Thereafter, having achieved form and definition, we can free ourselves from the page and go on to other things. That, to the nearest approximate metaphor, is what we are doing here in physical incarnation.

Our text is a little more specific than this. Our physical bodies, Fortune suggests, are like the molds used in casting. Once the hot metal has been poured into the mold and allowed to cool, the mold can be removed and thrown away, because the metal has taken on an enduring form. In the same way, our physical bodies confine the subtle levels of ourselves until they take on an enduring form, after which a physical body is no longer necessary—all its capacities for action and perception have been taken on by the next level up, and we have thereby unified the material and etheric sub-planes of the physical plane in ourselves. This in turn is simply the first of a long sequence of unifications, which will end with all the capacities of all our bodies on every plane being unified on the highest plane on which we are capable of existing.

This is the condition of the Lords of Flame, Form, and Mind, and it will be our condition ages from now when we have completed our evolutionary journey.

The same process also takes place on the level of the entire solar system. As each swarm of souls sweeps out to the periphery of existence, it brings with it certain patterns of movement that the Solar Logos has conceived. As they descend, the members of that swarm dance those patterns of movement, establishing tracks in space that proceed to influence the substance of each plane. Once they reach the physical plane, out here at the periphery, they awaken to objective consciousness, and begin to take an active role in the dance, embellishing it with their own epigenesis, and return dancing up the planes to the Solar Logos.

In this chapter, Fortune introduces a new metaphor for this process, building on metaphors she's used already in the context of the Greater Days and Nights of Brahma or God (depending on which version of the text you read). If the influences of the Logos at the center of the solar system are spreading outward, she suggests, this can be imagined as the extension of the center. The inward flow of each swarm of souls can thus be pictured as an outward flow of the center, a spiritualization of the planes, in which each plane gradually takes on the nature of the seventh plane. In a further metaphor that has seen a great deal of use in mystical writings, the solar system is gently reabsorbed into its god.

The symbolism of Days and Nights of Manifestation, which was introduced earlier in our text, returns here in a new form. Back in Chapter 3, we watched the Ring-Cosmos turning within the Ring-Chaos, creating a new Cosmic Day when the Ring-Chaos predominated and set a wave of changes in motion, and creating a new Cosmic Night when the Ring-Cosmos predominated and the changes settled down to stereotype themselves. In Chapter 29, while discussing the Law of Polarity, we revisited that image—but here, as so often before, Fortune shifts to a new set of imagery.

Imagine, she suggests, that as the forces of the created solar system flow back into the center at the end of the Cosmic Day, the center itself flows outward, a tide of pure spirit that sweeps out over all the planes of manifestation. Fortune refers to that tide as the Waters of Darkness, and describes that term as "a symbol of spiritual peace, cleansing, and regeneration." All the tracks in space that have been laid down during the Cosmic Day are filled with spirit and the positive evil in them is erased. Then the Waters of Darkness drain away to leave the planes of manifestation ready for the coming of dawn.

It's a potent image, and even more potent if you remember the immense role that Atlantis played in Dion Fortune's teaching. Central to the modern narrative of Atlantis is the vision of a mighty culture in the far past that descended into tremendous evil, and was then washed away by a close equivalent of the Waters of Darkness so that the fields of the world would be left clean for the coming of a new dawn. That image haunted many minds in Fortune's time. J.R.R. Tolkien, in papers published after his death by his son Christopher, wrote of a dream he had many times in which he looked across green lands toward the sea, and saw a mighty wave looming up to sweep over everything. In our time, when global warming threatens a hundred-meter rise in sea level worldwide, that image has lost none of its relevance!

The Waters of Darkness, then, are Waters of Evil only in a certain very nuanced sense. Light and darkness, good and evil, are the two poles of the creative process, the two hands of the Father in Fortune's Christian symbolism. A few chapters ago, she reminded us that what looks like life and death from our perspective may take on a very different appearance from the perspective of the inner planes, and she repeats that here: "the right [hand] sends out into manifestation and the left beckons back again; but you, looking as in a mirror, call right, left, and left, right." Apply that to the vision of the Waters of Darkness flowing over the fields of manifestation, and you have a theme that will bear many sessions of meditation.

The work of initiation depends on that outflowing, as our text explains, for beings who have already completed the descent into manifestation and the return to the center—the Lords of Mind, who are the initiators of our evolution, and those individuals of our swarm who have followed the path of evolution to its end ahead of the rest of us—proceed out from the center as heralds of the rising waters. Again, the echoes of the Atlantis legend are hard to miss; the initiators here fill the role of the seed-bearers who sailed from Atlantis in its last days to bear the secret teachings to new lands. Tolkien's Dúnedain, who sailed from Númenor to Middle-Earth with the White Tree and the nine Palantíri, are cut from the same cloth.

It's important here to remember that Fortune, like most occultists of her time, drew a firm distinction between the lesser initiations that could be conferred by magical lodges such as the one she headed, and the

greater initiations—or, in the language she uses here, Illuminations—
that are conferred by souls that have progressed far beyond the human
level. These latter do not take place in physical lodge rooms, and our
text gives the reason; they can only take place on planes that the Waters
of Regeneration have already reached. In our present phase of evolution, those waters have not yet begun to percolate through the cracks of
the material world, and so for the time being the greater initiations can
only take place when the initiate is in an out-of-body experience and
has risen, or been brought, to the necessary plane.

As we have already learned, however, there are at least two ways to
move toward the center—the way of evolution and the way of devolution, the way of the Right-Hand Path and the way of the Left-Hand Path
(in Fortune's specific and rather idiosyncratic sense of these terms). The
former, as we have seen, moves forward along the trajectory of our further development as souls; the latter moves back toward older, archaic
influences. Both these Paths respond to the attraction of the Center, but
those who take the Right-Hand Path have completed involution into
matter, undergone the initiation of the Nadir, and passed beyond it,
while those who take the Left-Hand Path turn back up the path of involution before they have finished it.

The Right-Hand Path is a path of unification, in which all the complexities of material existence are brought into the greater unity of the
spirit. The Left-Hand Path is a path of simplification, in which those
same complexities are discarded. The Right-Hand Path seeks whole-
ness, while the Left-Hand Path seeks that flawed image of perfection
that involves assigning all the problems of the individual to some portion of the self—sexual desire, say, or the thinking mind, or the ego—
and insisting that this portion of the self is irredeemable and can only be
cast aside. In Fortune's vision, the Right-Hand Path leads to realization,
while the Left-Hand Path leads only to dissolution. The former is the
path of love, the latter the path of death. "Therefore choose love and
live," our text ends.

If you've been paying attention, this will have you scratching your
head. Didn't an earlier chapter point out that death is life and life is
death, and didn't this chapter note that we confuse the right and left
hands of God, mistaking the light for the darkness and the darkness for
the light? Of course, they did. *The Cosmic Doctrine* does not offer anyone
a set of simple rules for simple minds. At the end of his enigmatic treatise *The Hieroglyphic Monad*—another essay meant "to train the mind

and not to inform it"—John Dee notes: "Here the common eye will see nothing but obscurity and will despair considerably." The same note could be appended here. Which path is life, and which is death? That, of course, is left for students to explore in meditation themselves.

Yet there's a hint woven into the structure of this last section of our text. As we've seen, *The Cosmic Doctrine* is meant to train your mind rather than to stock it with ideas that can be used in familiar ways. To go backward now—to think of what you have learned while reading the text as though it was a set of doctrines to be accepted blindly in the useless "Dion Fortune said it, I believe it, that settles it" manner—is to take the way of simplification and to enact, in a very small way, the Left-Hand Path. Do that and your efforts will be wasted, for the images and ideas you have studied will dissolve into mere opinions. To go forward now—to take the mental training you have received and apply it, through repeated study and meditation on *The Cosmic Doctrine* and other occult writings, by Dion Fortune and by other authors, including those who influenced her and those she influenced in turn—is to take the way of unification and to enact, in a very small way, the Right-Hand Path. Do that, and the work you've invested in the most important work of twentieth-century occult philosophy may just do what Dion Fortune meant her writings to do, and set your feet firmly on the first steps of the Path.

# BIBLIOGRAPHY

Barnett, Lincoln, *The World We Live In* (New York: Time, 1955).

Billington, Penn, and Ian Rees, *The Keys to the Temple* (London: Aeon Books, 2022).

Blavatsky, Helena P., *Isis Unveiled* (Cambridge: Cambridge University Press, 2012).

Doczi, György, *The Power of Limits* (Boston: Shambhala, 1994).

Fortune, Dion, *Applied Magic and Aspects of Occultism* (Wellingborough, UK: Aquarian, 1987).

——, *Mystical Meditations on the Collects* (London: Rider, 1930).

——, *The Cosmic Doctrine*, revised edition (Cheltenham, UK: Helios Book Service, 1966).

——, *The Cosmic Doctrine*, Millennium Edition (York Beach, ME: Samuel Weiser, 2000).

——, *The Esoteric Philosophy of Love and Marriage* (Wellingborough, UK: Aquarian, 1988).

——, *The Magical Battle of Britain* (Bradford on Avon, UK: Golden Gates, 1993).

——, *The Mystical Qabalah* (London: Ernest Benn, 1935).

——, *The Problem of Purity* (New York: Samuel Weiser, 1980).

——, *Through the Gates of Death* (Wellingborough, UK: Aquarian, 1987).

Fuller, Buckminster, *Synergetics* (New York: Macmillan, 1975).

Green, H.S., *Mundane or National Astrology* (London: Fowler, 1911).

Greer, John Michael, *Paths of Wisdom* (London: Aeon Books, 2017).

Hall, Manly Palmer, *The Secret Teachings of All Ages* (Los Angeles: Philosophical Research Society, 1928).

Hofstadter, Douglas, *Godel, Escher, Bach* (New York: Vintage, 1989).

Knight, Gareth, *Dion Fortune's Rites of Isis and of Pan* (Cheltenham, UK:
Skylight, 2013).

Lévi, Eliphas, *Doctrine and Ritual of High Magic*, trans. Mark Mikituk and
John Michael Greer (New York: Tarcher, 2017).

Lewis, C.S., *Out of the Silent Planet* (New York: Scribners, 1996).

Proclus, *The Elements of Theology*, trans. Thomas Taylor (London:
Prometheus, 1994).

Richardson, Alan, *Dancers to the Gods* (Wellingborough, UK: Aquarian,
1985).

Sagan, Carl, *The Demon-Haunted World* (New York: Random House, 1995).

Sallust, *On the Gods and the World*, trans. Thomas Taylor (Los Angeles: Philosophical Research Society, 1976).

Schopenhauer, Arthur, *The World as Will and Representation*, trans. E.F.J.
Payne (New York: Dover, 1969).

Sheldrake, Rupert, *A New Science of Life* (London: Paladin Grafton, 1988).

Smuts, Jan, *Holism and Evolution* (New York: Macmillan, 1926).

Tolkien, J.R.R., *The Fellowship of the Ring* (New York: Ballantine, 1965).

Whitehead, Alfred North, *Process and Reality* (New York: Free Press, 1979).

——, *The Concept of Nature* (Cambridge: Cambridge University Press, 1920).

# INDEX